*For George William Irwin who loved
fresh air and good company.*

Sociology and the Environment

A Critical Introduction to Society, Nature and Knowledge

Alan Irwin

Polity

First published in 2001 by Polity Press in association with Blackwell Publishers Ltd

Editorial office:
Polity Press
65 Bridge Street
Cambridge CB2 1UR, UK

Marketing and production:
Blackwell Publishers Ltd
108 Cowley Road
Oxford OX4 1JF, UK

Published in the USA by
Blackwell Publishers Inc.
350 Main Street
Malden, MA 02148, USA

ISBN 0-7456-1359-4
ISBN 0-7456-1360-8 (pbk)

A catalogue record for this book is available from the British Library and has been applied for from the Library of Congress.

Typeset in $10\frac{1}{2}$ on 12 pt Sabon
by Best-set Typesetter Ltd., Hong Kong
Printed in Great Britain by TJ International, Padstow, Cornwall

This book is printed on acid-free paper.

Contents

Preface

In an influential lecture delivered in 1991, Howard Newby[1] made two particular claims concerning the relationship between sociology and the environment. First, 'that environmental change . . . is as much a social science as a natural science issue'. As Newby anticipated, this assertion was likely to be 'highly congenial' to most sociologists. Certainly, it is fundamental to this book.

Secondly, and less congenially, Newby argued that 'the slender contribution of sociologists to the study of the environment has been, to put it mildly, disappointing'. More specifically, he asserted that sociology had been 'inhibited' in this regard by a 'deeply rooted set of theoretical and conceptual issues which must be overcome if sociology is successfully to rise to the challenge which I believe to be there'. This book offers a critical introduction to these theoretical and conceptual challenges and, in so doing, addresses the sociology–environment relationship at a basic level.

Newby substantiated his claims in a number of ways: by noting that the causes of environmental change lie in human societies, by exploring the 'technological determinism' at the heart of policy prescriptions and by discussing the rhetorical usage of 'scientific facts' within environmental discussions. All these points are important and will be discussed in these pages. Nevertheless, one of the most interesting aspects of Newby's lecture was its discussion of the question (which I paraphrase slightly): why, given the centrality of sociology to environmental questions, has sociology remained so silent?

Newby's own answer to this question takes us into territory that will be central to the chapters that follow: 'The very *raison d'être* of sociology has rested upon identifying and demarcating a disciplinary paradigm quite distinct from, and irreducible to, the natural and the biological. And, even to pick at this problem runs the risk of being tainted with an abhorrent political philosophy' (Newby 1991, p. 7). For Newby, environmental questions represent a fundamental challenge to the discipline precisely because they raise what can be termed 'foundational problems'. On that basis, the implications for the discipline are profound: '[T]he sociology of the environment ought not to be regarded as some esoteric, sub-disciplinary specialism, but rather [as] something which defines the sociological enterprise' (ibid.). In a finale to the lecture, which serves equally well as an overture to this book, Newby asserted: 'It is vital for all our futures that we lose no opportunity to acquire the appropriate knowledge about ourselves and our relationship to the planet' (ibid., p. 8).

Re-reading Newby's lecture today, a number of his observations remain valid. Although things are slowly changing, 'sociology of the environment' is still largely found 'in the outer reaches of a third-year undergraduate option where it can be safely marginalized alongside the sociology of development, or some such' (ibid., p. 6). One also suspects that many current sociology students – and staff too – would fail the 'Brundtland test' implied by Newby (i.e. of whether they have read – or perhaps even heard of – this influential report[2]). Equally, there is still a tendency for the 'social' dimensions of environmental problems to be seen as secondary within policy debates – as a set of 'soft' issues to be ironed out once the 'hard facts' have been collected.

On the other hand, and as Newby acknowledged, even back in the early 1990s there already existed a relevant sociological literature. This included environmental sociology[3] (especially in the United States) and, very importantly for this book, a concern with risk and environmental issues within science and technology studies (STS). It could also have been argued against Newby that, although twentieth-century sociology was indeed largely silent on environmental matters, the sociological heritage should not be dismissed altogether (even if it is, as we will discuss, highly 'questionable' in this regard). Certainly, various sociologists have defended the continued significance of the sociological classics for environmental issues and concerns.

In taking stock of the relationship between sociology and the environment today, it must especially be noted that a range of books has emerged since the early 1990s with titles such as *The Green Case, Social Theory and the Global Environment, Society and Nature, The Social Construction of Nature, Environmental Sociol-*

ogy, *An Invitation to Environmental Sociology* and *Ecology and Society*.[4] The list is long and getting longer every year – particularly if one includes publications which, whilst not primarily sociological in orientation, have important implications for the discipline and specifically for our understanding of the social–natural relationship (for example, the expanding interdisciplinary literatures on sustainability, eco-feminism and green philosophy). As Riley Dunlap has observed, the 1990s witnessed a 'dramatic resurgence' in the field and 'signs of its intellectual revitalization' (1997, p. 29). This book hopes to capture that spirit of intellectual renewal and revitalization at the start of a new century when environmental problems and environmental understandings seem more important than ever.

Nevertheless, and a decade later, the central challenge posed by Newby's talk remains: what should be the relationship between the discipline of sociology and the study of environmental issues, problems and concerns? In particular, it is still relevant to ask whether this area of study should simply take its place alongside other undergraduate options and specialty areas or whether instead more foundational challenges are being offered to the sociological canon. Does environmental sociology represent yet another sociological specialty or should it alter the whole complexion of the discipline? In the following chapters, we will witness a challenge not only to the interpretation of the 'natural' within sociology but also to the meaning of the 'social' in a world where nature and society are so closely intertwined.

In asking such questions we are challenging not only the intellectual assumptions of contemporary sociologists but also the prevailing sense of what defines environmental issues, problems and concerns. Any radical attempt to reconstruct the conventional relationship between society and nature will have consequences for how we view the environment and the modern environmental crisis. This in turn means that Newby's 'environmental challenge' to sociology may involve a more fundamental rethinking than is immediately apparent. Such a suggestion should not be seen as dismissive of contemporary environmental concerns (on the contrary). However, it does suggest that in offering a challenge to the discipline of sociology we are simultaneously and unavoidably challenging the conventional construction of environmental problems. Throughout *Sociology and the Environment*, we will be very conscious of this dual challenge both to sociology itself and to the definition of environmental concerns.

It follows from what has already been said here that the subsequent chapters are not primarily about the social dimensions of environmental change, nor are they designed to heighten sociologists' awareness of the environmental crisis (although along the way they should stimulate reflection on both these points). My goal instead is to ask more basic questions about the very definition of the 'natural environment' and the ways in which environmental matters are defined within everyday talk, within policy formulations, within the institutions of science and, very importantly, within sociology as a discipline. This book will not survey environmental problems, nor will it directly review the different ways in which sociological analysis can assist environmental action. Instead, it will specifically focus on the larger theoretical and conceptual challenge: how can the discipline of sociology usefully address questions of nature and the physical environment and what would this in turn mean for sociology?

As I hope to suggest, the crude notion that the environment is simply 'out there' and that 'it' then has certain social impacts is being replaced by a more complex and multi-layered sense of the different ways in which the natural world is constituted, contested and defined within institutional practices, environmental discourses and forms of expertise. Central to this exploration of institutional practices and 'contested natures'[5] will be the question of *environmental knowledge*: how do we know what risks we run and what environmental threats we face? Since nature cannot speak to society without our active interpretation and understanding, environmental knowledge is central to the social–natural relationship.

In raising such basic conceptual issues, it should be stated from the beginning that I write as a sociologist with a long-standing interest in this area but also as someone with an equally long-standing concern with issues of hazard, risk and the environment at a practical as well as theoretical level. In that sense, what follows is not just the outcome of reading a particularly fascinating area of literature but also of personal (often troublesome) experience in this area. The attentive reader will certainly be able to detect my own attempts to make sense of a set of problems that can never be just 'out there' but are 'in here' within our own thoughts and practices.

In one vivid illustration of this sociological complexity, I remember visiting a factory in the North of England during the early 1980s to discuss problems of occupational health with managers and local trade-union officials. Prior to my visit, I had studied a number of articles that chronicled the problems of cancer and lung disease and also the steps being taken at national level to control exposure. I certainly went with a clear sense of what the problem was – even if what should be done about it was less clear to me.

My cautious reception by management at the plant had been anticipated but not the positively hostile encounter with a senior trade-
union official. The message was clear: my sense of a significant hazard
was totally at odds with his sense of security, employment and an
exceptionally rigorous set of workplace controls. This is not (as we
agreed) to deny the general existence of health problems, but it does
suggest the different ways in which such issues can be constructed,
framed and understood – and also the relationship between these elements and the contexts of their enactment.

In line with that insight, my assumption of a major health issue
was matched by his notion that this was merely the temporary and
controllable side-effect of an otherwise successful technology. My
scepticism of the plant's management was countered by his sense of
an honest and caring group of people who were brought up, lived
and worked in the same small town as himself. My (inevitably partial
and selective) use of scientific evidence conflicted with his trust in
the technical competence of the company's medical staff (did I have
better formal qualifications than them?). In this one example, we can
see many of the issues of risk, knowledge and expertise that will be
specifically developed in this book. In particular, we can identify the
importance of *context* and of social *practices*, which may have profound implications for environmental understanding without being
primarily environmental in orientation. As we will discuss, risk issues
do not arise in a socio-cultural vacuum.

Looking back, I suspect neither of us shifted position during the
decidedly heated discussion. However, it does serve to illustrate the
embeddedness of such questions within the assumptions and understandings of everyday life (including, of course, my own). At least for
me, it especially emphasized the need not just to impose an outsider's
framework on a set of issues but to consider the 'local knowledges'
and contextual understandings involved (even if they sometimes
conflict with one's own preferences and judgements). Put differently,
our interpretation of the underlying reality of the situation differed
markedly. There was no single environmental truth upon which we
could agree – and, crucially, for reasons that are both social and
natural in character.

The encounter also raised far-reaching questions concerning the
analytical, political and ethical role of the researcher: to document
and analyse this as a case-study or to make a practical intervention?
Certainly, it was difficult for me to come away with the notion that
I had some unproblematically privileged concept of what the problems 'really' were. Meanwhile, existing sociological theory seemed
inadequate when applied to such a context. As I travelled back to

what now felt like the comfort and intellectual shelter of the university, I was left wondering what the best role for the sociologist should be in situations of this kind.

So what does this book offer? First of all, it focuses squarely on the social–natural relationship and its consequences for the social sciences (specifically, for sociology). Secondly, it places questions of environmental knowledge and expertise at the core of relations between the social and the natural. Whilst 'sound science' is often presented as a sufficient foundation for effective environmental action, we will consider some of the inherent difficulties of 'knowing' the scale and severity of environmental problems.

Thirdly, this book suggests that the sociological study of the environment is not just a matter of applying conventional social theory (in all of its abstracted glory) but also of reconstructing that theory. Accordingly, we will both review existing sociological debates (including the entrenched battle between realists and constructivists[6]) and explore new possibilities (especially the concept of 'co-construction'). This leads into a fourth point, that this reconstruction requires not just theoretical analysis but also empirical exploration and grounded discussion. For that reason, we examine an important range of institutional frameworks (including sustainable development and government decision-making) and everyday contexts (notably, the public reconstruction of environmental issues). I will suggest that these frameworks and contexts are not just *illustrations* of the social–natural relationship, but represent some of the *crucial processes and contexts* within which social–natural relations are enacted and practised.

Finally, we will consider both disciplinary and practical questions. Indeed, the whole argument is that we are unlikely to reach satisfactory conclusions about either unless we tackle both.

Constructing one's audience for a book like this is never easy. In the usual egocentric manner of academics, it is particularly hard to remember that one's own obsessions and enthusiasms are not universally shared. In taking up Newby's theoretical and conceptual challenge, I am potentially addressing everyone interested in the future of sociology although I recognize that the audience will consist particularly of those within the discipline with a special interest in environmental and scientific matters (a number that is steadily growing). I also very much hope to engage those within geography, political science and science and technology studies as well as the wider social sciences who wish to reflect upon the status of environmental claims and the relationship between the social and the natural within environmental disputes.

This book is certainly designed to help sociology and other students who are tackling courses in this area. Much of this material developed whilst teaching final-year undergraduate and also graduate students. Just as importantly, I hope to gain the attention of those who are pondering how best to interpret and act upon environmental concerns: whether in environmentalist groups, industry, government or simply through more personal contemplation of a topic that touches us all.

It must be said that this sociological field is both controversial and disputed. It is also dynamic rather than settled into a single paradigm or disciplinary framework. I have to confess that it is partly for this reason that I am attracted to it. However, it also follows that much of what I present here will provoke disagreement, criticism and debate (and rightly so). It is therefore appropriate that the following chapters are not primarily intended as a magisterial or all-encompassing overview. My aim instead is to encourage engagement, reflection and discussion regarding a key area of international concern. This is offered as a critical introduction to a set of important discussions and, as such, aims to stimulate and provoke rather than to place this challenging and exciting subject in one tidy corner of the sociological edifice.

As my publisher is only too aware, this book has a long and entangled history. Certain people in particular deserve gratitude for keeping me alive, alert and on-course and for making a real contribution to what follows: Peter Dickens (to whom I owe particular thanks), Susse Georg, Christine Hine, Elaine Mc Carthy, Anthony Murphy, Henry Rothstein, Peter Simmons, Frederic Vandenberghe, Gordon Walker, Steve Woolgar, Brian Wynne and Steve Yearley. Let me also thank students and colleagues in Human Sciences and CRICT at Brunel University for their endless supply of good ideas and, just as importantly, good humour.

Introduction

I have divided this Introduction into three integral sections ('Getting Started', 'Elements of an Environmental Sociology' and 'Overview and Book Structure') with a brief summary at the start of each. If you want to begin with a quick overview of the whole chapter, I suggest you read through the three summaries right now. Similar summaries will be found at the start of each subsequent chapter.

Getting Started

In the first section of this Introduction, different forms of social environment are considered before we move to the main focus of this book: the natural environment. At this point, the important duality between the 'social' and the 'natural' within sociology is identified and some of its consequences noted. The discussion then moves on to consider the 'questionable heritage' provided by the sociological classics when approaching environmental issues. The conventional social–natural separation is linked to the perceived need to establish a distinctive disciplinary identity for sociology, the historical lack of awareness of environmental problems but also the ideological difficulties for sociology of acknowledging a 'natural' basis for social life (as embodied, for example, within fascist thought). Finally, I suggest that recent sociological accounts are beginning to engage once again with social–natural relations and so offer a more productive direction for environmental sociology.

Right from the start, it must be said that the relationship between sociology and the environment seems impossibly broad and all-encompassing. After all, the environment represents the whole setting within which we spend our lives. Equally, the 'environment' as a term gets used in a number of contexts: the 'home' environment, the 'work' environment, the 'local' environment, the 'urban' environment, the 'global' environment and so on. How can any single book or course of study possibly cover such a range of 'environments'?

In practice, discussions of the environment tend to focus on quite specific contexts – the city and built environment, for example, within urban sociology; the work environment within occupational sociology or industrial relations. Generally, these environments are seen as separate from one another. They represent the discrete locations within which social life is conducted. However, it is important to consider the possible ways in which these different environments do more than just provide a backdrop to our lives: they also have the capacity to change lives. The move from older-style terraced housing to high-rise blocks (and, increasingly, back again) can be seen as having various deleterious (but also positive) effects on the quality of urban life. Workplace design can affect productivity and job satisfaction. These environments influence how we interact with the people around us, how high our stress levels are, even our very sense of happiness and well-being.

It is clear, therefore, that we cannot discuss the meaning of 'environment' without observing that we are not merely the passive victims of the environment. The environment is not just 'given'. It is also created and interpreted. High-rise blocks can be demolished, factories and offices can be rebuilt or reconfigured. Of course, we do not all have equal influence over such matters – and we may still find ourselves living and working in environments that we consider to be oppressive and injurious – but they are all ultimately *human* products and constructions.

There is another dimension to this basic point about the human (or, to be more precise, *social*) construction of environment. The environments discussed so far are not simply *fixed* in character. Instead, we read and construct them in different ways. One person's slum is someone else's proud home. One person's experience of the excitement of a great city is someone else's urban nightmare. We invest meanings in the world around us and those meanings make sense within the patterns of everyday life. This is not (of course) to deny that cities, housing estates and factories have a physical existence. However, it does suggest a subtle and overlapping relationship between the material and social worlds: a relationship that will be central to this book.

Certainly, people in my home town still talk nostalgically about the town-hall clock, which represented a central focus to the town centre – and many of them (including me) still look up to check the time even though the town hall was demolished long ago. The physical presence (or non-presence) of the clock, its height and architectural design are now less important than its persistent role within our memories and conversations. The clock ticks on through numerous anecdotes, jokes and everyday references.

However, what was 'read' by some people (at least in retrospect) as a symbol of local pride was obviously interpreted by others as an outdated eyesore, which should be replaced with a concrete-and-glass civic centre more appropriate to the town's changing image.[1] At this point, we can see how these different environmental constructions might serve as a basis for political and campaigning alliances which offer fundamentally different presentations of the issues.

The following chapters are centrally concerned with the question of just how different an account should emerge when we move from this set of explicitly human-made environments to the main focus of this book – what is generally referred to as the *natural environment*. As several commentators have noted, social scientific analysis has routinely distinguished between the above forms of human-built (or *social*) environments and the *natural* environment.

A definite dualism is at work here. The 'social' environment has been seen as legitimate territory for sociologists, whilst the 'natural' environment has been left to the natural sciences – a category that specifically excludes (or grants only a supporting role to) the social sciences. Whilst, for example, the workplace and home have been portrayed as appropriate settings for sociological analysis, the natural world – almost by definition – is regarded as asocial and external to human life. Indeed, much of sociology deals with what makes the social structure distinctively 'human' rather than 'natural'. On that basis also, the physical surroundings within which different societies are located are seen as less sociologically interesting than how people respond to the environment within which they live. Put differently, the natural environment may be presented as a backdrop to the dramas enacted by human beings – but certainly not as an actor itself.

Various assumptions have served to divide the natural environment from the more social environments considered so far. These will be discussed in greater detail in this and later chapters. For now, a few simple observations can be offered:

1. As the very term 'natural environment' suggests, issues of ecology, pollution and global environmental change have been considered as outside the competence of the social sciences: science offers a powerful means of understanding such issues so why should sociology get involved?

2. In line with this, the natural environment has generally been presented as outside human agency or intervention: the assumption seems to be that we can improve a city square (or even rebuild a town-hall clock) but we can hardly improve or rebuild a rainforest or wilderness.

3. There is an apparent sociological assumption that the social and the natural are separable even though one prevailing feature of contemporary social life is its blurring of such categories (national parks, canal-side walks, traditional villages and towns are examples here – they are often presented as natural yet are unavoidably also social in origin and character). As Simon Schama observes in discussion of the Yosemite National Park in California: 'The wilderness, after all, does not locate itself, does not name itself' (1995, p. 7).[2]

4. Issues of environmental destruction seem far removed from what is still largely the staple fare of sociology courses: what have species loss, acid rain or ozone depletion to do with mainstream social theory or key disciplinary concepts such as class, power and inequality?

5. Linked to the above, there may still be a lingering suspicion that environmental concerns are simply a flash in the pan – a passing concern that can easily be ignored. At the same time, research and teaching around such topics can be dismissed as an attempt to cash in on environmental awareness or perhaps as a distraction from more weighty intellectual matters (presumably, of the kind researched and taught by those making this accusation).

6. It has been suggested that any attempt to blur the lines between the 'natural' and the 'social' might undermine environmental activism and policy-making: how can we protect or preserve nature when it can no longer be distinguished from the social world?

As might already have been gathered, this book will not be sympathetic to such attempts at excluding the natural environment from sociological discussion. Instead, it will explore and challenge the very distinctions that have been built up between the social and the natural sciences. Going further, *Sociology and the Environment* will argue that in order to engage positively with environmental issues it will be necessary to reconsider many of the taken-for-granted assumptions within both the social and natural sciences.

Shortly, we will go on to discuss the kinds of intellectual challenge that environmental sociology represents to such established disciplinary assumptions. Before that, it is important to reflect a little further on the relationship between sociology and the analysis of environmental issues and concerns. What foundation for such a line of investigation can the discipline offer? How might 'classical' social theory help in dealing with these issues?

A Questionable Heritage?

It is sadly true that classical social theory has had an ambivalent and indeed problematic relationship to environmental issues. This is not to deny the significance of sociological analysis in this context. However, it is important to acknowledge from the outset that sociology (and especially social theory) provides us with what Redclift and Benton (1994) have termed a 'questionable heritage' in this regard.

Thus, substantial references to the environment are generally limited within classical social theory as represented by the usual triumvirate of Marx, Weber and Durkheim. More specifically, there has been an absence (at least until recently) of serious sociological discussion concerning the ecological implications of human actions and social development.[3] As Goldblatt puts this:

> The limitations of classical social theory for our purposes are, first, that it does not possess an adequate conceptual framework with which to understand the complex interactions between societies and environments, and second, that where it has addressed such issues it has focused on the ways in which human societies have transformed their environment without attending to the negative consequences of those transformations. (1996, p. 6)

Looked at from a larger historical perspective, there has certainly been a long-standing intellectual tradition of discussing the impact of nature upon society. However, with the emergence of sociology as a distinct discipline, such naturally driven arguments were generally downgraded. Thus, in the early essays and writings of Montaigne and Montesquieu (often heralded as the progenitors of modern social science) there was an extensive discussion of the impact of national climates on the form of various civilizations.[4] At a different level, early nineteenth-century theorists such as Auguste Comte and Herbert Spencer regularly built upon biological and, especially, evolutionary concepts as a basis for sociological explanation. Marx also argued that natural conditions (e.g. soil and climate) cause different social divisions of labour: 'The mother country of capital is not the tropical region, with its luxuriant vegetation, but the temperate zone' (1976, p. 649).

The shift in thinking away from these initial discussions of the 'impact of the natural upon the social' appears to emanate particularly from Durkheim and Weber. Thus, the first meeting of the German Sociological Association (held in 1910) featured a lively debate over whether sociological discussion should give any credence to 'natural' categories such as 'race' or biology. Max Weber was one of the most vigorous opponents of such elements being included within sociology. Stehr and Grundmann suggest that Weber took this line for at least two reasons. First, in order to give sociology a 'professional profile of its own'. Secondly, in order to develop a political outlook that was not dependent on 'naturalistic or biologistic concepts' (1996, p. 7).

Similarly, it was a central tenet of Émile Durkheim's definition of the discipline that social facts must be explained by other social facts – that suicide rates, for example, are caused by social forces rather than 'natural' elements such as climate or season. Durkheim, in other words, granted little significance to what we now know as 'Seasonal Affective Disorder', preferring instead to link suicide to the social condition of anomie. At this point, we can identify a sociological world-view that is explicitly premised on the separation between the social and the natural – with the social as the legitimate professional territory of the sociologist. As Redclift and Woodgate put this: 'For the "founding fathers" of modern sociology the natural environment was, on the whole, defined negatively as that which was not "social"' (1994, p. 53). Rather than providing a detailed account of the historical relationship between the social and the natural within sociology,[5] I want to consider briefly the broad characteristics of this sociological heritage and, in particular, the exclusion of the natural from questions of the social.

One important element within this disciplinary definition has been the attempt to separate our social from our biological selves – and hence to lay a foundation for the discipline of sociology. In that sense, sociology has become part of an intellectual (or, more properly, epistemological) division of labour, which constrains the possibilities for social theory to engage with questions of the natural. Instead, such questions are predetermined as lying outside the sociological domain. At the same time, the social was constrained so as to exclude issues that can be allocated to science (a demarcation that, as we will discuss, is being challenged by contemporary sociologists of scientific knowledge).[6]

Of course, such separations of the social from the natural, biological and scientific can be effective in terms of establishing disciplinary boundaries and gaining professional recognition from practitioners of other disciplines. Sociology has often felt particularly hard-pressed in this regard – especially when natural scientists are characteristically less hesitant about discussing social matters than sociologists are about engaging with the natural.[7] However, and as this book will argue, such a division of labour becomes profoundly problematic when confronting environmental questions. Certainly, the ambitious argument for an environmental sociology suggests the need to transcend rather than be constrained by established intellectual and disciplinary boundaries – even if, as we will suggest, this has significant implications for the discipline as a whole.

Linked to the conventional 'ring-fencing of the social', there has very often been a sense within orthodox sociological accounts that the natural no longer has major significance within everyday social life. Weber, for example, in his discussion of 'rationalization' as the characteristic trend of modernity,[8] considers the possible emancipation of human beings: 'from the cycle of the old, simple and organic existence of the peasant' (in Gerth and Mills 1993, p. 346).

For Weber, rationalization brought its own problems – but the distinction between the 'modern' and the 'organic' world is very apparent (and has echoed since throughout social theory). Indeed, many early sociologists were specifically driven to contrast pre-modern social structures (where natural constraints had a profound effect on everyday life) with modern social life (which had progressed beyond such natural constraints). The very notion of a transition (in Tönnies's well-known formulation[9]) from *gemeinschaft* (the old and traditional order) to *gesellschaft* (the modern way of life) is hinged upon this notion of a fundamental change in relations between the social and the natural.

At the beginning of the twenty-first century, the notion of the 'transcendence of the social over the natural' seems less straightforward both in social and environmental terms – as some contemporary sociologists such as Beck (1992) have argued. In other words, both the intellectual development of the discipline and a wider sense of 'environmental crisis' are necessitating a reconsideration of the basic social–natural divide upon which sociology has been founded.

Nevertheless, and as was briefly suggested in the Preface, the existence of this division does not necessarily render the sociological heritage irrelevant to the task at hand. Instead, there is much that can be retrieved from this tradition. Thus, it may be true that Marxist thinking has typically focused on the social conditions of capitalism rather than on the significance of relations between the social and natural. In this, sociological thinking may well have been reflecting the abiding concerns of its historical period of conception:

> [T]he classical social theorists were historically late enough to witness not simply the escape of modern societies from their organic constraints, but also their dynamic capacity to transform the natural world. . . . Yet they were too early to register fully the implications of those transformations; far from transcending ecological constraints, modern societies were rapidly acquiring new ones of their own making. (Goldblatt 1996, p. 5)

However, Marx had much to say about the appalling health and safety conditions experienced by workers in the nineteenth century (1976, ch. 10). Equally, Engels wrote powerfully about the squalor of working-class housing in industrial cities such as Salford and Manchester (1968). Marx and Engels also made reference to the negative impact of capitalism on natural resources and the urban environment. Goldblatt suggests that these were 'at best illuminating asides rather than core areas of concern or investigation' (1996, p. 5). Nevertheless, as we will see, Peter Dickens has developed (and criticized) ideas taken from Marx and Engels in order to suggest a 'green social theory' that draws upon 'critical realism'.[10]

There seems considerable further scope for such development of established social theory. Weberian notions of 'disenchantment' have implications for understanding current notions of an 'environmental crisis' – and not least in terms of the intimate connection between 'crisis' and the character of modernity. So far, however, relatively little sociological attention (with notable exceptions such as Goldblatt, Dickens and Benton) has been devoted to the task of recasting and reworking classical social theory.

In making such general arguments, it must also be considered that the conventional sociological separation of the social and natural may be due not only to reasons of sociological imperialism (i.e. in order to establish a distinct base for the discipline) or historical contingency (since these issues were simply not on the intellectual agenda), but also to the possibly constraining effects of many arguments concerning the natural on sociological thinking. Thus, and as Mary Douglas (1977) has suggested, nature is often evoked as a powerful justification for established customs and modes of behaviour: boys (it used to be argued) are naturally aggressive, while girls are just as naturally neat and compliant; certain 'races' (defined again as if these were naturally given) are naturally intelligent/hard-working/dominant; it is natural for society to be divided into rich and poor. Significantly, a reification of the natural and an emphasis on its significance for the organization of social life has been central to fascist thought. As Mark Neocleous expresses this: 'The Nazi "blood and soil" doctrine, for example, is suggestive of an intimate connection between the blood of the people (nation) and the soil of the land (culture), expressing the unity of a racial people and its land' (1997, p. 76). In this way, there can indeed be a 'green thread' running through fascist ideology.[11]

One of the prime challenges for the sociological imagination has been to attack such claims to the natural and to identify their social roots (in, for example, prevailing notions of 'race' or gender). Feminist scholarship has been especially influential in its general opposition to the argument that gender inequality can simply be explained by reference to 'natural differences' between men and women (Buckingham-Hatfield 2000). Sociological thinking, therefore, has generally been dismissive of the natural – or, rather, it recognizes its power within everyday discourse but characteristically aims to uncover its social roots. Certainly, an essential feature of any sociological training is to encourage scepticism every time the phrase 'it's only natural' is used as justification for an argument or course of action.

These sociological challenges to natural claims have inspired significant developments in the discipline. However, such an approach can also lead to a characteristic awkwardness in addressing, for example, questions of our biological rather than social beings. Rather than viewing such factors as being in interaction with one another, the tendency for sociologists has been to keep them firmly apart and to maintain a focus on the social dimension.[12] In this way, questions of the natural have been set aside from the main business of sociology – for disciplinary and, at times, ideological reasons.

In the particular case of the natural environment, the division of labour between the social and natural sciences appears especially fixed. The natural has been debunked in areas of life that sociologists have predetermined as social (e.g. with regard to gender or racial stereotypes) but left unchallenged with regard to what is still seen as the 'natural world' – presumably on the grounds that the judgements of natural scientists are value-free and asocial in character. As Dickens outlines the situation:

> We have a dichotomous understanding, one based on science, the other on social theory. So, while social theory can certainly continue to make major contributions, the danger is that it will do so within its comparatively watertight disciplinary compartments. Much the same could be said of the sciences. (1992, p. 2)

It is possible to detect not only a dichotomous understanding but also a characteristic *sociological inconsistency* in this treatment of the natural world.

It is here that more recent sociological accounts (of the kind discussed in the next section of this chapter) are of particular value in more systematically challenging the dichotomy between 'science' and 'social science' – and the distinction between the social and natural upon which this dichotomy depends. Thus, rather than separating scientific from sociological accounts as if these were simply given, it becomes relevant to examine their interaction and mutual dependence. Accordingly, we will consider theoretical accounts – and notably the sociology of scientific knowledge and notions of the 'risk society' – which together suggest that it may no longer be possible to separate either the social from the natural or the sociological from the scientific (as a variety of writers from perspectives as different as Beck 1992, Dickens 1992, Haraway 1991 and Latour 1992 now argue). The collapse of such established dualities also has important consequences for our understanding of the environmental crisis.

Such an interim conclusion suggests an ambitious path for the sociological study of the environment. Along the way, we will need to reconsider our sense not only of the natural but also of what it means to use the term 'social'. Both are likely to be changed by a study of their interaction. In this, we will also be moving beyond the kind of environmental sociology that simply calls for society and nature to be seen as interconnected. Instead, we will be taking a closer and more sceptical look at the dynamic and changing construction (what we will term *co-construction*) of these categories.

Elements of an Environmental Sociology

Now that the main characteristics of the historical relationship between sociology and the environment have been briefly sketched out, the second section of the Introduction presents some central topics for analysis and discussion. These include questions of epistemology, social theory, the operation of social institutions and, very importantly, the relationship between the social and the natural. Taken together, these questions reinforce the point that what is needed is not simply the further application of existing sociological understanding (what can be presented as a 'sociology of the environment' approach) but a more radical reassessment of the discipline and its treatment of the natural environment ('environmental sociology'). Rather than simply dusting off the 'sociological toolkit' and applying it to a new set of problems, a fresh perspective is required.

Three contemporary sources of inspiration for such a sociological treatment are presented: the concept of 'sustainable development', theories of the 'risk society', and emergent work within science and technology studies and the sociology of scientific knowledge. These provide the focus for the next three chapters of this book. Before this, however, it is important for us to consider four sociological interpretations of what it means to conduct environmental sociology – all of which have tried to move beyond the disciplinary constraints presented so far. Crucially, each of these tackles the question of how we should understand the relationship between the social and the natural (and hence the relationship between sociology and the environment). As presented here, these interpretations are: the call for a new ecological paradigm, critical realism, the social construction of environmental problems, the concept of social nature. Discussions between these four interpretations of environmental sociology provide important conceptual background to the rest of this book and locate subsequent discussions in their contemporary sociological context. Finally, this section indicates the book's intention to move beyond the entrenched sociological debate over whether the natural world is either real or constructed.

It follows from these introductory comments that issues of the environment pose a fundamental challenge for sociology and its theoretical foundations. Incorporating the environment within sociological discussion means reassessing the whole relationship between the social and the natural and the disciplinary structure that has been built upon this. As Benton puts it succinctly: 'The really difficult problems only *start* here' (1994, p. 29; italics in original).

Expressed like this, the attempt to provide a critical introduction to the relationship between sociology and the environment seems daunting for both the reader and the author. How can we possibly get started on such a journey? Do we have any idea what an environmental sociology would resemble? Of course, it would be easier if this book limited itself to a discussion of environmental issues and their social dimensions. It is not difficult, for example, to suggest that environmental change might have major social consequences and to consider the possible character of these. Equally, various aspects of the natural environment can be considered in terms of their relationship to established social theory.[13]

This important but inherently less ambitious 'sociology of the environment' suggests an interesting pathway but misses the most challenging and rewarding sections of the route. Instead, I will suggest a more ambitious road towards an environmental sociology that addresses foundational matters of the discipline as well as significant but applied matters. In so doing, we should be presented with fresh sociological insights but also a better understanding of how to deal practically with matters of environmental policy. Specifically, the strong case for an environmental sociology raises questions that take us to the heart of the discipline, including:

- matters of *epistemology*: how do we come to 'know' about environmental problems? what constraints are there on our environmental knowledges?
- *social theory*: how can environmental issues inform – and be informed by – the classical themes considered so far and also more recent areas of theoretical debate?
- *social institutions and institutional practices*: what can we learn from this area of inquiry concerning the capacity of existing institutions – whether in the public or private domain – to cope with emerging social and political challenges?
- crucially, the relationship between the *social and the natural*: how should sociology deal with problems, questions and concerns that are presented as either 'natural' or 'social' in character? The following chapters present this relationship as fundamental to the disciplinary engagement with environmental issues and concerns.

A number of recent developments in sociological understanding and in public debate provide an important stimulus for what is to follow in terms of the treatment of the social–natural relationship – and together suggest the need for a more radical approach than that implied by the development of another 'sociology *of*'. These again will be discussed in greater detail as we proceed. For now, let me simply introduce some of those that have been especially significant in shaping the ensuing discussion – and with which the first three chapters of this book will commence.

A major stimulus to environmental sociology is provided by the contemporary experience of environmental concerns – and particularly the complexity and controversy that surround environmental issues. It seems – especially given the scale of possible harm and the level of social change being called for – that this is not just 'business as usual'. National and international disagreements over, for example, acid rain or global warming strongly imply the need for fresh social scientific insights. As chapter 1 discusses, environmental action represents a major challenge to existing institutions and methods of decision-making. This challenge seems far from trivial in social scientific terms. It indicates instead the need for revised patterns of national and international collaboration, new industrial practices, changing citizen behaviour and the development of new environmental values.

Specifically, since the 1980s the international debate over *sustainable development* has had a major effect on environmental awareness and action. However, and as Wolfgang Sachs has argued, sustainability extends far beyond the technicalities of environmental action: '"Sustainable development" is the late twentieth-century expression for "progress". It extends the long-standing hope for universal social improvement into an era faced with a divided world and a finite nature' (1997, p. 71). The language of sustainability, therefore, emphasizes social–natural relations even if, as we will see, it characteristically places these within a rather rigid framework.

Such themes of progress and social improvement lead us directly to a recent body of sociological writing which explicitly links contemporary risk discussions with the changing structure of modernity. For Ulrich Beck, we are now entering the *risk society*, where problems of environmental damage and physical safety have assumed the status formerly granted to social class. Environmental divisions in society are now at least as significant as matters of material or social inequality. Very importantly, Beck (1992) stresses that the social transformation into 'late modernity' is not simply a question of increased risk but rather of our heightened awareness of such physical threats. The risk society thesis suggests a close interconnection between environmental awareness and our declining confidence in modernity and its institutions. This argument, and the issues it raises concerning the link between social and environmental change, represent an important stimulus to a thoroughgoing environmental sociology. In particular, Beck's work offers an approach to risk and the environment that goes far beyond the mere application of existing social theory. Instead, it provokes discussion about the inseparability of the social and the natural within the late-modern world. As such, it embeds risk and environmental matters deep in the mainstream of sociological thinking – and in a manner so far unparalleled.

One important question to emerge from Beck's account of the late-modern transformation concerns the status of science within environmental debates. He suggests that a major stimulus to environmental concern is precisely a loss of faith that science can provide environmental solutions. Rather than necessarily serving as our environmental saviour, science is intimately connected to the modernistic assumptions of control that have created environmental collapse. This suggests that environmental sociology must centrally consider the character of scientific knowledge and its contribution to environmental concerns.

This aim is substantially assisted by the emergence over the last twenty-five years of a *sociology of scientific knowledge* that has taken a challenging – and necessarily critical – look at the development and validation of science. Typically, this perspective has built upon careful empirical research to explore the social processes that lead to the emergence of facts and theories about the natural world. Such research suggests that science has had a particularly problematic relationship with matters of risk and environmental threat – where controversy and uncertainty have often been very apparent.

Work in the sociology of scientific knowledge (and, more generally, in science and technology studies) has not assumed that the facts of environmental issues simply speak for themselves. Instead, the emphasis has been on how environmental phenomena are constructed by scientists and on the ways in which claims to environmental knowledge are developed and maintained. Going further, research in this area has considered the kinds of environmental knowledge possessed by non-expert groups – environmental campaigners, local people, citizen coalitions – and the relationship between this form of knowledge and the understandings of science.

These approaches to expert and non-expert (or 'lay') environmental knowledges suggest a fresh sociological perspective on environmental issues. In particular, environmental knowledge becomes a central topic for sociological analysis: what counts as 'knowledge' in such situations? How are knowledge claims constructed and defended? Rather than simply assuming that science can present us with an objective view of the natural world, the technical definition of environmental issues becomes an essential constituent of environmental sociology.

Already, we can identify new questions and potentially illuminating perspectives within sociology and the natural environment. However, it is also important that we take stock of the recent literature that has directly attempted to build up a systematic and progressive approach to environmental sociology.

Revisiting the Sociological Heritage: Contemporary Debates over the Social and the Natural

Insofar as academia is capable of having a stand-up row, it is over this issue that sociology has become most heated. (Dickens 1996, p. 72)

As has already been emphasized, questions of the social and the natural lie at the very heart of the relationship between sociology and the environment. As we have also seen, sociology's focus on the realm of the social – on the explanation in Durkheimian terms of social phenomena by other 'social facts' – and refusal to accept the full significance of the natural within social life has held back the development of a thoroughgoing environmental sociology. However, this observation – which is now accepted by most sociologists working in this domain – raises once again the social–natural relationship that is central to this book. How can the discipline move on in specific terms? Put more formally, *how should we theorize the relationship between the social and the natural within environmental problems, issues and concerns?* As a basis for future discussion and empirical study, this section takes a closer look at four important positions and perspectives within contemporary sociology.

Before embarking upon these, it is worth pausing to emphasize one key sociological debate over the social–natural relationship: that between realism and constructivism. Put in starkly polarized fashion (which, as I will later suggest, is *not* the most appropriate formulation), should we consider the environment to be external to social life (as 'objective reality') or is it constructed by social relationships and forms of understanding (and in that way should be seen as a social construction)? 'Constructivism' (or 'constructionism' as it is sometimes termed) in this context indicates a sociological approach that is broadly agnostic concerning truth claims about the environment, but instead considers how (and what) we claim to 'know' about the natural world and how we invest meaning in the settings in which we live. In that way, the very manner in which the natural world becomes defined and analysed represents an important focus for sociological attention.

Expressed very crudely, 'realists' have been critical of what they sometimes represent as the empty and misplaced theorizing of constructivists. Equally, the realist charge has been that by undermining the reality of environmental problems, constructivists fail to develop an adequate analytical framework, and ultimately deny the separate existence of the natural from the social. Constructivists have suggested in response that realist approaches miss out on one of the most important aspects of environmental debate: the manner in which particular issues rise to prominence and are seen to be 'real'. Constructivists also argue that their accounts bring more rather than less 'reality' to environmental problems – and especially in terms of the social and institutional processes that lead to their emergence.

Environmental debates are certainly not unique in raising such matters. There are strong parallels, for example, in contemporary feminist debates: is gender 'given' or is it constructed and shaped within everyday life? However, the intention in this book is to avoid the sterility of arguments that suggest *either* that the environment must be a 'real' problem *or* that it is a social construction. Whilst the former (extremely crude) form of realism suggests that environmental problems simply impact upon society, the latter (equally crude) form of constructivism suggests that the planet on which we live has no material status. As the following chapters argue, neither of these positions seems especially productive in sociological terms. Instead, each seems to lead to an ultimately irresolvable and unproductive debate. Whilst this book unashamedly draws especially on the constructivist sociological tradition, it does so in a self-critical fashion and in a spirit of renewal.

Specifically, I will argue that neither the natural nor the social can be given paramount status but that instead a process of *co-construction* needs to be recognized and explored. In this way, we will avoid both objectification of the natural world and social relativism. Before getting further into these points, however, we need to review the main elements of the realist-constructivist debate as it has taken place so far.

Catton and Dunlap: the case for a 'new ecological paradigm'
One of the most significant statements of the need for an 'environmental sociology' came from the US sociologists Catton and Dunlap. Writing in 1978, they defined this field as 'the study of the interaction between the environment and society' (cited in Dunlap 1997, p. 21). As Dunlap subsequently described their overall stance: 'We ... contended that examining such interaction would require overcoming sociology's traditional and deep-seated reluctance to acknowledge the relevance of the physical environment for understanding contemporary societies' (ibid.). The call was therefore an ambitious one for nothing less than a paradigmatic revolution in sociology. As the authors expressed this (Catton and Dunlap 1980), the human exceptionalist paradigm within the discipline must be replaced with the new ecological paradigm. The human exceptionalist (later renamed 'human exemptionalist') paradigm assumes that people are fundamentally different from other creatures, that they can determine their own destinies and that there are no constraints on human society. Catton and Dunlap were not denying that human beings possess exceptional characteristics, but were rejecting the proposition that these exempted our species from ecological constraints.

The new ecological (or 'environmental') paradigm, meanwhile, presents human beings as just one part of a larger ecosystem and considers that human affairs are influenced by nature as well as society. Equally, the biophysical environment sets material limits to human action.

As Martell observes, Catton and Dunlap were basically presenting a 'call to arms' for a broadly ecological sociology. They put it as follows in 1978: 'the necessary research will only be done by minds that have freed themselves from the obsolescent world view and disciplinary traditions' (cited in Martell, p. 171).

In making this claim for a new ecological (or environmental) paradigm, Catton and Dunlap were hoping to facilitate a sociological approach that would consider the impact of, for example, resource issues on society (in other words, the impact of the natural upon the social) and also the opposing relationship: how social processes affect the natural world around us. The now familiar criticism being made of mainstream sociological studies was that they do not accept the significance of environmental variables within sociological study. Instead, Catton and Dunlap advocated an analytical framework, which gave due emphasis to categories such as population, technology and environment. Once one moves beyond an 'exemptionalist' paradigm and recognizes the intimate link between people and the natural world, the relevance of the physical environment to humans can be fully recognized. In so doing, sociologists must acknowledge not just that 'human activities are causing a deterioration in the quality of the environment' but also that 'environmental deterioration in turn has negative impacts on people' (Dunlap 1997, p. 27).

Critical realism and the greening of social theory

Peter Dickens began his 1992 discussion of *Society and Nature* with a summary of Catton and Dunlap's plea for a 'new ecological paradigm for a post exuberant sociology'. He observed: 'Unfortunately . . . Catton and Dunlap did not provide a clear picture of what this paradigm might look like. And it is probably true to say that, despite increasing concern with environmental and ecological issues, social theory has still not adequately responded to Catton and Dunlap's challenge' (1992, p. xiii). Dickens's response to the challenge – along with authors such as Benton and Martell – has been to advocate 'critical realism' within the sociological interpretation of environmental problems. In offering this particular theorization of the social–natural relationship, Dickens claims to be offering a more solid analytical basis for the 'new ecological paradigm' and certainly a more developed perspective. Drawing upon Marx and Engels's dialectic mode of analysis, critical realism argues for the existence of 'relatively enduring generative structures' which 'underlie the manifest phenomena of everyday life' (Dickens 1992, p. xv)

Simply put, realism (in line with Catton and Dunlap's appeal) emphasizes the importance of the natural within social life and views nature as possessing independent powers. However, and as critical realists stress, 'nature' cannot directly speak to 'society'. Instead, natural processes must be identified, defined and measured by human beings. In that way – and at least to some extent – the natural is mediated through society (and particularly through the institutions of science). Martell (1994) has succinctly summarized this position in terms of four key points:

1. *Dialectics and realism*: drawing upon Marxist theory, Dickens presents the relationship between society and nature as mutually constitutive but with independent objective potentialities.
2. *Stratified knowledges*: entities in the world are not observable in some unmediated fashion. As Dickens put it, 'All concepts have evolved from human societies. Therefore all knowledge must in some sense be a social construction. No knowledge has fallen out

of the sky with a label attached pronouncing "absolute truth"' (1996, p. 71). Very importantly, however, acknowledgement of the social construction of knowledge does not mean that knowledge is *only* socially constituted. Objects have real characteristics and tendencies – even if humans are obliged to discern these through the variable interpretation of observable phenomena. In that way, critical realism adds a theoretical depth to Catton and Dunlap's call for an environmental sociology that explicitly recognizes social–natural relations. As Martell expresses his closely related position, 'I have argued for realism as a perspective which, unlike social constructionism, recognizes causal powers in nature but, unlike environmentalism, sees nature as mediated through social processes' (1994, p. 183).

3. *A unified science*: social theory and biological/ecological theory need to be brought together instead of, in Dickens's terms, 'consistently talking past each other' (1992, p. 18). The simple dichotomy between 'science' and 'social science' needs to be relaxed – with important consequences for sociology but also for disciplines such as biology and physics.

4. *The early Marx*: Dickens builds his analysis upon Marx's dialectical method and claims that 'Marx and Engels are arguably the only writers to have developed a science of the kind that is now needed for an adequate understanding of environmental issues' (ibid., p. xiv). Among the main themes he develops are that:

> Nature is integral to people's bodies. There is therefore no logical way in which nature can be treated as separate from people . . .
>
> Nature is socially constructed. It is always modified by people. And, in the process of changing nature, people change themselves . . .
>
> Under capitalism, nature is privately owned and exploited. People therefore find themselves becoming alienated or estranged from the nature on which they work. They also become alienated from their own species. (ibid., p. xiv)

Critical realism, therefore, aims to explore the complex relationships between, on the one hand, the 'causal powers of nature and the material processes involved in those powers' (Dickens 1996, p. 83) and, on the other, the 'particular ways in which people communicate to one another about those powers and processes' (ibid.). In making this distinction, a limited form of social construction is granted, since nature does not have a voice of its own. Such an approach can be seen as a distinctively sociological response to Catton and Dunlap's

call to arms – and one that does not confine itself to the exemptionalist paradigm.

The social construction of environmental problems
As has been suggested, the challenge to recognize the power and significance of the natural within social life has provoked a discussion
over how this relationship should be theorized and interpreted.
Whilst Catton and Dunlap's call seems initially straightforward, critical realists such as Dickens have opened up to inquiry the precise
relationship that should exist between an independent nature and the
constructions of nature developed within societies. In so doing, critical realism grants a significance to the social construction of natural
knowledge but is careful to argue that this does not deny the existence of an objective natural world. As Dickens expresses this: 'the
fact that knowledge is socially constituted does not entail that knowledge is *only* socially constituted. In other words, there exist powers
and mechanisms in society which are not simply a product of language and discourse' (1996, p. 72).

At this point, we turn to a sociological perspective, which explicitly styles itself as 'social constructivist' (or, depending on the
author's preference, 'social constructionist' – we will treat these terms
as identical in meaning). As an illustration of a 'social problems'
approach to social constructivism/constructionism, we can look at
John Hannigan's 1995 book, *Environmental Sociology*.

For Hannigan, what 'constructionist analysis has in common is
a concern with how people assign meaning to their world' (1995,
p. 33). Central to this 'social problems' approach is the insight that
environmental problems do not just materialize by themselves. Environmental concern varies over time. Certain problems are seen to be
more pressing than others at particular points. In order to get onto
both a personal and an institutional agenda, such problems must be
'constructed'. Someone needs to persuade others that the problem
in question deserves particular attention and that something must
be done. In this general way, and although there are certain unique
features to environmental problems, they have much in common
with other social problems – for example, child abuse, homelessness,
HIV/AIDS or juvenile crime: 'From a sociological point of view, the
chief task here is to understand why certain conditions come to be
perceived as problematic and how those who register this "claim"
command political attention in their quest to do something' (ibid.,
pp. 2–3). According to this approach, the 'successful' construction of
an environmental problem requires six factors:

- scientific 'authority for and validation of claims';
- the 'existence of "popularisers" who can bridge environmental-ism and science';
- media 'attention in which the problem is "framed" as novel and important';
- the dramatization of the problem 'in symbolic and visual terms';
- economic 'incentives for taking positive action';
- the emergence of an 'institutional sponsor who can ensure both legitimacy and continuity'. (ibid., p. 55)

Presented in this way, environmental issues are not just 'facts about nature'. Instead, their emergence depends upon successful *claims-making*. In sociological terms, it is less important to inquire how real a problem is than to explore the processes whereby certain problems come to acquire 'real' status at particular moments and in particular contexts. At this point, the difference (at least in terms of emphasis) between Hannigan's approach and that taken by Dickens should be clear. Typically, this process of the social construction of an environ-mental problem will involve pressure-group activities, scientific state-ments, governmental actors, media accounts and public evaluations. Central to sociological investigation will be the processes whereby environmental conditions are assembled, presented and contested (Hannigan 1995, pp. 41–52).

To take the example of international action on acid rain, *assem-bling the claim* involved the scientific community but also Swedish government officials and articles in the press. All of these were impor-tant in building public awareness and, crucially, distinguishing acid rain from wider air pollution problems. *Presenting the claim* involved 'framing' the environmental problem in 'dramatic, even apocalyptic' terms – a process helped by the phrase 'acid rain' itself, but also images of 'dying' lakes and forests. Such a claim was then vigorously *contested*, since the evidence was partial and circumstantial rather than conclusive (a common characteristic of environmental prob-lems). As Hannigan summarizes this sociological framework: 'What is ultimately most significant here is the process through which envi-ronmental claims-makers influence those who hold the reins of power to recognise definitions of environmental problems, to implement them and to accept responsibility for their solution' (ibid., p. 185). However, it is important to emphasize that Hannigan is not denying the reality of environmental problems. He explicitly rejects an 'extreme constructionist position' (often presented as 'radical' – or 'strong' – relativism). The position instead is that both real and imagi-nary problems need to be socially constructed if they are to find a place on the environmental agenda. For the sociologist, engaging in discussion over the reality of problems is less useful (and less relevant) than exploring the processes of their social construction. Whilst both the environmental problems and critical realist approaches acknowledge the existence of a natural world, the key difference at this level lies in the degree of sociological significance they attach to this.

Constructivist perspectives on 'social nature'

The fourth category of contemporary research into relations of the social and the natural incorporates wider perspectives, which relate broadly to the constructivist tradition but which aim to avoid the familiar social–natural dichotomy (and hence portray themselves as transcending the realist–constructivist debate). As the 1998 collection, *Remaking Reality*, presents it, we are now dealing with a 'social nature' that is 'ordered up, manipulated and constructed, as well as animate, unpredictable and consequential' (Braun and Castree 1998, p. xi). Rather than attempting to maintain a nature–society duality, the interdisciplinary contributors (who include geographers, an anthropologist and an environmental psychologist as well as two sociologists) seek to explore the manner in which nature (or natures) has become the focal point for a 'nexus of political-economic relations, social identities, cultural orderings, and political aspirations of all kinds' (Castree and Braun 1998, p. 5). Instead of presenting a nature–society split, this perspective emphasizes the extent to which such categories are continuously constituted through one other. It follows from this perspective that nature cannot just be singular: we are dealing with a range of different constructions and meanings rather than a simple objective reality. Nature cannot be separated from culture and, more specifically, it cannot be separated from cultural struggles and differing cultural understandings:

> Nature is multiple; its social production proceeds according to no single temporality, occurs with no one underlying logic, follows no unified plan. Accordingly, struggles over the social production of nature are multifaceted; they occur at various levels, involve a large cast of actors (not all of which are human), and follow a plurality of social and ecological logics that cannot be reduced to a single story. (ibid., p. 34)

Macnaghten and Urry make a closely related argument in their book *Contested Natures*: '[T]here is no singular "nature" as such, only a diversity of contested natures; and . . . each such nature is constituted through a variety of socio-cultural processes from which such natures cannot be plausibly separated' (1998, p. 1). This account explicitly rejects the 'doctrine of environmental realism' and its notion that modern rational science can understand the environment in such a way as to 'transcend the more superficial and transitory patterns of everyday life' (ibid., p. 1). Instead, Macnaghten and Urry emphasize the significance of specific *social practices* that 'produce, reproduce and transform different natures and different values' (ibid., p. 2). Such practices embody forms of knowledge and understanding and possess a number of 'constitutive principles'. These practices are discursively ordered, embodied, spaced, timed, and involve models of human activity, risk, agency and trust.

In one illustration of this approach, Macnaghten and Urry explore the social production of the English countryside during the eighteenth century and its relationship to the changing pattern of industrialized society – including rural depopulation and the increasing power of the rural landowning class to shape the landscape. New forms of leisure activity emerged – especially hunting, shooting and fishing – and a fashion developed for touring the English countryside and visiting ostentatious country houses. By contrast, urban environments were portrayed as 'unnatural' and contaminated: 'So while the countryside came increasingly to be desired because of its visual qualities mediated through the representation of space via the notion of landscape, the industrial town was seen as thoroughly polluted, as unnaturally invading all the human orifices' (ibid., p. 175). Presented in this way, 'nature' is not external to social life and practices but inextricably entangled with it. Rather than attempting to separate nature (as defined by scientific institutions) from society (as we experience it within everyday life) and then seeking to examine their interaction, this approach views the apparently natural world as the outcome of particular social contexts and cultural understandings. In so doing, we move beyond a 'social problems' perspective and into a more complex presentation of everyday social practices and their reconstructions of the natural. There is no singular nature for claims-makers to select from, but rather a plurality of natures embedded in daily life.

According to this constructivist perspective on the social–natural, there is indeed no 'nature' that can be separated from the cultural settings and webs of meaning that define and give it significance. As the social historian Simon Schama puts it: 'Instead of assuming the mutually exclusive character of Western culture and nature, I want to suggest the strength of the links that have bound them together' (1995, p. 14). In Schama's terms, our whole appreciation of landscapes and wilderness is inseparable from 'nature myths' and 'social memories'. Whilst we may conventionally present the workings of human perception and human imagination as quite separate from the natural environment, the argument is that 'landscape is the work of the mind. Its scenery is built up as much from strata of memory as from layers of rock' (ibid., p. 7). We do not simply observe raw nature in a cultural vacuum. Whether gazing at the Yosemite Valley, the English Lake District or Central Park (or, we might add, an urban housing project or an industrial wasteland), our view is framed by our own expectations, myths and social prejudices. To take one of Schama's examples:

> Central Park was always supposed to answer to both arcadian myths that have survived in the modern memory: the wild and the cultivated; the place of unpredictable exhilaration and the place of bucolic rest. . . . The woods and trails of Upper Manhattan are certainly not the only lair where ancient myths and demons, best forgotten . . . have returned to haunt the modern polis. (ibid., p. 570)

Discussion

Whilst this section has presented the main points of the realist–constructivist debate in environmental sociology, it probably has not brought out the heat of these exchanges. For realist critics, constructivism is inadequate in analytical terms since it cannot offer a coherent distinction between the social and the natural but instead wilfully blurs these categories. It also risks denying the existence of environmental problems and hence leads to a non-engagement with environmental concern and what has been termed 'environmental quietism'. In that way, constructivism (at least of the 'radical' kind) is seen as incompatible with environmentalism – and indeed could be used to undermine strong environmentalist claims for the protection of the natural world.

In response, constructivism fiercely defends the merits of its conceptual stance and denies the charge of quietism. Whilst a constructivist stance might indicate the need for great caution when claiming to 'speak for nature' (since knowledge claims are characteristically represented as partial, heterogeneous, contested and conditional social judgements), this reflexive awareness does not necessarily deny the possibility of environmental intervention. Instead, it can be argued that constructivism opens up the cultural choices, economic judgements and ethical assumptions at the heart of environmental decision-making.

Rather than attempt to resolve this discussion in general and abstract terms, the following chapters will consider these contrasting perspectives as they have been developed in environmental practice and particular sociological and institutional frameworks: including those of sustainable development and regulatory responses to environmental problems. In this way also, this book will keep its promise of interpreting abstracted theoretical debates through empirical cases and examples. As noted earlier, the debate over whether nature is real or constructed may be unresolvable in abstract terms – and may well have become unproductive in sociological terms. Much of the discussion in this book will be devoted to fresh perspectives and new possibilities.

Overview and Book Structure

Finally, I offer a specific guide to the remaining chapters. As should be quite clear by now, we will explore the relationship between sociology and environmental issues in both disciplinary and practical terms. In so doing, the aim is to encourage engagement and debate – and, specifically, to suggest an open-minded and inclusive approach to the environment that does not endlessly re-create the social–natural duality. One central element within this approach is the treatment of environmental questions not just at the general and abstract level but also in terms of more particular processes, contexts and challenges (including public responses, questions of institutional policy-making and governance, technology and innovation). Very importantly, chapters 4–6 should not be seen as conventional surveys and case-studies or applications of established theory. Instead, they represent an attempt to explore the embedded and contextualized character of environmental practices.

Rather than keeping to the conventional sociological format of beginning with a theme or issue and then developing a review illustrated by case-studies, this book purposefully adopts a more grounded approach. In that way, it aims both to consider areas of significant theoretical debate (for example, over late modernity and the sociology of scientific knowledge) and to develop these ideas through the closer analysis of public, institutional and technological practice. My argument is that this allows a more revealing exploration of society, nature and knowledge than can be gleaned from general 'theory first' discussion alone. Crucially, a closer inspection of specific forms of environmental practice allows us to step beyond the crude social–natural division. Whilst it may be possible to maintain a simple dichotomized approach at an abstracted level, such a dichotomy crumbles when confronted with the hybrid and co-constructed character of social and environmental processes and practices.

Sociology and the Environment is not yet another book that attempts to summarize the scale of environmental problems, nor does it offer an overview of 'environmental issues'. Equally, this book does not work consistently through all the substantive topics that might be covered by 'sociology and the environment'. In what follows, the aim instead will be to develop a broader sense of new conceptual possibilities for an environmental sociology (specifically regarding questions of the social and natural) and also of the potential sociological contribution to our understanding of environmental issues. Whilst social theory can bring new perspectives and ways of thinking, it will also be important to consider how it might itself be transformed as a consequence of environmental engagement. At the same time, it will be necessary to address the policy and practical implications of sociological analysis – not least because 'environmental practice' cannot be separated from 'environmental understanding'.

The first three chapters develop the sociological analysis of these issues by focusing on the three areas of current social and environmental debate that have already been briefly presented: the notion of 'sustainable development'; arguments initiated by contemporary sociologists (and notably Beck) over the 'risk society'; and the central question of 'environmental knowledge' and the sociology of scientific knowledge. In this way, we will explore three important frameworks for the construction of social–natural relations.

We then move on to consider a number of more specific topics, including communities at risk, the nature of environmental policy-making and the relationship between technology and the environment. These topics will allow us to explore the relationship between society, nature and knowledge in greater depth.

Looking at this structure a little more closely, chapter 1 begins with the challenge of sustainability and, more particularly, debates over one of the more problematic – and yet most-used – terms within contemporary environmentalism: 'sustainable development'. The definition of 'sustainability' is slippery indeed and certain commentators have suggested that the concept owes its widespread appeal to this flexibility of interpretation. Rather than attempting to impose a definition, our intention will be to explore the challenges and contradictions of contemporary environmental debate. How has 'sustainability talk' managed to construct an apparent unity out of a divergent set of environmental voices? More particularly, we will consider the implications for sociology of this framing of social–environmental relations.

At first glance, it might appear eccentric for such an ambitious sociological discussion to begin with a *policy*-oriented debate. Surely sociologists should keep themselves to more established territory such as the growth of environmental politics or the history of environmental philosophy? Rather than beginning at a grand level of abstraction, my argument is that it is necessary to adopt a more specific and a more contemporary approach. Chapter 1, therefore, aims to explore the characteristic assumptions and institutional practices that frame current environmental discussions. In selecting sustainable development as a starting-point, I am aware that this will be a relatively familiar topic to some readers but one that, in my experience, is very unfamiliar to many sociologists. Chapter 1 aims to bring together descriptive material and sociological analysis in order to offer something new to both audiences. Equally, the argument is that sociological discussion indeed needs to be situated in current environmental and institutional debate rather than, as is more typical, selecting such topics as seem appropriate to the sociological tool kit.

So as to gain greater critical distance on the sustainability 'framing' of environmental discussions, chapter 2 takes us to a contrasting, and explicitly sociological, framework for environmental understanding. Rather than suggesting ways in which current global institutions can cope with environmental concerns, the 'risk society' thesis argues that modernistic institutions serve only to increase problems. Accordingly, environmental issues both raise and are raised by a set of deep-rooted social concerns over relations of knowledge, risk and trust.

Sociologists have identified structural changes within the current condition of modernity. Matters of risk and environmental concern cannot be dismissed as the mere side-effects of social progress but instead suggest profound questions for the very direction of modernity and its institutions. As with the discussion of sustainable development, we will need to maintain a critical perspective on what counts as 'knowledge' and on the relationship between the social and the natural within these theoretical discussions. Equally, it will be necessary to consider the implications of 'risk society' discussions for the wider relationship between sociology and the environment.

A third framework for sociological interpretation of social–natural relations is introduced in chapter 3. The sociology of scientific knowledge (SSK) not only challenges the 'naturalistic' (i.e. science-structured) agenda that generally dominates sociological analysis of environmental matters, but also deconstructs the conventional separation of the social from the natural. Once again, the definition of 'environmental knowledge' becomes an important area for sociological investigation – especially in a context where scientific knowledge claims seem to be increasingly characterized by uncertainty and indeterminacy. Such a perspective also has important consequences for our understanding of the wider relationship between sociology and the environment.

The SSK approach developed here leads away from generalized sociological claims about the social and the natural and towards an emphasis on the hybrid and co-constructed character of environmental issues and concerns. Rather than granting priority to either the social or the natural, we need to examine the particular construction of these categories within specific cultural, institutional and ecological settings.

One characteristic of discussions on sustainable development and the risk society is that they both attribute specific and important roles to public groups: as resources for local environmental action; as citizens of late modernity who embody the contradictions and uncertainties of our historical period. Meanwhile, the SSK-based approach outlined in chapter 3 has dealt with issues of environmental knowledge in the laboratory and in technical decision-making structures but has, until recently, said less about public assessments and lay reconstructions of environmental issues, problems and concerns.

In chapter 4, we consider two examples of the public interpretation of risk and the local environment. As we do so, we suggest the inherent limitations of sweeping sociological generalizations and also of institutional attempts to exhort the public to 'respond' in a specific manner to predetermined environmental problems. We also identify the close relationship between environmental and other concerns within the conditions of everyday life. Accordingly, this chapter emphasizes the importance of a *contextual* approach to the analysis of environmental concerns.

Chapter 5 develops this analysis further through the study of what may appear for many sociologists to be an unglamorous and 'applied' area: environmental decision-making and the establishment of environmental policy. On the one hand, it will be argued that this represents a crucial arena for the creation and resolution of environmental conflicts. On the other, and as with the previous discussion of 'environmental publics', we consider the construction of environmental problems within particular social and institutional settings. As the third of the cases in chapter 5 emphasizes especially, at the heart of what may appear to be universal regulatory systems are at work local negotiations and contextual variations. From a sociological perspective, this suggests that cultural assumptions and institutional choices lie at the core of what might otherwise appear technical and standardized procedures. In making this point, we can also suggest a potentially important practical role for sociological analysis within policy-making processes: namely, unravelling and identifying the human judgements upon which environmental action ultimately depends.

The third empirical treatment in this book takes us into another non-traditional area for sociological exploration: technology. Rather than simply abandoning this area of socio-technical activity to other disciplines, it is argued that conventional notions of technological determinism need to be replaced with a contextualized and grounded understanding of people's 'sense-making' activities. Zonabend's (1993) powerful study of those who live and work with the nuclear industry is drawn upon so as to argue that the technology in question is not simply given but is varyingly constructed and experienced. Whilst treatments of sustainability often assume that social and environmental impacts are inherent in technologies themselves, this chapter suggests the social and cultural processes through which impacts are constructed by different actors. In that way, the judgement of technical consequences is not simply given but will be actively interpreted in a manner commensurate with social and cultural understandings. Such understandings in the Zonabend case crucially include a sense of self-identity and local history.

Chapters 4, 5 and 6 might initially appear simply as an assortment of case-studies. Equally, they can be presented as a curious departure from what has become the staple fare of 'sociology of the environment' discussions. However, this appearance should not distract from the radical sociological agenda that is being suggested here. In different ways, these chapters explore the social, cultural and contextual judgements that lie at the heart of environmental problems and concerns. Whether in the case of public assessments, institutional decisions or technological consequences, the emphasis is on the development of a sociological approach that is both contextually grounded and alert to the hybrid nature of contemporary environmental practices. In this way, sociological analysis is not constrained – but rather challenged and provoked – by the established intellectual boundary between the social and the natural. Equally, this boundary will be presented as a shifting contextual construction and as itself a focus for empirical investigation.

Chapter 7 briefly refocuses and develops these empirical and theoretical discussions before addressing two key questions: how should we conceptualize the relationship between the social and the natural? and what does this mean for environmental policy and practice? At this point, we will return to the realist–constructivist debate and consider co-construction as a dual process of the social and the natural being varyingly defined with environmental discussions.

So what should the reader learn from the following chapters? Certainly, I hope that an improved grasp of the social significance of environmental issues will be developed. More than that, I want to convey a sense of the two-way relationship between sociology and the environment. Whilst sociological understanding can help us deal with environmental concerns, the environment as an issue can help us reconsider and enhance sociological theories and practices. As with so many journeys, the place from which we started can look very different when we eventually return. That in itself may be sufficient justification for the route ahead. Meanwhile, it is time to turn from this programmatic treatment and consider more closely sustainable development as a challenge both to social institutions and to sociological understanding.

1

Sustainability as Social Challenge

[I]n the end, sustainable development is not a fixed state of harmony, but rather a process of change in which the exploitation of resources, the direction of investments, the orientation of technological develop-ment, and institutional change are made consistent with future as well as present needs.

World Commission on Environment and Development 1987, p. 9

[S]imply giving something a name does not indicate that it can actually exist viably.

Yearley 1996, p. 131

Having devoted the Preface and Introduction to a discussion of explicitly sociological themes and issues, in this chapter I offer an apparent change of focus: the discourse of sustainable devel-opment. However, the point is not to get caught up in the detail of 'sustainability talk' nor to offer a definitive history of the concept. Instead, the invitation is to explore one important and contemporary 'framing' of environmental issues and to consider the particular construction of 'society, nature and knowledge' that it offers.

In addition to providing a general context to environmental discussion, this account of the social–natural relationship will serve as a foundation for discussion in the following chapters. It will be suggested that, whilst the agenda of sustainability opens up an important role for social scientific analysis, it does so within a simple realist model of the need to connect envi-ronmental problems (as defined by scientific institutions) with social challenges (especially those of social equity and of co-ordinated international action).

So far in this book, we have considered issues of sociology and the environment only at the most general of levels. In practice, and here we come to one of this book's main arguments, environmental questions and concerns are not represented to us (nor, indeed, by us) in such an abstract or disembodied fashion. Instead, they are characteristically packaged (or 'framed') in particular ways by institutions and organizations such as government bodies, industries and environmentalist groups. It is therefore entirely appropriate that we begin by considering what has become the dominant contemporary framing of environmental issues. As Maarten Hajer presents the underlying issue: 'Environmental discourse is an astonishing collection of claims and concerns brought together by a great variety of actors. Yet somehow we distil seemingly coherent problems out of this jamboree of claims and concerns' (1995, pp. 1–2).

In this chapter's discussion of the Brundtland Report and the concept of sustainable development, it will not be the intention to catalogue international activities in this area. Equally, the chapter is not intended as a critique of sustainability. The aim is rather to explore the discourse of sustainability in broad terms – and, specifically, to consider its treatment of environmental knowledge, institutional practice and social–natural relations. In so doing, we will be in general agreement with Castree and Braun:

> [W]hat counts as 'nature', and our experience of nature (including our bodies), is always historical, related to a configuration of historically specific social and representational practices which form the nuts and bolts of our interactions with, and investments in, the world. Discourses like 'sustainability' are important to the extent that they organize our attitudes towards, and actions on, nature. (1998, p. 17)

Hajer's more blunt assessment should also be borne in mind:

> [T]he present hegemony of the idea of sustainable development should not be seen as the product of a linear, progressive, and value-free process of convincing actors of the importance of the Green case. It is much more a struggle between various unconventional political coalitions, each made up of such actors as scientists, politicians, activists. (1995, p. 12)

This 'hegemony' has taken particular form as a 'globalist perspective',[1] which aims to reconcile the perceived need for environmental protection with a desire for continued economic and industrial development. Put differently, sustainable development represents the marriage of developmentalism (the commitment to continued economic development) and environmentalism.[2] Such a reconciliation is neither

obvious nor straightforward – nor is it without its critics, who see it
as a centralizing approach, more concerned with 'business as usual'
than radical change, and as rooted in a Northern perspective on environment and development. The discourse of sustainability emphasizes the notion of 'commonality' (what Brundtland terms a 'human
family'). Alternative perspectives have challenged this sense of 'commonality' by suggesting that sustainable development might be better
understood as a form of environmental imperialism.

This creates a situation where, on the one hand, it is possible to
portray sustainable development as a hopelessly divided concept,[3]
whilst at the same time noting that leaflets and publications from
disparate organizations often end up looking remarkably similar. One
important characteristic of 'sustainability talk' therefore is the way
in which an apparently unitary discourse (complete with pictures of
dolphins, smiling children, the rainforests and 'Spaceship Earth') has
been created out of the 'environmental jamboree'.

To illustrate the 'sameness' of sustainability discourse, Myers and
Macnaghten quote one environmental leaflet: 'We all want clean air
and a healthy place to live. We all want a healthy environment – not
one scarred by the effects of industry. We want to protect the environment from abuse today and in the future' (1998, p. 339). What
is noteworthy here is that this statement could just as readily have
been made by Friends of the Earth or a government agency (in fact,
the leaflet was produced by the chemical company, ICI). The point
is that all these organizations are drawing upon a similar stock of
images, concepts and 'commonplaces'[4] – at least when dealing with
general audiences. However, it is important to be aware of what is
left out as well as included within this form of environmental discussion. As Hajer has observed, the language of 'one big united effort'
may serve a useful institutional role in setting an international agenda
but it can also exclude alternative accounts of environmental matters
– and perhaps disempower those understandings that do not trans-
late into a globalist perspective (1995, p. 14).

In this chapter, we will be interested in the tensions and ambivalences embedded within this superficially bland term – in other words,
in the relationship between the discursive representation of sameness
(across environmental problems, issues and concerns) and its underlying strands of difference. In so doing, we will also be acquainting
ourselves with the complex social debates and political struggles that
lie at the heart of contemporary environmental policy-making.

James O'Connor has described the underlying tensions within the
concept of sustainability: 'behind a seeming convergence of vocabu-
lary is a . . . gap between green and capitalist discourse, with both

sides talking past each other' (1994, p. 156). Sharachandra Lélé has powerfully made a similar point:

> Sustainable development is a 'metafix' that will unite everybody from the profit-minded industrialist and risk-minimizing subsistence farmer to the equity-seeking social worker, the pollution-concerned or wildlife-loving First Worlder, the growth-maximizing policy maker, the goal-orientated bureaucrat, and therefore, the vote-counting politician. (cited in Dobson 1998, p. 33)

In this chapter, I want to suggest that, whilst the language of sustainability is undoubtedly slippery, ill-defined and self-contradictory, this should not detract from a consideration of its sociological significance. On the contrary, the variable construction and application of this term within environmental discourse make it all the more suitable for sociological analysis. In particular, I want to consider the institutional definition of sustainability within one important document. The 1987 Brundtland Report focused international debate on sustainable development and provided a new agenda for environmental discussion.

In what follows, I am not going to attempt the heroic (or probably just hopeless) task of tidying up the definitions of sustainability, nor of producing a full intellectual and institutional definition of the term. Rather than seeking to pin down sustainability, the focus will be on what the prevailing discourse of sustainability tells us about the meanings of environmentalism and the character of environmental debate. The tensions within 'sustainability talk' can in that way serve as an introduction to the varying and contested construction of contemporary environmental issues and concerns. On that basis, we will be especially sensitive to certain underlying themes within sustainability talk. These include:

- a presentation of the kinds of social and institutional *change* being required (in terms of both scale and form);
- notions of *globality* and, linked to this, of *togetherness* in the face of environmental threat (both embodied within the notion that this is our common future);
- an argument for *democracy, empowerment and participation* as an essential means of achieving sustainable development;
- and, at the broadest level, an evocation of the *crisis* with which we are confronted.

In specific reference to the main themes of this book, we will identify:

- a definition of 'sustainable development' that explicitly brings together *social* (especially political and institutional) and *environmental* concerns – albeit in a form that ultimately maintains a strict social/natural distinction;
- a set of particular science-centred assumptions about *environmental knowledges* (of how we know what we claim about environmental concerns) which have important consequences for the social element within sustainability discourse;
- the importance of social and institutional *practice* for social–natural relations.

Taken together, these themes indicate a broadly based 'global problematique' (as the Club of Rome termed it), which suggests considerable scope for sociological analysis. Sustainability talk is interesting both for what it includes and for what it omits. What makes this all the more interesting (and again paradoxical) is that one key characteristic of sustainable development has been its explicit commitment to equity and participation.

The Emergence of Sustainability Talk

Sustainable development needs to be set in some historical context in order to explain its emergence and influence. However, in this brief account such contextualization cannot be offered in any detail.[5] Instead, a short introduction will be offered before we discuss the Brundtland Report itself.

In describing sustainability talk in this and the following two sections, I am aware that parts of the material may be familiar to readers who have already studied the Brundtland Report. However, and as discussed in the Introduction, experience suggests that such material is often unfamiliar (perhaps surprisingly) to many sociologists – as Newby's comments cited in the Preface also indicated. In such a situation, and given the need to establish sustainability as a basis for future discussion in this book, I can only request the temporary indulgence of Brundtland-aware readers – and threaten them with less familiar material ahead.

Although various claims have been made for the first usage of the term 'sustainable development',[6] it seems likely that the genesis of the concept stems from the 1970s when environmental awareness was becoming established in its modern reincarnation worldwide.[7] Redclift, for example, traces the term back to the 1974 Cocoyoc Declaration on environment and development (1992, p. 32). This stated that the purpose of development 'should not be to develop things, but to develop man' (cited in Reid 1996, p. 45). This emphasis on the social and human, as well as explicitly environmental, challenge certainly anticipated Brundtland's definition of sustainable development. Other commentators have identified the 1972 Stockholm Conference on the Human Environment as the event that first put the environment on the international political agenda.[8]

The Brundtland Report can also be represented as emerging out of a steady stream of international reports on environmental issues, which commenced in the late 1960s. For example, *Blueprint for Survival* was published in 1972 by *The Ecologist* magazine. This was followed (also in 1972) by *Limits to Growth*, which, as the title implies, argued that current patterns of development would lead to major social, industrial and resource problems within the following century – unless, that is, a new condition of 'ecological and economic stability' could be established that was 'sustainable far into the future'.[9] This report was criticized in a number of ways – and not least for its deterministic model and alleged failure to consider social and political factors. However, it did serve to suggest that there may be a fundamental contradiction between economic growth and the limited resources of the natural world.

These concerns about environment and development became the focus of a series of international conferences and meetings, including those held in Stockholm (1972) and Cocoyoc, Mexico (1974). The Stockholm meeting, organized by the United Nations, was attended by representatives of 119 countries and 400 Non-Governmental Organizations (NGOs). The Stockholm conference accorded international status to environmental issues – even if in so doing it also opened up a possible conflict between the North and the South. Was the new environmental agenda a covert means of holding back developing nations?

The term 'sustainable development' did not actually come to prominence until 1980 when it was proposed by the International Union for the Conservation of Nature (IUCN) as part of the World Conservation Strategy (WCS). The WCS defined the broad goal as integrating 'conservation and development to ensure that modifications to the planet do indeed secure the survival and well-being of all people'. In anticipation of the Brundtland Commission's best-known definition of sustainable development (discussed in the following section), 'conservation' was defined as 'the management of human use of the biosphere so that it may yield the greatest sustainable benefit to present generations while maintaining its potential to meet the needs and aspirations of future generations'. In this way, sustainable development is built on the notion that conservation and development are mutually dependent rather than opposed to one another.

As Pickering and Lewis (1994) observe, the IUCN report was criticized in a number of ways. Discussion centred on whether it was 'anti-development'. Inevitably also, debate considered whether the WCS was attacking the symptoms rather than the causes of environmental degradation (what Redclift calls the 'political and economic forces behind unsustainable practices' (1992, p. 21)). The report's argument that poverty was a key factor working against sustainability also attracted considerable attention: does such a conclusion suggest 'victim-blaming'?

Reid describes the report more generally: 'WCS reflects both the utilitarian and moral strands of environmentalist thinking of the 1960s and 1970s' (1996, p. 41). He continues:

> Both world conservation and global environmentalism offer 'solutions' that can be applied on a global scale. They tend to be presented as the obviously right thing to do, and therefore non-controversial. However, far from being apolitical, they reflect Northern bias. Their perspective is that of Northern interests . . . in largely Southern resources; their diagnoses are validated by Northern science on whose findings they are based, and their implementation would require Northern technology and expertise. (ibid., p. 42)

Already we can see that what may appear self-evident to one viewpoint can appear quite different from other perspectives – and especially given the growing debate over the 'Southern' perspective on these issues (a category that itself requires some deconstruction).

Very importantly for the institutional history of sustainable development, a fresh international perspective began to fuse with the concept of environmental crisis from the late 1970s onwards. This was driven by the sense of an alternative – but possibly related – crisis: that of world poverty and the requirement for a 'new international economic order'. Accordingly, the UN established three independent commissions to explore various aspects of the crisis: the Independent Commission on International Development Issues (which became known as the Brandt Commission) in 1977; the Independent Commission on Disarmament and Security Issues (the Palme Commission) in 1980; the World Commission on Environment and Development (the Brundtland Commission) in 1983. Each of these dealt with difficult questions of the global balance of power and relations between 'developed' and 'developing' nations. Each also represented an attempt to develop a global agenda for the resolution of international conflict. It would appear that only the Brundtland Report still commands attention today.

As expressed in the Brundtland Report, sustainable development offers the promise of reconciliation between apparent irreconcilables: economy and ecology, equity and survival, technological development and long-term interests, international policy-making and local action. That the concept of sustainability should gain any level of international acceptance would appear most remarkable given these fundamental points of tension within the term itself. The Brundtland Report represents an intriguing mix of the specific and the ill-defined, and between the pragmatic and the idealistic. This combination may allow 'sustainability talk' to find a common voice whilst also being riven by deep disagreement over specific measures and strategies. It is for this reason that more critical groups consider the concept to be diversionary and shallow.

The Brundtland Report

Our report . . . is not a prediction of ever increasing environmental decay, poverty and hardship in an ever more polluted world among ever decreasing resources. We see instead the possibility for a new era of economic growth, one that must be based on policies that sustain and expand the environmental resource base. And we believe such growth to be absolutely essential to relieve the great poverty that is deepening in much of the developing world. (WCED 1987, p. 1)

The Brundtland Commission was asked to present a 'global agenda for change'. More specifically, the General Assembly of the United Nations called for the Commission to:

- propose long-term environmental strategies for achieving sustainable development by the year 2000 and beyond;
- recommend ways in which greater international cooperation and also the achievement of commonly held objectives might occur;
- help define 'shared perceptions' of the issues and of the consequent required action.

The members of the Commission came from some 21 countries covering both the developed (e.g. USA, Japan, Germany) and the developing worlds (e.g. Colombia, Zimbabwe, Ivory Coast). One key feature of the Commission's operation was its broad definition of both 'development' and 'environmental issues'. As the Commission's Chair, Gro Harlem Brundtland, herself argued:

> The environment does not exist as a sphere separate from human actions, ambitions, and needs, and attempts to define it in isolation from human concerns have given the very word 'environment' a connotation of naivety in some political circles. The word 'development' has also been narrowed by some into a very limited focus, along the lines of 'what poor nations should do to become richer'. (WCED 1987, p. xi)

The point instead was that economic growth and environmental protection are not only compatible but mutually dependent. This interlinkage of the environment and development was tied in to the Commission's much-repeated definition of sustainable development: 'Sustainable development is development that meets the needs of the present without compromising the ability of future generations to meet their own needs' (ibid., p. 43). However, 'social equity' cannot just be a matter between generations but must 'logically be extended to equity within each generation' (so that *intra-* as well as *inter-* generational equity was central to sustainable development). At the very heart of the Brundtland Report we have, therefore, a concern with issues of equity, poverty and power.

Before analysing this construction of sustainability, it is worth considering the Brundtland Commission's assessment of the scale of the challenge to environment and development. The Report noted four main environmental challenges: *poverty* ('there are more hungry people in the world today than ever before in human history, and their numbers are growing' (ibid., p. 29)); *growth* ('environmental problems linked to resource use will intensify in global terms' (ibid., p. 32)); *survival* ('Nature is bountiful, but it is also fragile and finely balanced' (ibid.)); the *economic* crisis ('environmental degradation is eroding the potential for development' (ibid., p. 35)). On that basis, and as the Report puts it: 'we are serving a notice – an urgent notice based on the latest and best scientific evidence – that the time has come to take the decisions needed to secure the resources to sustain this and coming generations' (ibid. p. 2).

We can see that these challenges incorporate a strong *social* element – or, more accurately, they explicitly mix social, environmental and developmental elements in such a way as to suggest their mutual interdependence and potential compatibility. In so doing, the concept of sustainability is drawing upon both modernistic and environmentalist rhetoric in a fashion that suggests their basic reconcilability (and, indeed, mutual support). These points become very clear in the 'strategic imperatives' proposed by the Commission. These include: reviving (economic) growth; meeting essential human needs; ensuring a sustainable level of population; reorienting technology and managing risk; merging environment and economics in decision-making.

In summarizing the requirements of sustainable development, the Commission called for changes to what it described as a number of 'systems' (for example, the political, social and technological systems as separately defined). Without such changes, it would be impossible to achieve 'harmony among human beings and between humanity and nature'.

In its third section, the Report considered 'Common Endeavours'. This re-emphasized one underlying theme of the whole report – that sustainable development requires *international* action and agreement. Nations are dependent upon each other, the problems cannot be tackled by nation-states acting in isolation. This is especially true with regard to the 'global commons' – such as the oceans, outer space and Antarctica. It also applies to other pollution issues, such as global warming or ozone depletion, where significant changes cannot be made by any nation acting alone.

'Common Endeavours' extend to political tensions and military conflict. Thermo-nuclear war, for example, would have devastating environmental consequences – as also do other contemporary forms of warfare. Environmental damage within Vietnam, the Gulf states and Bosnia may seem a minor side-effect when contrasted with human suffering (although this depends upon the value placed on 'natural' as opposed to 'human' destruction), but it can present long-term consequences for agricultural, industrial and living conditions.

The Commission also portrayed environmental stress as itself a source of conflict – for example, famine can lead to mass migration and the heightening of political and ethnic tensions. The future effects of global warming might well include social upheaval and international tensions. Moreover, the Report sees an international 'arms culture' as creating a 'destructive logic' directly counter to the aims of sustainability. At an immediately practical level (if such an unlikely policy shift can be considered 'practical'), the reallocation of military budgets towards social and environmental purposes would be of enormous assistance. The Report noted, for example, that implementing the UN Action Plan for Desertification would have cost

$4.5 billion a year for the last two decades of the century – the equivalent of 'less than two days of military spending' (WCED 1987, p. 303).

Finally, in terms of 'Common Endeavours', the Brundtland Commission presented a series of proposals for institutional and legal changes: 'The time has come to break out of past patterns'.

> The onus for action lies with no one group of nations. Developing countries face the challenges of desertification, deforestation, and pollution, and endure most of the poverty associated with environmental degradation. The entire human family of nations would suffer from the disappearance of rain forests in the tropics, the loss of plant and animal species, and changes in rainfall patterns. (ibid., pp. 308–9)

The institutional changes called for are not intended to be a quick fix, but rather suggest 'some pathways to the future'. They include 'getting at the sources' of the problems in institutional terms; strengthening environmental protection and resource management agencies; establishing a Global Risk Assessment Programme; increasing the role of the scientific community and of NGOs in setting policies; reassessing and reformulating environmental law 'in harmony with the unchanging and universal laws of nature'. As the Report concluded:

> The Commissioners came from 21 very different nations. In our discussions, we disagreed often on details and priorities. But despite our widely differing backgrounds and varying national and international responsibilities, we were able to agree to the lines along which institutional change must be drawn.
>
> We are unanimous in our conviction that the security, well-being, and very survival of the planet depend upon such changes, now. (ibid., p. 343)

Since Brundtland

The Brundtland Report has stimulated numerous international activities since 1987. Notably, in June 1992 more than 100 world leaders and 30,000 other participants gathered in Rio de Janeiro for the UN Conference on Environment and Development – the 'Earth Summit'. This represented a major world event and certainly served as an important focus for argument and debate over the meaning of sustainable development both generally and with regard to specific issues of international concern.

The Rio Declaration approved 27 principles 'on the goal of establishing a new and equitable global partnership'. Agenda 21 offered a 40-chapter 'sustainable action plan for the 21st century', covering a whole host of actors (including women, indigenous people, farmers and business people) and issues (for example, poverty, seas, forests, waste management, human health). Agenda 21 represents a framework within which governments must operate in order to achieve an environmentally and socially sustainable environment. Social equity and wide public participation are central to this framework.[10] Rio also produced a Climate Change Convention and a Biodiversity Convention along with agreements on a range of other issues and a 'commitment' to reduce global poverty.

However, the Rio meeting raised many problems regarding the notion of sustainable development – and especially its ability to bring harmony from a range of otherwise discordant voices. Perhaps the most significant of these disagreements revolved around the notion of 'commonality' between the peoples of the world. The concept of a 'human family' was threatened by a number of dualities – between rich and poor, North and South, developing and developed, governments and non-governmental organizations. Disagreements emerged both with regard to substantive issues (such as the Climate Convention) and within the agenda-setting process itself. Specifically, it was alleged that Northern concerns were being granted higher priority within the Summit than Southern ones. Disputes of this kind suggest once again that the official commitment to equity does not prevent a sense of exclusion for certain groups. At the same time, we see the importance of the micro-politics of environmental conflict (notably, concerning what gets discussed, when and where).

What was equally apparent during these heated discussions was that national positions were not dictated by membership of any North/South bloc. As Reid observes (1996, pp. 194–5), Bangladesh and Egypt (both low-lying territories) took a very different stance on the Climate Convention from Saudi Arabia and Kuwait (with their major oil revenues). At this point, we begin to see the complex and shifting alliances that may be concealed by the apparent commitment to 'sustainability talk'.

Rio has been followed by further discussions, arguments and agreements. The Biodiversity Convention was ratified in 1993. The Climate Convention was ratified in 1994 – to widespread disbelief from NGOs that the target of stabilizing worldwide CO_2 emissions would actually be achieved.[11] Conventions have also been established on desertification and on the Law of the Sea. Meanwhile, the UN Commission on Sustainable Development (created in 1992) meets annually and has provided a focus for governmental and NGO activities.

In 1997, world leaders met again for the sequel to the 1992 Earth Summit. By this time, both positive and negative changes could be identified: environmental progress was reported in some countries (with the new British Prime Minister Tony Blair particularly proud of his country's success in reducing carbon dioxide emissions) but there were also gloomy accounts (with carbon dioxide in the atmosphere increasing overall). As the UN Development Programme's administrator somewhat predictably expressed it in 1997: 'If there's one big failure . . . it's the failure of the rich to live up to the commitment they made at Rio to help the poor countries deal with their environmental issues and their developmental issues simultaneously.'[12]

Meanwhile, parallel activities at a national level have attempted to put the principles of Brundtland into practice. Numerous countries have now established their own national commissions for sustainable development. Local Agenda 21 activities have been taking place worldwide. To take the example of Britain, a national strategy on sustainable development has been published and reviewed on a regular basis.[13] In 1994, a Government Panel on Sustainable Development was established.[14] Other initiatives such as 'Business in the Environment' or 'Going for Green' have attempted to operationalize and encourage notions of 'sustainability'.

Throughout these discussions and initiatives, the central tensions, contradictions and ambiguities of the term have remained. As the former British Prime Minister John Major expressed this with apparent innocence in the 1994 strategy for sustainable development: 'Sustainable development is difficult to define. But the goal of sustainable development can guide future policy' (quoted in Myerson and Rydin 1996, p. 19).

As noted above, it seems possible to be ignorant of 'sustainability' or unclear as to what it actually means. However, it is very difficult to be *against* it. Instead, more subtle struggles are now taking place over how it should be defined in any particular context. Is it a matter of 'inter-generational equity' or green economics? Is it about NGO engagement or governmental stewardship? Is 'business as usual' sufficient, or is more radical change required? Can it serve as a basis for action or is it essentially a series of pious statements to international meetings? Opinions differ markedly over the kind of challenge represented by sustainable development. As Reid expresses this:

Despite its concern about the impact of development on people, Brundtland's emphasis on economic growth and its faith in an amended international economic order have provided the elites who dominate the international community with a pretext for viewing sustainable development as the latest version of 'development', rather than as a new concept that challenges orthodox assumptions and means a radical departure from conventional thinking and practices. (1996, p. 229)

Meanwhile, it is impossible to avoid the observation that the international conferences are not themselves without environmental consequences, as literally thousands of participants have flown across the globe to attend lavishly sponsored meetings in air-conditioned conference centres. In one typical illustration of this, Concorde ('the world's ultimate gas-guzzler'[15]) was chartered to take the British Prime Minister and Foreign Secretary to New York for the June 1997 conference. It has been estimated that the British delegation alone to that conference was responsible for more than 30 tonnes of carbon dioxide emissions.

The Sustainability Problematique

'[S]ustainability' could be called the post-modern equivalent of a grand narrative, replacing the modernist grand narrative of progress which held sway for much of the twentieth century. Sustainability is our way of seeing the present in the perspective of the future and provides a societal story-line for justifying change. (Myerson and Rydin 1996, p. 23)

This chapter has focused on the manner in which 'sustainability talk' attempts to interconnect the otherwise disparate themes and concerns of modern environmental discussion. We have noted the contestations and ambivalences within the superficially unitary character of this discourse. We have also observed the broadly defined character of the sustainable development concept and the way in which this definitional breadth bestows a degree of flexibility upon its interpretation and implementation. In so doing, we have also implied the social complexities of international environmental debates depending as they do on a variety of shifting alliances and ideological expressions. At the same time, we have suggested that the definition of sustainable development is far from rigid. Dobson (1998), for example, has identified three main conceptions of sustainability, which differ markedly in terms of *what* they seek to sustain and *how* they aim to achieve this. In this way, he distinguishes between the wider topic of environmental sustainability and the more particular framework offered by sustainable development of the kind discussed in this chapter.

This discussion has also identified a number of aspects of 'sustainability talk', which together give it substantial resilience in the face of the distinctly centrifugal tendencies of international discussion. These have included:

1. A quasi-religious sense of 'togetherness' and 'globality' as the 'human family' struggles to deal with its problems.
2. Linked to this, an argument for inter- and intra-generational equity – only the full participation of all can deal with this crisis.
3. Although this has largely been taken for granted rather than openly debated within sustainability discussions, a stress on *science* as the best means of identifying and gauging, but also responding to, environmental problems. A large part of the optimism within the Brundtland Report stems explicitly from this faith in our scientific and technological capacities. From a sustainability perspective, such capacities provide a solid foundation for the necessary social and institutional changes: 'We can move information and goods faster around the globe than ever before; we can produce more food and more goods with less investment of resources; our technology and science gives us at least the potential to look deeper into and better understand natural systems' (WCED 1987, p. 1).
4. An argument for change, which marries the radical with the incremental. Change is needed urgently, but that change can be brought about without, for example, abandoning economic growth. This model of change also marries the local with the global. Different levels of social and institutional action fit seamlessly together rather than being in contradiction or tension.
5. A crisis that is real and yet bound up with social and institutional arrangements. The environmental crisis in that way mirrors (and accentuates) a sense of social and economic crisis. As Ulrich Beck has expressed this: 'It is not something external but itself that society encounters in the hazards that convulse it' (1995b, p. 159). Nevertheless, and despite acknowledgement of the social roots of environmental crisis, 'sustainability talk' differentiates between the two forms of crisis and so stops short of the more radical account offered by Beck (as the following chapter will discuss).

Above all, we have suggested that 'sustainability talk' is not simply a straightforward response to an external 'crisis' but an *actively created* framework for discussing our period in history. Sustainable development is all-inclusive in its coverage. It brings together democratic principles, faith in science and technology, a view of the future, an assertion of the moral responsibility of those alive today, and a sense that we are part of a global family.

However persuasive or attractive this combination as a set of ideals, the point is that it represents a carefully negotiated worldview emerging from a series of high-level international meetings rather than simply a pragmatic and 'obvious' response to pressing environmental concerns. It is not necessarily cynical to suggest that the discourse of sustainability is especially appealing to governmental and industrial officials – and, of course, to many politicians looking for an issue that is global in significance but not overtly divisive. Sustainability offers a note of radicalism (and both localism and globalism) but without challenging the centrality of existing institutions. Environmental imagery also suggests that sustainability is a concept that we can all feel good about – and in that way is a possible counterweight to international conflict taking place elsewhere.

Equally, it is important to be aware that the particular form of institutional response that is proposed with regard to environmental problems depends very much on the manner in which these problems are initially constructed. Brundtland's presentation of global problems that need global solutions leads directly to a particular form of environmental politics. In one illustration of this, Hajer considers the widespread usage within sustainability discourse of one of the most powerful and pervasive of environmental images: the view of planet Earth as seen from outer space. This image was one important (arguably *the* most important) product of the 1960s space programme:

> The confrontation with the planet as a colourful ball, partly disguised by flimsy clouds, and floating seemingly aimless in a sea of utter darkness, conveyed a general sense of fragility that made people aware of human dependence on nature. . . . Indeed, the image . . . caused a cognitive elucidation through which the everyday experience of life in an industrialized world was given a different meaning. (1995, p. 8)

The point here is that this ubiquitous image represents environmental reality to us in a structured and manufactured manner. Such a representation of our planet encourages us to 'see' the world (and, therefore, to think and act) in a suitably global fashion. Equally – and notably when this image is manipulated in order to demonstrate the extent of environmental devastation – such images present a reality to us, which we cannot see, smell, hear, touch or taste for ourselves. The lack of unmediated common-sense awareness of planetary fragility or ozone depletion obliges us to rely upon such environmental representations. At the same time, the very existence of such images emphasizes the centrality of science and technology to contemporary environmental awareness. We are reminded that what is often presented as 'hard environmental reality' depends upon sophisticated representations and hard-achieved constructions. We have no neutral or disembodied means of seeing either global environmental problems or our human 'togetherness'.

None of this suggests that sustainability is a conspiracy. The whole institutional and international process is so inherently unmanageable that the exercise of control by any one interest group seems improbable. Nor is this chapter intended to be dismissive of the efforts of so many actors and organizations. However, it is reasonable to view the concept as the outcome of a particular 'framing' of the environmental imbroglio and, moreover, as the product of a particular (albeit complex and international) social and institutional context. In Hajer's terms, it offers a 'story-line' through which various actors are positioned 'and through which specific ideas of "blame" and "responsibility", and of "urgency" and "responsible behaviour" are attributed' (1995, p. 65). However, it is also a story-line grounded within its own social and historical setting.

This chapter has argued that the linkages between a sense of environmental crisis, calls for inter-generational equity and the notion of togetherness are not simply given but instead are actively constructed. Despite the common-sense appearance of 'sustainability talk', *the environmental crisis does not simply impact upon our lives but is mediated and reconstructed within a host of social institutions and through the kinds of discursive formation considered here.*

Addressing sustainable development in explicitly *sociological* terms, it becomes apparent that the Brundtland framing implicitly poses various questions and issues for sociological research. These include social action with regard to environmental concerns and the operation of international institutions.

However, there are also very clear limits to the social within this policy perspective. Characteristically, sustainability talk suggests that social and institutional action must be based on the deliberations of science. Whilst supporters of sustainable development might acknowledge that science has encountered various difficulties in dealing with environmental issues, science is nevertheless considered the best hope for reaching environmental solutions.

From a sociological perspective, therefore, a certain division of labour stems from the framing of environmental issues within the 'sustainability problematique'. Sociology can follow once scientific analysis has defined the underlying problems. The task of sociological analysis on that basis is to deal with matters of social response to environmental problems but not to enter more fundamental discussion of what constitutes an environmental problem in the first place.

A similar point can be made about the perspective on international institutions which is developed within sustainability discussions. Whilst it is acknowledged that these institutions have struggled previously to cope with environmental matters, hope for the future is nevertheless entrusted in just these institutions. The possibility that the kinds of international forum encouraged by the Brundtland Report might actually contribute to unsustainable practices does not enter within this framework. In making this point, of course, the reforming drive of sustainable development should not be underestimated or trivialized.

In analytical terms, sustainable development can be represented both as one institutional response to a set of social and environmental concerns, and as a particular *construction* of those concerns. Whilst the framing of environmental challenges in this way is certainly powerful, it is also necessary for us to establish a critical distance on this problematique. As this chapter has suggested, we need to be especially sensitive to the assertion of particular forms of *environmental knowledge* (based largely on one reading of science), of *institutional practice* (based on existing institutions) and of the relationship between *the social and the natural* (based on the notion that these are closely related but ultimately separable). All these points will be challenged as we move to a second framing of societal–environmental relations: Ulrich Beck's treatment of the 'risk society'.

Before concluding this chapter, it is also important to draw attention to the style of sociological argumentation being developed here. Rather than reducing the complexities of environmental debate to preconceived sociological categories in order to demonstrate the validity of established forms of sociological analysis, the aim has been to draw out one contemporary construction of environmental problems. In this way also, institutional framings of the issues come to be seen not simply as matters of 'applied' interest but as central to our exploration of environmental action.

The point is not to be dismissive or over-critical of conventional frameworks such as sustainable development. On the contrary, the sustainability movement is an important source of inspiration for environmental sociology. However, we do need to consider the implicit assumptions, ambivalences and contradictions upon which such frameworks depend.

2

The Risk Society Thesis: The End of the World As We Know It?

Just as earlier generations lived in the age of the stagecoach, so we now and in future are living in the hazardous age of creeping catastrophe. What generations before us discovered despite resistance, and had to shout out loud at the world, we have come to take for granted: the impending 'suicide of the species'.

Beck 1996, p. 40

'Risk society' means an epoch in which the dark sides of progress increasingly come to dominate social debate. What no one saw and no one wanted – self-endangerment and the devastation of nature – is becoming the motive force of history.

Beck 1995a, p. 2

Beck's framing of 'society, nature and knowledge' takes us deep into contemporary social theory. In this chapter, particular attention will be paid to Beck's argument that environmental problems are 'thoroughly social problems' and also to his analysis of science as a problematic means of 'knowing' the environmental crisis.

Beck's radical sociological account offers a strongly contrasting framework for the social–natural relationship to that offered by sustainability talk. Rather than presenting nature as external to society, late modernity indicates a world where the social and the natural have become inseparable from one another. In so doing, Beck portrays a scale of social and institutional crisis beyond that suggested by the sustainability agenda. His treatment of social–natural relations moves us into more ambiguous and complex territory, where neither the social nor the natural can be seen as independent or self-contained.

As can be gathered immediately from the quotations at the start of this chapter, the perspective adopted here indicates a considerably more radical role for sociological analysis than tinkering with existing institutions or considering the political implications of the latest scientific thinking on the environment (to caricature the Brundtland agenda). Ulrich Beck's exploration of the 'risk society' raises instead a fundamental set of problems for both science and political institutions in dealing with environmental issues. His account also suggests a profound role for the 'social' and for sociological investigation within what he portrays as the current environmental crisis.

Towards the end of chapter 1, we quoted Beck to the effect that society 'encounters itself' within environmental and hazard discussions. In this chapter, we will explore the character of this 'encounter' and consider what it means both for sociology and for the contemporary treatment of environmental concerns. I will not attempt to summarize all the key elements of Beck's analysis (a task as hopeless as tidying up the definitions of sustainable development). Instead, I intend to offer a general sense of his account and its implications for sociology.

To put it simply, whilst the concept of sustainable development suggests that scientific/technological development and the 'institutional system' can cope (at least after significant modification), Beck's account is of a world where everything is open to question, where every aspect of life is imbued with doubt and uncertainty, and where the very sense of 'science, truth and progress' upon which the Brundtland Report ultimately depends is being challenged and found wanting. In that way, there appears no separating the social and economic from the environmental crisis: 'The transformation of the unseen side-effects of industrial production into global ecological trouble spots is therefore not at all a problem of the world surrounding us – not a so-called "environmental problem" – but a far-reaching institutional crisis of industrial society itself' (Beck 1996, p. 32). On that basis, Beck's work has special importance for the relationship between sociology and the environment. As Goldblatt observes: 'The distinguishing feature of his work is to place the origins and consequences of environmental degradation right at the heart of a theory of modern society, rather than seeing it as a peripheral element or theoretical afterthought' (1996, p. 155). In this chapter, we will explore the basic features of this influential attempt to link social theory with environmental issues and concerns, and consider the implications for both sociology and social practice.

Ulrich Beck and the 'Risk Society'

It is rare for any book in sociology to attract the kind of attention accorded to Ulrich Beck's *Risk Society* (1992). Originally published in German in 1986, more than 60,000 copies were sold within five years of its appearance. The German weekly magazine, *Der Spiegel*, devoted four pages to a review of this sociological best-seller. Beck himself has been involved in numerous seminars, conferences, management presentations and even talk shows. As he acknowledges, the nuclear accident at Chernobyl – which took place after the book's completion but before publication – added particular significance and topicality (and also unprecedented publicity) to the 'risk society' concept. For many readers, sociology had demonstrated its predictive as well as analytical powers.

In addition to the wide dissemination of Beck's work since the 1980s, a series of books by the British sociologist, Anthony Giddens, has also been addressing related themes and issues. This has served to build sociological interest in the risk society thesis and encourage debate in Britain and the United States as well as in Germany. Commencing with *The Consequences of Modernity* in 1990, Giddens has explored the relationship between our period of history (which, in broad agreement with Beck, he terms 'high-' or 'late-'modernity) and our sense of self-identity (of who we think we are). More recently, Giddens (1994a) has considered the political consequences of the changing social structure – changes that have important implications for ideology and practice on both the conventionally defined 'right' and 'left'.

These two social theorists[1] have attempted to interlink an otherwise divergent set of phenomena (in Giddens's case including shifts in political structures, individual lifestyles and sexual behaviour) with the changing framework of contemporary social order (otherwise known as 'modernity'). More particularly for our current discussion, the debates initiated by these two authors suggest fresh possibilities for interconnecting sociology and the environment – and in a fashion that goes beyond the restricted notion of 'social and institutional' dimensions as suggested by sustainable development. In this chapter we will focus on Beck in particular, since environmental issues are at the core of his theoretical treatment.

Beck's analysis of the 'risk society' suggests that centralized institutions such as national governments are fundamentally incapable of responding to contemporary environmental and risk concerns. Instead, these institutions are largely trapped within the very sets of assumptions that have generated the current crisis for modernity. Beck's argument therefore is that the challenges currently being faced cannot be resolved by a mere reorientation of current policy directions and patterns of technological development:

> the problems emerging here cannot be mastered by increased production, redistribution or expansion of social protection – as in the nineteenth century – but instead require either a focused and massive 'policy of counter-interpretation' or a fundamental rethinking and reprograming of the prevailing paradigm of modernization. (1992, p. 52)

This sociological account argues that the current sense of environmental crisis is not just (or even necessarily) a response to the emergence of a set of problems 'out there' (in an external 'real world'). Risk concerns have always existed, so why are these seen to be a particular problem right now? Instead, the crisis coincides (and is inextricably linked) with a wider *social* malaise: a loss of faith in centralized institutions and the assumptions of 'progress' upon which these are based. However, this malaise is also a source of liberation and new opportunities. In the 'risk society', many of the old restrictions on thought and behaviour cease to apply.

An acceptance of such a broad sociological perspective would have important consequences not just for our grasp of the relationship between sociology and the environment but also for the realm of politics and for environmental policy-making. In addition to challenging the institutional base upon which the Brundtland agenda depends, the wider phenomenon of radical doubt and uncertainty makes many environmental claims – based upon an apparent sense of certainty and self-confidence in their own predictions – appear backward-looking and outdated. When government departments or environmentalist groups attempt to give us the 'facts' regarding a particular issue, they are speaking the language of certainty, which, at least for Beck, belongs to a bygone age.

From a risk society perspective, the social and sociological challenges of sustainability cannot be met within a conventional (or 'modernistic') world-view. Instead, environmental issues are bound up with a wider set of social, personal and institutional problems which evade any single solution, since all the solutions generate new, and even more difficult, problems of their own.[2] In the emerging social structure, the new realities are difficult to grasp. They simply slip through the fingers of our 'conceptual hands'.

All this makes Beck a difficult thinker to summarize. However, what is more important than any of his specific points is the fresh sociological perspective that he brings. In the following section, I will present an overview rather than a summary, with special emphasis on the themes that run through this book: including the social significance of contemporary risk concerns, the new challenges being presented to science within environmental disputes, changing relations between the social and the natural, and the problems being created for established institutions.

The Risk Society Thesis

> The system of coordinates in which life and thinking are fastened in industrial modernity – the axes of gender, family and occupation, the belief in science and progress – begins to shake, and a new twilight of opportunities and hazards comes into existence – the contours of the risk society. (Beck 1992, p. 15)

'Panoramic' best describes Beck's account of our current state of societal development. Beck offers a sweeping vision of modernity and the changes that it is currently undergoing. Working in the broad intellectual tradition of Weber, Habermas and German sociology – but heavily influenced by the German greens – Beck covers almost every aspect of social life. Whilst our current concern is with the specifically environmental aspects of his analysis, this cannot be understood without some grasp of his wider framework (reinforcing also the fundamental position of the environmental crisis within his account of societal change).

This breadth can make *Risk Society* and Beck's other publications difficult to digest – a digestive problem exacerbated by his admitted tendency to develop his thinking as he writes. Quotation from Beck is a particularly dangerous enterprise, since he tends to rephrase and reconsider his own arguments within each text. At the same time, quotation often seems the only way of capturing not only his particular points but also his distinctive style and expression. Typically, and as noted by Goldblatt (1996, ch. 5), Beck attacks problems from various different angles so that the pattern only emerges after substantial reading. Equally, Beck (like Giddens) is a prolific writer who continues to develop his thinking through a series of books and essays.

Risk Society combines abstract analysis with very specific examples and case-studies. Beck's sense of humour and enthusiasm for aphorisms ('The devil of hunger is fought with the Beelzebub of multiplying risks' (1992, p. 43)) can distract, stimulate or delight depending on the reader's temperament and state of mind. It should be noted too that Beck does not write in a categorical or magisterial style but deliberately opens up questions and challenges the reader to respond (and in that way the style fits precisely with the substantive thrust of the argument).

Overall, *Risk Society* and the publications that have followed might best be read as a set of essays with a common theme: a series of sociological and critical excursions into the current, and changing, condition of modernity. As Beck puts the most general terms of the argument: 'Just as modernization dissolved the structure of feudal society in the nineteenth century and produced the industrial society, modernization today is dissolving industrial society and another modernity is coming into being' (ibid., p. 10). Beck's work can be seen as criss-crossing, exploring and probing the terrain which the dissolution of 'industrial society' is now opening up. Very importantly, this new form of modernity – known as 'late modernity' or the 'risk society' – is essentially an outcome of the *success* of modernity. Thus, in Western society (and Beck is very much focused on the prosperous countries of the world) scarcity is no longer a major issue within everyday life. However, in a wide number of other areas – such as gender and the family, the workplace, class relations and our treatment of risk and environmental issues – major problems are being generated. These problems have no immediate or obvious solution. Instead, they provide a new source of doubt, uncertainty and confusion. This is described with regard to gender relations: 'Suddenly everything becomes uncertain, including the ways of living together, who does what, how and where, or the views of sexuality and love and their connection to marriage and the family' (ibid., p. 109).

The process for Beck is one of modernity becoming *reflexive*. The problems and constraints of everyday life are no longer externally imposed (for example, by the natural world and its resource limitations). Instead, we enter a secondary phase of modernity, which frees us from the constraints of some supposed natural order (e.g. which once dictated that fathers go out to work whilst mothers stayed at home with the children) whilst also raising new challenges and problems (the loneliness and anomie that can follow when each one of us behaves as an autonomous individual). Rather than taking our family structure and gender role for granted, in late modernity we must *choose* how to live: 'The option of not deciding is tending to become impossible' (ibid., p. 116).

Similar changes are taking place across the class structure where fixed socio-economic relations are giving way to 'pragmatic alliances in the individual struggle for existence' (ibid., p. 101). Such alliances include green politics and environmental campaigns that do not fit the conventional and bureaucratized patterns of parliamentary democracy. In typical Beck – but also Weber-inspired – style, this is referred to as the 'rationalization of rationalization', since it represents a secondary 'rationalization' following the initial social transformations brought about by 'classical' (or 'industrial') modernity. In both cases, 'rationalization' refers to a transformation in the relationship between our characteristic style of thought and our way of life. The overall process is one of *individualization* in which we are each obliged to reflect upon our personal experiences and make our own decisions about how we wish to live: 'the basic figure of *fully developed* modernity is the *single person*' (ibid., p. 122; emphasis in original). Class and gender identity can no longer be simply ascribed. They are consciously negotiated and selected.

It is important to stress that these new social circumstances do not represent the collapse of modernity but rather the consequences of its development. This process is especially apparent with regard to the place of *science* within contemporary life. Originally, science took a position alongside 'truth' and 'progress' as a guiding principle of social development. Science could once offer an improvement on previous living conditions and a solution to the problems of existence. Now, the problems with which science must deal are increasingly those that have been created by science itself. As Beck puts it:

> Scientific civilization has entered a stage in which it no longer merely scientizes nature, people and society but increasingly itself, its own products, effects and mistakes. Science is no longer concerned with 'liberation' from *pre-existing* dependencies, but with the definition and distribution of errors and risks which are *produced by itself*. (ibid., p. 158; emphasis in original)

Nuclear power represents an especially clear example of this phenomenon. Scientific (and technological) development produced the Chernobyl reactor; now we depend on scientific analysis to control the consequent risks and to inform us about the effects of low-level radiation. This scientifically produced risk is all the more troublesome for us since we cannot see, smell, hear or touch it. Instead, we must rely upon the statements of experts. Yet, the very occurrence of events such as Chernobyl reduces our confidence in these same experts.

In late modernity, we depend upon science but must also fight against it. Either way, the simple notion of truth seems naïve and problematic, since the truth as seen from one perspective may not be the same as that seen from another – as evidenced by the contrasting reaction to Chernobyl from Friends of the Earth, the British nuclear industry and the Soviet authorities.

This phenomenon of modernity dealing with the problems created by modernity itself appears to be the defining characteristic of 'reflexive modernization'. In that way, the 'reflexive' process is above all one of 'self-confrontation' (Beck 1996, p. 28). Individuals and institutions are now forced to deal with the consequences of social action. What were once side-effects are challenging the core of our everyday assumptions. In line with this, science's 'monopoly on rationality' has begun to break down in the face of the new set of risks and challenges created by science itself.

This 'new phase' may be especially clear with regard to nuclear power, but also applies to many other forms of late-modern threat in which science serves as both the source of the problem and the offered solution. Genetically modified foods, chemical hazards and global warming are further examples of this 'reflexive' process. In such a situation, citizens become wary of the latest form of progress and of environmental solutions based on the logic of science. In sharp contrast to the Brundtland agenda of sustainable development, Beck presents science as having 'become the protector of a global contamination of people and nature' (1992, p. 70). However, in the 'new ambiguity' science constantly takes on contradictory positions. All aspects of society are now open to redefinition and simultaneously take on multiple forms.

The crisis at the heart of the risk society, then, is not primarily an abstract or intellectual crisis. Instead, at least for Beck, it comes about through the 'automatic operation of autonomous modernisation processes' (1996, p. 28), as described below. Modernization, from this perspective, has 'burst the categories' that it itself created – pitching us all into a new period of doubt and uncertainty. Beck's account is primarily concerned with broad social-structural changes rather than the philosophical or psychological experience of radical doubt (although, and as Giddens has argued, these phenomena are linked).

As Beck describes it more generally, the concept of 'risk society' suggests 'systemic and epochal transformations' in three main areas (see Beck 1996, p. 29):

1. The relationship of modern industrial society to the 'resources of nature and culture' (ibid.) – a category that includes 'nature external to human beings and human cultures' as well as 'cultural life-forms' (such as the nuclear family). Accordingly, our relationships both to conventional ways of life and to the natural world are being challenged and changed.
2. Very importantly, the relationship of 'society to the hazards and problems produced by it'. In particular, these hazards 'upset the basic assumptions of the previously existing social order' – and cause special problems for politics and decision-making (ibid.). Risks go beyond the insurable since they cannot be limited in terms of time, place or social group. Equally, they cannot be compensated for. As Beck puts this 'the injured of Chernobyl . . . are not even all *born* yet' (1996, p. 31; emphasis in original). In other words, we no longer have a means of redressing the imbalances caused by risks. Instead, they represent a constant undermining of the normalities of everyday life.
3. The collapse of 'collective and group-specific sources of meaning' places new pressures on individuals to 'live with the most diverse, contradictory global and personal risks' (1996, p. 29). Each of us must somehow confront this loss of certainty and the awareness that every aspect of life is open to challenge: 'The driving force in the class society can be summarized in the phrase: *I am hungry!* The movement set in motion by the risk society, on the other hand, is expressed in the statement: *I am afraid!* The *commonality of anxiety* takes the place of the *commonality of need*' (Beck 1992, p. 49; emphasis in original).

As can be gathered, the contemporary sense of risk and environmental threat is of primary importance amongst these new fears. However, the coincidence of rising environmental concern with changes in class, gender and family relations – and also with a larger crisis for our sense of 'Science, Truth and Progress' – suggests that this threat is just one part of a transformed social structure. Our sense of 'external threat' – in the form of environmental issues and concerns – is, therefore, linked to a wider questioning of 'techno-scientific rationality'.

The absence of clear and unequivocal knowledge systems makes the concern with risk all the more problematic and pervasive:

Everywhere, pollutants and toxins laugh and play their tricks like devils in the Middle Ages. People are almost inescapably bound over to them. Breathing, eating, dwelling, wearing clothes – everything has been penetrated by them . . . Their invisibility is no proof of their non-existence; instead, since their reality takes place in the realm of the invisible anyway, it gives their suspected mischief almost unlimited space. (Beck 1992, p. 73)

These physical risks assume global significance since they do not accept divisions of, for example, class or location. To quote one of Beck's hallmark aphorisms: 'poverty is hierarchic, smog is democratic' (ibid., p. 36). Put more broadly:

[T]he risk society (in contrast to class society) develops a tendency to unify the victims in global risk positions . . . friend and foe, east and west, above and below, city and country, south and north are all exposed to the leveling pressure of the exponentially increasing risks of civilization. . . . To that extent the risk society controls new sources of conflict and consensus. The place of *eliminating scarcity* is taken by *eliminating risk*. (ibid., p. 47; emphasis in original)

It follows from this analysis that, in the risk society, our ideas of the natural cannot be kept apart from the social concerns of our time. In a statement that is highly relevant to this book, Beck argues that:

Environmental problems are *not* problems for our surroundings, but – in their origins and through their consequences – are thoroughly *social* problems, *problems of people*, their history, their living conditions, their relation to the world and reality, their social, cultural and political situations. . . . At the end of the twentieth century nature *is* society and society is also '*nature*'. Anyone who continues to speak of nature as non-society is speaking in terms from a different century, which no longer capture our reality. (ibid., p. 81; emphasis in original)

Beck suggests that nature is nowhere 'left to itself' within the structure of late modernity. Instead, it has become a cultural product. On that basis also, risk concerns stand as the focus for a variety of social, institutional, scientific and moral concerns: 'Statements on risk are the moral statements of scientized society' (ibid., p. 176).

Nature only assumes an appearance of reality through human interference and especially through the activities of science. How would we be aware of such phenomena as global warming or acid rain without the intervention of scientists? Nature does not speak for itself but must instead be interpreted and constructed through institutions and social actions. The media too have an important role to play here, since images of nature (in 'its beauty and its suffering') must be brought to people before they are likely to become concerned.

In such a situation, it is hardly surprising that politics and social movements should also take a new form – what Beck often refers to as the 'unbinding of politics'. There are a number of changes at the level of 'sub-politics'.

First of all, Beck argues that existing institutions generally struggle to come to terms with the profound challenges of environmental threat. Instead, they are accused of 'organized irresponsibility': 'On the threshold of the twenty-first century, the challenges of the age of atomic, genetic, and chemical technology are being handled with concepts and recipes that are derived from the early industrial society of the nineteenth and early twentieth centuries' (1995a, pp. 24–5). Given this general orientation, official institutions may be more likely to amplify than resolve the problems.

Secondly, according to Beck, environmental issues have not emerged onto the public agenda as a consequence of 'the cathedrals of power in business, science, and the state', but through the efforts of diverse and splintered groups such as environmental coalitions, campaigning groups and local networks. As we have already noted, Beck refers to these as 'pragmatic alliances in the individual struggle for existence' and seems to see in them a possible model of 'democratic subversion' for the future.

Thirdly, in drawing attention to these new forms of political action – forms that have largely bypassed conventional democratic processes involving party politics, parliament and the civil service – Beck also observes what he considers to be a lack of attention to one key player within the risk society: 'In relations to the state, industry possesses a double advantage, that of the *autonomy of investment decisions* and the *monopoly on the application of technology*' (1992, p. 212; emphasis in original). Put more generally, we have reached a social condition where: 'The division of labor thus leaves the industries with the primary decision-making *but without* responsibility for side effects, while politics is assigned the task of democratically legitimating decisions it has *not* taken and of "cushioning" technology's side effects' (ibid., p. 213; emphasis in original).

Whilst the agencies of the state and various 'pragmatic alliances' struggle to influence the risk society's direction, the 'structuring of the future is taking place indirectly and unrecognizably in research laboratories and executive suites' (ibid., p. 223). Meanwhile, other parties are obliged to live off the 'crumbs of information that fall from the planning tables of technological sub-politics'(ibid.).

Accordingly, Beck has called for an opening-up of technological processes to democratic criticism and challenge. This is not a question of turning back to old institutional forms but rather of building towards a *new* modernity. This might mean 'insisting that those who create the risks take responsibility for them' (1995a, p. 74). It would also involve 'supporting and extending the counter-control and counter-influence possibilities of sub-politics' (ibid., p. 75). Nevertheless, and as Beck has concluded on a more pessimistic note: 'No one knows . . . how, whether and by what means it might be possible to really throttle back the self-endangering momentum of the global risk society' (1996, p. 42).

Beck does not offer a clear and specific agenda for the new era, since the whole point of his argument is that we have no solid foundation upon which to build this. Whilst sometimes offering the possibility of a positive scenario, his serious academic aim is to draw attention to the 'dark side' of the current social structure and its treatment of risk and environmental crisis.

Re-examining the Risk Society

[R]isks are industrially produced, economically externalized, juridically individualized, and scientifically legitimized. (Beck 1995a, p. 127)

The first reaction to this rapid summary of Beck might well be a degree of disorientation. Although the notion of an environmental crisis seems familiar to us, Beck's portrayal of a world based on doubt, ambivalence and individualization is decidedly more troublesome than that provided by the Brundtland Commission. This is especially the case, since Beck deprives us of the very fixed points upon which we would most obviously depend in dealing with this crisis: namely, our faith in science, in national and international institutions and in the established structures of everyday life. Beck's account even deprives us of the familiar notion that 'nature' represents a world external to society.

Conventional accounts stress the role of science in providing a rational basis for environmental policy. However, Beck argues that, whilst science may have an important role to play, it cannot be looked to for clear solutions. Instead, reflexive modernization raises major questions about science and its role in generating environmental problems. Equally, while the Brundtland agenda calls for increased governmental activity and cooperation, Beck argues that governments struggle to cope with the profound challenges. The conventional sense of an external environmental crisis suggests that institutions need somehow to 'respond' to this. Beck portrays a pervasiveness and depth of crisis that almost defy the human imagination and hence our abilities to cope. Building especially on cases such as nuclear risks and global warming, he presents a situation where the scale and pervasiveness of threat override other social divisions (and notably class).

Beck's account takes us into an unsettling world where risk has become paramount but our bearings have been lost, and where the usual solutions (more science, stricter regulation and tighter institutional control, further technological development) only create greater problems. On the one hand, the side-effects of modernity have become central. On the other, the problems are not just about risks and environmental threats but go to the core of the social structure as we shift towards late modernity.

In this way, risks are an 'explosive problem', since the institutions that claim to have the problems under control are failing badly and the situation is only getting worse. Risk issues are destabilizing and delegitimizing the very institutions that have been set up to control them. Meanwhile, modernity's attempt to brush these problems aside and treat them as if they were merely temporary set-backs is becoming visibly inadequate and publicly unconvincing.

Of course, and as we saw in the previous chapter, this has not stopped international organizations from attempting to deal with the crisis by creating new institutions and striving to strengthen their grip on the situation. However, Beck's analysis does offer some insight into why citizen groups might oppose international initiatives of this kind: isn't sustainable development an attempt to re-establish modernity rather than to seek a fundamental transformation? Equally, Beck's analysis suggests why institutions might repeatedly fail in the task they are setting themselves. They are basically attempting to reimpose the very form of rationality that created the problems in the first place.

For Beck, this represents an institutional crisis for industrial society. The issue has moved beyond 'what do we do about the environment?' and been transformed into 'how are we to live in the new social conditions?'. This latter question is all the more complex when the new conditions are only barely discernible. Moreover, it seems characteristic of the new risks that we cannot detect them through our senses – we cannot see or smell nuclear radiation, low-level chemical pollution or mad cow disease. In such a situation of the 'disempowerment of the senses', we are all the more vulnerable to the very institutions that have created the conditions of environmental collapse.

In this labyrinth of the risk society, we need to find new ways of thinking and acting. The best possibility for Beck of dealing with ubiquitous risk is a redefinition of both political and technological action:

> We must reverse the prevailing practice of developing and financing new technologies first, and then investigating the effects and the hazards, and finally publicly discussing them under the guillotine of manufactured objective constraints. Only in that way could we minimize the hazards *and* open the possibilities for people to have a say in the matter. This time . . . the political and democratic opening of hazard technocracy is also a way to prevent the hazards. (1995a, p. 110; emphasis in original)

At a superficial level, this call for democratization is reminiscent of the Brundtland Commission's demand for greater social equity and empowerment. Further reflection suggests just how different these perspectives are – especially since Brundtland offers a much more restricted notion of the depth of the challenge being faced and consequently of the form of democratic discussion required.

In specifically sociological terms, we can view Beck as offering a profound challenge whilst also drawing theoretically upon the 'founding fathers'. The concept of risk is accorded major explanatory status. Science and expertise become a key topic for sociological discussion. Existing concepts such as social class are downgraded, since there is from Beck's perspective no 'ecological proletariat'. Most generally, Beck presents a world of turmoil, change and ambivalence in which the standard sociological tool-kit may no longer apply:

> What does the social researcher do when it is no longer clear how far fundamental concepts such as occupation, family, social class, or social stratum still fit reality; when it is no longer clear whether unemployment is a social problem or the first step toward freedom from labor society? (ibid., p. 114)

At the same time, Beck explicitly draws upon a sociological tradition that encompasses Habermas and the Frankfurt School but also Weber and the 'disenchantment of the world'. In particular, Beck can be seen as grappling with well-established questions of social order and of the continuities that are maintained beneath the apparent maelstrom of late modernity.

Although his work often touches upon quite specific examples of environmental damage and industrial catastrophe, Beck is self-consciously engaged in debate with both classical and contemporary social theory, and focused on the large-scale structure of modernity. Paradoxically perhaps, his challenge to the discipline emerges from one major tradition within it and in particular from a concern with large-scale social change and equally large-scale generalizations concerning institutions and social processes. In that sense, Beck himself can be presented very much as a product of the modernity that he criticizes in such depth.

Beck recognizes that, as Hajer puts it, 'sociological theory is essentially a product of industrial society' (1995, p. 37, fn. 53). Beck also argues that this causes major problems for sociological analysis, since, as we noted in the Introduction, the conceptual tools of the discipline struggle to grasp the new relationship between the social and the natural. Nevertheless, his critique of, for example, knowledge and expertise causes some difficulties for his own form of sociological analysis. Surely sociology must be open to the same general critique as is being addressed to the natural sciences? If scientific discourse is open to challenge, then the same would appear to be true of sociological accounts of the kind offered by Beck.

A similar point applies to Beck's reliance on scientific expertise to identify the scale of physical risk facing us all. How can such certain claims be built on what is otherwise presented as uncertain evidence? Whilst Beck is aware of this difficulty, it also represents a tension point for this form of sociological argumentation.

As might be anticipated, there has been a substantial critical response to Beck. Given the wide-ranging character of his account, these criticisms are inevitably also broad. In what follows, I will briefly list some of these criticisms before going into greater depth on two interlinked aspects of Beck: his use of 'modernity' as an analytical category and his treatment of the social–natural relationship.

At a blunt level of criticism, it is not too hard to suggest that particular aspects of Beck's case may be overstated or just plain wrong. Thus, it can be claimed in response that individualization has not overwhelmed modern life, that family structures remain stubbornly in place (even if in modified form). Equally, Marxist critics – but also empirically inclined researchers – have suggested that social inequality and exposure to hazardous environments are still closely related despite Beck's claims for the 'boomerang effect' (whereby the middle classes can no longer avoid the consequences of environmental degradation).

Beck has also been accused of offering a very Western (and specifically German) view of both risk and the social structure. How can he talk about the end of hunger when so many people worldwide are starving?[3] Equally, his notion of the 'unbinding of politics' may be based upon experience of German politics (and especially the partial success of the green movement) rather than that of other nations where the traditional political parties are still centre-stage.

At a more general level, there has been a reaction to Beck's emphasis on the 'bads' of modernity. Is he perhaps exaggerating the level of threat and also the contemporary awareness of such issues? Beck may indeed be building too much on such dramatic cases as nuclear power, rather than considering the more mundane treatment of smaller-scale, but possibly more pervasive, risks such as local pollution incidents and factory accidents. His treatment of risk is certainly sweeping and generalized. Whilst there is no denying the relevance or pervasiveness of risk and environmental concerns, it does not necessarily follow that these are *central* to contemporary social life.

Somewhat ironically, for certain environmentalists Beck's bleak message can be unpalatable since it offers a largely pessimistic account. At the same time, talk of 'reflexive modernization' might be seen as getting in the way of practical action, since, from the viewpoint of environmental activists, it might obfuscate and confuse rather than suggest a way forward. Environmentalists might, therefore, be critical of the practical implications of Beck's account. Meanwhile, for defenders of modernity, Beck seems to ignore the high level of public support for new technologies. Here he stands in contradiction to alternative accounts that stress the new technological possibilities (for example, linked to information technology, cyberspace and tele-working). Is his message of modernity in collapse perhaps overstated and over-reliant on the philosophy of the 'deep Greens'? On that basis also, is he perhaps over-critical of science and technology and insufficiently aware of the progressive potential of the new technologies?

This point about a possible over-emphasis on the bads of modernity takes us into a general characteristic of Beck: his tendency to make broad statements and to plunder illustrative examples rather than building his case upon more grounded empirical observations.

Thus, it is possible to make illustrative use and rhetorical play of specific disasters such as Chernobyl, but this is not the same as documenting and exploring the anxieties and concerns of particular groups of citizens. In Beck's analysis, various social phenomena and social groups are described and summarized – whether public groups, scientists, governmental institutions or industry – in complex and interesting ways. However, we learn less about the specifics of the social processes involved or the particular viewpoints and rationales of those social actors who are being invoked. As one empirical socio-logist (and rather harsh critic) put it, 'feature writers à la Beck' need 'neither data, nor data analysis'.[4]

These points take on special significance when we consider the large-scale concepts employed by Beck: concepts such as science, social institutions and, as the biggest generalization of all, modernity. Beck does indicate the multifaceted nature of all of these. However, one is left with a decidedly homogeneous notion of, for example, science (what we can term an 'essentialist' treatment, as if science only represented one body of thought and social practice). It seems to follow from Beck's account that science is an independent force, which impacts upon society. Such an approach will be strongly con-tested in the next chapter.

Modernity, likewise, features in an undoubtedly sophisticated but also shadowy manner throughout Beck's account. What explanatory status should we grant this term? How exactly is it being defined and in what particular ways does it manifest itself within everyday life? The clear danger with the treatment of modernity (as with science) is that it imposes an inflexible sociological framework upon a mass of competing experiences and social tendencies.

Thus, Beck's portrayal of a sceptical public for scientific and technological 'progress' builds upon the notion that, in previous times, the public was acquiescent in the face of change. In this way, Beck is presenting a structural account rather than adopting a more diverse and pluralistic approach to the publics and their assess-ments and understandings of socio-technical change. In historical terms, this approach seems both restricted and potentially mislead-ing (by, for example, downplaying nineteenth-century public con-cerns over technological developments). As a treatment of the public response to risk and environmental issues it appears very limited. The assumption seems to be that citizens comply with the dominant trends of history rather than exercising their own agency and forms of knowledge.

There is, then, a tendency for Beck, whilst acknowledging the complexity and ambiguity of social phenomena, to accommodate them within singular, and inevitably rigid, categories. Even while he is opening up the contradictory nature and uncertainties of the risk society, he is also constructing the 'global risk positions' of late modernity from his own theoretical position. In so doing, a serious discussion of Beck raises the question of whether an alternative and more contextualized sociological approach might be possible – one that begins with specific social phenomena rather than simply presenting them as illustrations of a larger framework.

The theoretical status of such overarching terms as 'modernity' and 'late modernity' is certainly open to sociological challenge. Beck is drawing an explicit contrast with a previous classical age without substantial historical evidence to support this. He is also attempting to impose a generalized framework upon an inevitably complex range of personal and institutional experiences. The clear problem with such a perspective is that it reduces diversity and variation to a more constrained analytical structure. In so doing, this sociological framing plays down the significance of specific social and environmental contexts.

The generalized approach also raises issues for Beck's treatment of environmental risks and threats. The Brundtland Report adopted a straightforward (and straightforwardly realist) stance that the environment represented an 'external' threat (albeit one largely created by social and technological development) to which societies now need to respond. Beck, however, presents environmental threats as simultaneously social *and* natural in character.

On the one hand, this suggests a more important role for sociology than simply analysing the non-technical aspects of the environmental crisis (since the interpretation and selection of environmental threats can now be viewed as a social process rather than simply being left to science). On the other, it does indicate an ambiguity within Beck's position – an ambiguity that seems to place him midway between a realist and constructivist position. Put simply, Beck's talk of an environmental crisis is used to lend significance to his arguments: 'In the modernization process, more and more *destructive* forces are being unleashed, forces before which the human imagination stands in awe' (1992, p. 130; emphasis in original). At the same time, the 'globalization of risks' is presented as a 'social dynamic'.

Beck's argument here hinges on the difficulty of apprehending (or knowing) the risks that surround us. Whilst environmental risks may be 'real' (in the sense that they exist outside of human apprehension), there is no straightforward way of comprehending them, since the new categories of risk (for example, nuclear or chemical contamination) are neither 'visible nor perceptible'. In such a situation, the 'sensory organs of science' (ibid., p. 162) are needed in order to decide whether the hazards exist – even whilst these sensory organs are open to challenge and may serve to support particular social and institutional interests. In a world where we have no common-sensical way of knowing what risks we run, hazard assessment becomes a combination of scientific rationality, institutional deliber-ation and the efforts of new political and environmental organiza-tions. Beck is not denying the existence of a real crisis but is instead drawing attention to the moral and political character of its con-struction. As he puts this: '*Cultural norms and cultural willingness to perceive* decide which damage is accepted and which is not' (1995a, p. 124; emphasis in original).

Beck also views the selection of either a constructivist or realist perspective as a *pragmatic judgement*: 'a matter of choosing the appropriate means for a desired goal'. Rather than confronting an 'either–or option' or a 'matter of belief', the sociologist should be able to employ whichever framework is most appropriate to the task at hand: 'I can be both a realist and a constructivist, using realism *and* constructivism as far as these meta-narratives are useful for the purpose of understanding the complex and ambivalent "nature" of risk in the world risk society we live in' (1999, p. 134).

In the next chapter, we will consider these questions of science and the social construction of environmental threats in greater depth – and with specific reference to an emerging tradition within sociology which stresses the importance of an empirical and actor-oriented perspective. Whilst the approach taken in the next chapter is there-fore rather different from that of Beck, we will see that related themes of uncertainty and ambivalence arise. We will also develop the point that such questions, as Beck has convincingly argued, are central to a sociological understanding of environmental problems and concerns.

Despite the critical points above, Beck's approach suggests a soci-ological engagement with environmental matters rather than a retreat to more conventional theories and concepts. As he expresses this in typically disarming fashion: 'I cannot cast off the peculiar naiveté of believing that sociology should have something to do with understanding the society in which it acts' (1995a, p. 117). Whilst Beck's analysis may provide some problems for those committed to environmental action, it also suggests one model of a sociologi-cal approach that leads to the critical discussion of environmental strategy.

We have suggested in this chapter that Beck's exploration of the contemporary character of modernity does not represent an endpoint for sociological analysis but a route into a series of important questions about environmental concerns and the form of sociological explanation that is required to deal with these. Accordingly, Beck's analysis will be reviewed and developed as this book continues. At this point, we move to a third important framing of the relationship between sociology and the environment: the sociology of scientific knowledge.

3

Science and the Social Construction of Environmental Threat

[O]ur technology and science gives us at least the potential to look deeper into and better understand natural systems. . . . We have the power to reconcile human affairs with natural laws and to thrive in the process.

World Commission on Environment and Development 1997, p. 1

The origin of risk consciousness . . . is truly not a page of honor in the history of (natural) scientists. It came into being against a continuing barrage of scientific denial, and is still suppressed by it. . . . Science has *become the protector of a global contamination of people and nature.*

Beck 1992, p. 70

This chapter introduces a third framework for the relationship between society, nature and knowledge. Central to the sociology–environment relationship is the role of science *as a means of apprehending, defining and measuring environmental problems.*

The sociology of scientific knowledge (SSK) has explored science as a social and institutional process. *Rather than prejudging the validity of scientific claims to truth and objectivity or reaching sweeping assertions about science, SSK adopts a sceptical and symmetrical approach to all knowledge claims – including those of science – which attempt to speak for nature. This has the effect of challenging the fixed duality between nature and society, and presenting environmental problems as profoundly* hybrid *in character. SSK has also emphasized the importance of social and cognitive practices in the constitution of environmental knowledge.*

Rather than directly engaging in abstract discussions over the social and the natural, the SSK perspective advocates the inves-

tigation of specific and detailed scientific interactions with environmental matters. Three examples of such interactions are presented in this chapter.

Given the centrality of scientific discussion to environmental issues, science and technology studies (STS) in general and the sociology of scientific knowledge (SSK) in particular have potentially major implications for sociology and the environment. By tradition, sociology has a tendency to beat a retreat when technical matters appear over the environmental horizon. What can sociologists possibly have to say about science? For an SSK-based approach, however, the empirical and theoretical study of science represents a core element within the sociological analysis of environmental concerns. This suggestion in turn has profound consequences both for environmental understanding and for the discipline of sociology.

Certainly, it is difficult to engage with the contemporary treatment of environmental issues without encountering scientific analysis and argumentation. Given the difficulties discussed by Beck of identifying and measuring environmental problems (since we cannot necessarily touch, hear, see, taste or smell them and since, in any case, they may extend beyond the boundaries of not only our senses but also of previous human experience), science has become a crucial means of apprehending these potential problems and of thinking the unthinkable. As Beck argues, science is *the* characteristic means by which modern societies deal with the identification and assessment of environmental problems.

The Brundtland Report makes very few direct references to science. However, one important operating assumption within sustainability talk is that institutional change needs to take place in line with scientific and rational principles (or scientifically defined 'natural laws', as described in the chapter's opening quotation). Science is, almost common-sensically, seen from this perspective as the best means of interpreting and defining environmental challenges. With proper financial and technical support, science can continue to increase its understanding of environmental processes and so provide a solid foundation for social and institutional action. According to this approach, science identifies and gauges environmental problems. The task of institutions is then to respond appropriately. In that way also, scientists can play a crucial part in helping governments build towards sustainability. If such a 'naturalistic' perspective on environmental issues is accepted as the starting-point for sociological analysis, then a number of possible lines of investigation emerge. Sociologists might consider various topics, including the 'social challenges' of sustainability, concepts of global and intergenerational equity, and likely 'social responses' to environmental problems. However, there is a clear distinction being drawn between such social elements and the basic scientific task of defining and quantifying environmental threats. The task of sociology effectively begins once the scientists have completed their separate mission.

Beck is generally more critical of the part played by scientific expertise within environmental disputes. Certainly, he suggests a far wider set of issues for sociological analysis. A fundamental reassessment of the relationship between modernity and environmental destruction is required. Whilst Beck acknowledges the important part played by the 'sensory organs' of science, he also portrays the relationship between science and environmental protection as profoundly ambivalent in character. Science serves as the protector of contamination. It often stands on the side of modernistic institutions against the anxieties of citizens. Science and technology become *causes* of mistakes and problems rather than their solution (Beck, 1995a, p. 52).

Science is generally presented by Beck as being out of control. Accordingly, it has become necessary to 'install brakes and steering gear' into science – with the first step towards this being 'the revival of the ability to learn and the ability to admit errors' (ibid., p. 93). Whilst Brundtland presents the problem as being the need for *more* science and for greater institutional responsiveness to its environmental warnings, Beck views the *quality and direction* of science as a major issue. Science needs to change, to acknowledge criticism and to admit uncertainties if it is to cope with the new social and environmental challenges.

Beck's approach offers the possibility of sociology adopting a critical perspective on scientific issues. He points out the, almost hegemonic, influence of scientific thinking within environmental debates. Thus, scientific arguments are often used to stifle other voices within environmental discussion and, especially, those of ordinary citizens. Beck also considers the social impacts of science and the possible relationship between scientific arguments and various social interests. Notably, he moves sociological analysis on from the 'social challenges and social impacts' approach suggested by the sustainability perspective and considers instead the role of scientific analysis in formulating and 'framing' environmental debates.

The starting-point for an SSK approach to the relationship between science and the environment is to note the very *schematic* picture of contemporary science (and of the environmental consequences of science) presented by both Beck and Brundtland. Beck discusses the ambivalent character of science and presents us with a number of illustrations to reinforce this message. Discussions of sustainable development consider science to be a force for rationality and progress. Neither approach offers a more detailed account of science itself nor an indication of *how* scientific knowledge is generated and legitimated within hotly contested social contexts. In other words (and to adopt the language of SSK), we are offered little sense of science as *social process*.

This social process includes relations between scientists – for example, between the different occupational and disciplinary groups that might be involved in analysing environmental problems. Seen from the perspective of SSK, it may be highly significant whether a scientist works in an academic department or an industrial consultancy – or whether she is a plant biologist or a nuclear engineer. Equally, the manner in which individual scientists make sense of environmental issues becomes an important topic for analysis.

Rather than just assuming that the processes of scientific knowledge production are sociologically mysterious, irrelevant or uninteresting, SSK has viewed these processes as sites for detailed empirical investigation. How do specific scientists construct their accounts? How might the accounts offered by particular scientists relate to the social circumstances of their development? How do scientists attempt to persuade other scientists of the validity of their analyses? How in turn have scientists persuaded *non*-scientists of the validity and 'truthfulness' of these claims to natural understanding? By this point, the contrast with Beck's structural analysis should be quite clear.

Whilst the schematic (or 'textbook') account typically treats science as a 'black box' with inputs (institutional support and funding) and outputs (scientific theories and 'facts'), SSK perspectives have specifically attempted to explore the nature of 'laboratory life' (Latour and Woolgar 1979) in all its heterogeneity and social complexity. Equally, whilst the conventional sociological approach has adopted an 'essentialist' treatment of science (i.e. based on the rather self-serving picture of science offered by textbook accounts of its growth and development), the sociology of scientific knowledge has largely been *constructivist* in orientation.

'Constructivism' within an SSK context indicates a sociological approach that *is broadly agnostic about the validity of the truth claims of scientists but instead considers how such claims come to be seen as valid statements about the natural world.* Rather than simply stating that scientific accounts become accepted as facts because they are 'true' (a somewhat unhelpful and circular formulation, which denies any significant role for sociological investigation), constructivism typically analyses the social and institutional processes through which statements acquire 'truthful' status. In that way, and put provocatively, truth is not assumed to be an input to scientific discussion but is instead presented as the *output* from scientific and institutional processes. As Grint and Woolgar put it: 'Research in social studies of science and technology has repeatedly and overwhelmingly demonstrated how truth is the contingent upshot of social action rather than its prerequisite' (1997: 166).

By what rhetorical and discursive devices do scientists attempt to persuade colleagues and wider audiences of the solidity of their claims? In what ways is the definition of knowledge affected by the social circumstances of its development? What different relations have developed between the sponsors of research and the kinds of knowledge produced? An SSK approach generally replaces any fixed notion of scientific determinism (i.e. that science simply follows a predetermined path of discovery and the development of 'facts') with a more fluid and dynamic interpretation of the active processes through which scientists 'make sense' of the natural world.[1] Turning explicitly to the subject of this book, we can begin to see how a sociological approach to scientific knowledge might be of special relevance. Given the importance of science within environmental discussion, the argument that scientific knowledge does not simply mirror an external real world of nature but is *socially constructed* becomes extremely important both in terms of interpreting environmental discussion and for sociology itself. SSK suggests that *the 'facts' of environmental matters do not speak for themselves: instead, they are actively created and interpreted. Similarly, nature can no longer be represented as an external category. Statements about the natural world represent social and institutional constructions.*

In the case of environmental matters, we are confronted with a wide array of institutional actors and processes when attempting to establish the state of nature. These include industries deciding about innovation policy, governments making decisions about public safety and environmental protection, campaigning groups considering which problems to select and how to persuade public audiences of their significance. This social complexity puts particular strain on scientific understanding. We are very far from the closed world of the laboratory. Instead, scientific and sociological interpretation must deal with a diverse network of scientific facts and political actors, industrialists and concerned scientists, campaigning groups and natural phenomena, even non-humans as well as humans.

The key point about the SSK perspective is that it doesn't automatically privilege scientific accounts over those offered by other concerned groups. Nor does it assume that certain scientific claims should be prioritized over others. Instead, SSK offers a *symmetrical* and *sceptical* account of knowledge claims and the social processes of their construction. It has also been characteristic of an SSK approach that it focuses analytical attention not on the development of sweeping generalizations and broad frameworks but on the specifics of 'science in action'.[2] The contexts within which knowledge is produced are not simply an irrelevance or a matter of marginal historical interest (as 'textbook' accounts of science suggest). Instead, social, institutional and cognitive processes are central to the constitution of scientific understanding.

In keeping with that empirical tradition, we can take a look at issues of science, risk and the environment as they have arisen in three recent cases: civil nuclear power, BSE and chemical hazards. These cases have been selected so as to illustrate the SSK perspective and the characteristic issues raised. Within each of these examples, we can observe science as playing a significant role within the social construction of environmental threat. At the same time, each case offers serious difficulties for science: difficulties that can only be fully understood once we move outside the 'essentialist' framework encountered so far. Rather than simply portraying science as embodying a 'rational' (in the language of sustainable development) or 'modernistic' (Beck) response to environmental concerns, we can begin to explore the diverse character of modern science and its relationships with various groups active in the environmental arena.

Science in Environmental Action

Civil Nuclear Energy

The health and environmental effects of the international nuclear energy programme represent one of the main examples employed by Beck in exploring the contemporary treatment of 'unthinkable' risks. The significance of nuclear risks has been emphasized by a series of accidents at nuclear power plants (notably, Windscale, UK, in 1957; Three Mile Island, USA, in 1979; Chernobyl, Ukraine, in 1986). Equally, international controversies have occurred over the environmental impact of low-level radiation from nuclear power plants, the long-term disposal of nuclear waste and the relative environmental risks of nuclear power compared to other forms of energy production (for example, coal- or oil-based systems). Throughout these discussions, nuclear power has been distinguished by the steadfast opposition of its critics (for whom it represents the unacceptable face of modern technology) and the equivalent enthusiasm of its supporters (who argue that, despite occasional problems, it represents a relatively safe form of energy generation).

In line with Beck's analysis of late modernity, it is possible to view scientific research as being implicated both in the development of this technology and also in the public and institutional discussion of its health and environmental consequences. In that sense, current discussions of nuclear power can be viewed as a clear example of 'reflexive modernization': the logic and methods of science being applied to the product of a previous generation of scientists (so that science is literally 'encountering itself' within environmental disputes). However, rather than viewing nuclear technology in such general and abstracted terms, there are a number of specific features of civil nuclear power that give it particular sociological interest when viewed from the SSK perspective.

One immediate point concerns the *variety* of technical expertises that exist in this area. Rather than simply discussing 'nuclear science', it is possible to identify a series of sub-disciplines and specialties in operation – from chemical and nuclear engineering through to epidemiology, from physics to animal toxicology, from medicine to mathematics. Typically, each possesses its own intellectual and institutional structure. Right from the start, therefore, we encounter the fundamental point that nuclear science can usefully be disaggregated into a range of particular bodies of expertise, each operating on rather different principles and with different foci of attention. The epidemiological analysis of health records is a very different activity from engineering calculations of the probability of pressure-vessel failure – even if both can be loosely described as 'scientific' in character.

Secondly, and linked to this general point, there is the question of the *institutional location* of nuclear debates. The sociology of scientific knowledge suggests the need to encompass the social variety of groups that have been involved in technical argumentation in this area: from government departments to the nuclear industry itself, from environmentalist groups to people who work in the industry, from international bodies to local communities living close to nuclear power facilities. Each is likely to have its own social and, closely linked to this, technical evaluation of, for example, the safety of commercial nuclear power stations. In that way, we can begin to explore the different uses of science made by different groups, but also the ways in which such groups serve to generate knowledge and expertise concerning these issues.

Thirdly with regard to nuclear power, we can see that assessments of the scale of nuclear risk are by no means unanimous. Science is instead *differentiated and divergent* in its appraisal. One characteristic of Beck's approach to these matters is that science can be portrayed as, for example, resisting public awareness and critique. A more agnostic approach to scientific truth claims in this area would observe clear *disagreements and discrepancies* within scientific accounts. It is hard to place science on any side in the dispute, since – and especially in the United States – scientists have represented (and constituted) a variety of pressure groups and concerned institutions. Once again, a detailed account of science in this area would suggest a more complex and dynamic picture than its essentialist representation would suggest.

One further characteristic of the scientific evaluation of nuclear power has been its contentious relationship with matters of *public policy and decision-making*. Whilst dominant social institutions have indeed employed scientific argumentation as defence for their policies (for example, decisions in the 1970s to proceed with nuclear facilities), it has also been clear that these decisions have come under widespread attack and criticism from various campaigning organizations (and notably environmentalist groups such as Friends of the Earth and Greenpeace). Typically, such groups have employed the language of science in making their case against civil nuclear energy.

Taking these points together, we can begin to see that the relationship between science and the assessment of nuclear risks is considerably more complex and multifaceted than a simple study of science and modernity might suggest. Rather than offering a homogeneous presentation of science, this discussion has indicated that nuclear expertise actually covers a range of forms. In addition, the scientific debates have not been static but highly dynamic in character, with an overlapping relationship between technical analyses and those offered by various pressure and campaigning groups (who may themselves have technical expertise to offer). All this means that the interpretation and construction of natural law (to adopt the terminology of the Brundtland Commission) has been a highly contested and often partisan activity, as various groups employ the language of science to defend their own position. This would also suggest that sponsoring more scientific research will not necessarily resolve the controversy – and indeed that further research input might only exacerbate existing disagreements (Collingridge and Reeve 1986).

It would appear simplistic to portray science as the 'protector of global contamination', since the very existence of global contamination is not agreed by all parties, and scientists can be found on almost every side within this long-running area of controversy and debate. Rather than simply accepting scientific claims to offer natural laws for political interpretation, an altogether more complex and overlapping relationship can be identified between 'science' and 'policy'.[3]

Bovine Spongiform Encephalopathy (BSE)

These questions of science and the environment become clearer if we now move to a second case of science–environment relations. The British treatment of BSE (or mad cow disease) has vividly illustrated the problematic relationship that can develop between scientific evidence and risk issues. The major debate here has concerned the possible connection between Creutzfeldt–Jakob disease (CJD) in humans and contaminated beef. This controversy has notably involved the United Kingdom but also various other nations in a complex set of arguments about the possible risk of a barely understood causative agent. When the controversy arose in Britain in the late 1980s, scientific analysis struggled to come to terms with this potentially devastating threat, since no established framework existed for its assessment and analysis. Meanwhile, government ministers and civil servants offered public reassurances based on scant evidence.

This situation opens up a number of issues for the science–environment relationship, not least concerning the *burden of proof* that should be applied in such cases. Put succinctly, does an absence of evidence indicate evidence of absence? In this case, one side could reasonably argue that there was no evidence of BSE crossing the barrier between species. On that basis, the existence of a problem in cattle does not mean that a human health problem will arise. The other side could make equal use of scientific logic to suggest that there was no evidence that the agent would *not* cross this boundary.

As in the nuclear case, therefore, we can observe scientific evidence as being characterized by *uncertainty* and perhaps also *indeterminacy* (see Wynne 1992). With regard to BSE, there have certainly been fundamental technical questions raised about the mechanism of causation (just what is the link between diseased cattle and human CJD?), about the best methods of control (how far-reaching do we need to be in culling affected – or even possibly affected – cattle?) and about the likely scale of any human epidemic (with estimates ranging from a relatively small number of deaths to a 'whole generation' being lost). There have been no simple or straightforward scientific answers to these questions, since such issues stand at the very boundaries of scientific understanding and do not fall within any single discipline or specialty.

A further characteristic of the BSE debate, and one that this debate shares with various other risk and environmental issues, is the extreme difficulty of *separating the social from the scientific* within technical appraisal and assessment. Whilst science generally claims to deal in the facts of such matters and to exclude social assumptions and value judgements, the sociology of scientific knowledge has challenged this distinction. In the case of BSE, apparently factual assessments of risk depend upon social and institutional assumptions about conditions of animal husbandry and whether specified farming and abattoir precautions will actually be put into practice. A similar point can be made with regard to the nuclear case. Sophisticated calculations of risk must always depend upon social and institutional judgements as to the likelihood that safety procedures will actually be followed or that component parts have been correctly manufactured and fitted. In each case, the judgements of scientific experts are premised upon what is effectively a social assessment of how the risks involved will be managed and whether officially sanctioned procedures and practices will actually be observed. Discussing four other examples of risk management, Wynne (1989) has presented these embedded (but unacknowledged) social judgements as a form of 'naïve sociology' at the core of expert analyses.

In the case of BSE also, we can observe the difficulty of making any fixed distinction between *the social and the natural*. For now, we can simply note that the simple characterization of this case as representing the 'scientific' analysis of a 'natural' problem is flawed in numerous ways, since no easy line can be drawn between what is 'scientific', what is 'natural' and, indeed, what is 'social' in a case like this. If we take the cows on which all of this debate has centred, then the obvious approach would be to view these as natural creatures (a view that might seem especially obvious to town-dwellers like myself, brought up on various butter and cheese commercials featuring 'happy cows' in green fields). However, even the most cursory analysis suggests that these happy, indeed laughing, cows are far from the reality of international farming practice. Equally, the creatures in question appear no more natural than Dutch tulip fields or US national parks. The modern cow is the product of generations of human-controlled cattle-breeding, feeding and housing. Looked at in this way, it is very difficult to see where the social element of factory farming ends and the natural begins. Instead, both are part of the same web of human and animal interaction. Scientists might claim to be studying natural phenomena, but this category is not so unambiguous as a conventional account would suggest.

Finally in this section, we can simply observe the public difficulties that have arisen for government bodies (and the UK Ministry of Agriculture, Fisheries and Food, MAFF, in particular) in dealing with the social and scientific dimensions of this risk crisis. A number of sociological observers have noted the problems for *public trust and credibility* that have arisen.

Put bluntly, the usual institutional tactic of offering public reassurances and representing oneself as confident in the validity of one's own judgement has tended to backfire in the BSE case and raise even further problems of institutional legitimacy. Whilst this does not suggest that scientifically based government messages have been dismissed or rejected, it does open up discussion of the critical publics for scientific information and the possibility that such official statements will be interpreted in a sceptical manner. One aspect of this public reception will typically involve a judgement as to *who* is conveying a particular message and their perceived interest in this matter. The close relationship between the government department and the meat industry has drawn particular public comment in this case – despite the view of many farmers that the government was actually causing their industry great problems because of its inactivity.

The examples of BSE and nuclear power broadly suggest the problematic character of scientific knowledge (or, more accurately, scientific knowledges) in this area. The separation of 'scientific' from 'social' assumptions is especially difficult in both these cases. A scientific assessment of nuclear power plant operation or of the likely success of various animal culling practices appears to be unavoidably a matter of social as well as technical judgement. Equally, whether one views a low probability event (such as a major nuclear disaster) as so unlikely that it is irrational to worry or as a risk that might just occur seems a matter of social and professional judgement. Science emerges on that basis not as a socially independent agent but as itself an embodiment of social as well as technical values and assessments.[4]

Chemical Hazards and Pollution

As a third example of relations between science and the environment as seen from an SSK perspective, we can focus on discussions, especially since the 1960s, over chemical pollution – in other words, environmental risks and concerns relating to the products and processes of the chemical industry. Chemical hazards take a number of forms – from large-scale disasters such as that at Bhopal, India, in 1984, to the more everyday risks of living close to chemical installations during their daily operation. Equally, chemical products have been implicated in a whole series of environmental and health disputes: food additives, workplace chemicals and medicines have all been at the centre of arguments around cancer risks and various other long-term health problems. The operation of the chemical industry has also generated a series of local controversies over the siting of chemical facilities and the air and water pollution caused by existing installations.

In order to illustrate the issues, we can select one particular example within the chemical field: the case of pesticides (or 'agro-chemicals', as they are known more generically within the chemical industry). Since Rachel Carson's classic early-1960s onslaught on the environmental effects of pesticide usage, *Silent Spring*,[5] pesticide producers have been obliged to consider carefully the impact of their products on the environment. Such impacts have so far included damage to eco-systems and animal populations, and also a possible link to human health effects as a consequence of consuming low levels of pesticide residues within foodstuffs and drinking water. Scientific evidence has played a growing part both in the regulation of risk and in the development of new agrochemicals. Certainly, scientists have become centrally involved in decisions over whether it is worthwhile for a company to proceed with a particular product if, for example, it appears unlikely that it will gain regulatory approval on environmental grounds.

At this point, we can identify the emergence of what has been termed 'regulatory science' – forms of science developed especially within industry and with direct relevance to industrial concerns (see Irwin et al. 1997b). Whilst certain commentators have tried to draw a distinction between this form of scientific activity and 'academic science', it should be noted that academic practice is also changing. At MIT, for example, some 20 per cent of research funds are provided by industry.[6] We need, therefore, to be generally aware of the *changing conditions of scientific practice*.

This is not to deny the intellectual quality of regulatory scientific work or to suggest that industrially sponsored science is always 'applied' in nature (much basic research – including Nobel Prize-winning science – has emanated from the larger industrial laboratories). However, it does draw attention to the institutional contexts within which contemporary science is conducted – contexts that inevitably accord special significance to knowledge that is of practical as well as 'intellectual' value. This point is especially important given that research in the area of agrochemicals is overwhelmingly funded by industry itself. This, of course, raises questions about the relationship between funding sources, the location of research and the kinds of scientific work that are conducted. All of this is highly relevant given the issues of public trust that were raised in our previous discussion of BSE. The industrial basis of regulatory science may provoke a particular scepticism from public groups. For this reason, there is a sociological need, rather than simply discussing the relationship between 'science' and environmental concerns, to consider the *social and institutional contexts* within which modern science is produced.

We can also identify not only a variety of institutional contexts and scientific disciplines but also a *scientific division of labour*, which covers both routinized testing (especially the administration of chemical samples to animals in order to test for health effects) and sophisticated theoretical analyses of possible pathways of chemical contamination. 'Science' in this area includes the submission of dossiers for regulatory approval and, very importantly, the operation of scientific committees, which decide what tests should be run and what kinds of evidence are required before open release can occur. In that way, the possession of scientific expertise also serves as an important influence over the form of public and regulatory controls relating to specific hazards.

Finally then, we can note the *highly differentiated character* of scientific activity in this area of risk and environmental threat. Whilst the term 'science' may conjure up a range of specific images in the minds of non-scientists (including mad professors and sinister peddlers of doom), the more disaggregated approach sketched here portrays a complex set of activities – in terms of physical location, intellectual division of labour, forms of activity and disciplinary approach. This differentiation suggests a social complexity to scientific activities but also an overlapping relationship with social, institutional and environmental concerns. In abstract terms, it may be possible to separate the assessment of agrochemical risk from matters of industrial innovation, regulatory policy or public concern. As the sociologist takes a more specific look at the social and intellectual processes involved in reaching such assessments, these distinctions appear increasingly meaningless.

Where does the 'science' end and the 'industrial economics' begin when deciding whether it is worthwhile to develop a new pesticide? Are regulatory checks based on 'science', or on a sense of what is politically acceptable to various competing parties? Is the toleration of routine testing on laboratory animals a scientific or a social judgement? The answer to such questions is generally to suggest that these factors are not separate but overlapping. As we have seen with all three cases, once we move into the specific contexts of scientific development and scientifically based decision-making, large-scale categories of society, nature and knowledge melt into one another.[7]

Perspectives from the Sociology of Scientific Knowledge

All of culture and all of nature get churned up again every day. (Latour 1992, p. 2)

Bruno Latour begins his provocatively entitled *We Have Never Been Modern* with the 'proliferation of hybrids'. His opening section discusses a newspaper article concerning the hole in the ozone layer over the Antarctic. For Latour, what is most interesting about the article is precisely the way in which it combines chemists and industrial organizations, heads of state and refrigerators, inert gases and ecologists:

The same article mixes together chemical reactions and political reactions. A single thread links the most esoteric sciences and the most sordid politics, the most distant sky and some factory in the Lyon suburbs, dangers on a global scale and the impending local elections or the next board meeting. The horizons, the stakes, the time frames, the actors – none of these is commensurable, yet there they are, caught up in the same story. (ibid., p. 1)

Building on this and related cases, Latour argues that what we are witnessing is the collapse of existing categories such as 'Economy', 'Politics', 'Science', 'Culture'. Whilst current styles of thought and academic disciplines still insist that it is possible to divide the world into established divisions, in more and more cases (and environmental examples demonstrate this especially well) we are dealing with 'hybrids', which cut across these conventional boundaries:

> Press the most innocent aerosol button and you'll be heading for the Antarctic, and from there to the University of California at Irvine, the mountain ranges of Lyon, the chemistry of inert gases, and then maybe to the United Nations, but this fragile thread will be broken into as many segments as there are pure disciplines. (ibid., pp. 2–3)

Each of our three case-studies exemplifies this process of 'hybridization'. To take the case of BSE, a very similar story could be told of infected cows and human deaths, of government committees and scientists at the laboratory bench, of abattoir practices and weekend shoppers deciding what to have for Sunday dinner. As the quotation at the beginning of this section suggests, nature, culture and science get churned up in stories such as these.

As we also noted above, the overall effect is to transgress boundaries – or rather to deny the validity of such boundaries. Science depends upon social assumptions. It becomes impossible to determine whether a cow is natural or social. Instead, we are dealing with changing rather than fixed categories. Scientists claim to offer an account of the natural world, yet struggle with the uncertainties generated (especially since the problems encountered do not fit easily within any established disciplinary structure). The overall effect is to render these different elements inseparable. As Latour expresses it, they are bound together by a 'fragile thread' so that scientific questions of the risk of BSE are 'hooked up' with issues of the public credibility of governmental institutions, and the troublesome image of a tottering cow immediately raises questions of what to purchase during a trip to the local grocery store.

As Latour and colleagues working in an SSK tradition are keen to argue, one consequence of the existence of such hybrids is that matters of science and technology are not at all marginal to understanding contemporary social life but are instead absolutely central. Established disciplinary boundaries are struggling to keep apart what the hybrids tell us cannot be separated. How can the sociological, scientific, political or economic dimensions of the cases discussed in this chapter ever be studied independently of one another? An acceptance of this argument would have profound consequences for our understanding of environmental issues, for the discipline of sociology and, as Latour ambitiously argues, for the ways in which 'we moderns' view the world in which we live.

What this chapter has already demonstrated is that environmental issues are not separable in scientific (or any other) terms from a wider range of concerns and questions. Equally, SSK suggests the need for flexibility and open-mindedness in the face of environmental claims-making. For a sociological perspective simply to take the current claims of governments, environmentalists or scientists as given would be to miss one of the most fascinating elements of environmental debate: *the manner in which environmental 'hybrids' are constructed, contested and defended in particular social, scientific and institutional settings.*

SSK suggests not just an analytical perspective but also a particular methodology and especially the need to examine the *contextualization* of environmental claims and to adopt a *situated* approach to environmental concerns. Rather than trading in broad abstractions, the approach aims to consider differing environmental constructions and the particular groups of social actors which assist in their formulation and defence. It remains in this chapter to bring some of these points together and consider directly how an SSK perspective might assist our understanding of sociology and the environment.

Scientists, Social Scientists, Mad Cows and Environmentalists

The first, and most striking, characteristic of an SSK-based approach to environmental issues is its *refusal to limit sociological analysis to the study of social challenges and social impacts.* Rather than assuming that an unproblematic scientific assessment of environmental issues is available (i.e. the 'facts' of environmental degradation), this sociological perspective views the very *definition* (or 'framing') of environmental problems as a key aspect of analysis. In that way, the business of deciding what counts as environmental fact becomes a legitimate (indeed essential) topic for sociological inquiry. The sociology of scientific knowledge adopts a sceptical perspective on all claims to environmental knowledge and to possession of the facts. This means that scientific statements and assessments will not simply be taken at face value but will instead be examined in terms of their construction and reception.

In the case of BSE, the contested claims made by different scientific authorities become the starting-point for sociological analysis. Rather than sidelining questions of scientific uncertainty or the difficulties of extrapolating theoretically on the basis of limited human data, the SSK perspective is keen to explore and analyse just these issues. Science is not 'black-boxed' but represented as an important site of institutional and technical negotiation.

Secondly, and linked to this, the approach outlined in this chapter conveys a sense of *scientific variety and heterogeneity*. Whilst it may be helpful at times to view science as characterized by a particular world-view and approach, it seems more generally appropriate and productive to consider scientific differences as well as similarities. Thus, occupational and disciplinary divisions between scientists may produce substantial variations in terms of the scientific accounts offered.

This point was especially clear within the case-study of agrochemicals. Different disciplinary and occupational groups of scientists may be led to identify different sets of problems and to approach them with rather different social and cognitive assumptions. In that way, the toxicological testing of chemicals on animal populations is not at all the same as the epidemiological study of human health and illness or the theoretical investigation of basic pathways of environmental damage. What seems unavoidable for scientific investigations is that professional assumptions must be made about the relevance and significance of specific forms of data to the risk assessment of a chemical. These assumptions will obviously vary, but key issues include the relationship between animal-based evidence and human health, and the identification of particular causative agents (e.g. a suspected chemical) from the large range to which humans are exposed.

In the case of pesticides, this has meant that there have been clashes over the safety of specific chemicals based largely on the kinds of evidence put forward by different scientific groups. In at least one instance – and as chapter 5 will discuss – US regulatory authorities were prepared to deem a substance as carcinogenic (cancer-causing) based on animal evidence, whilst the equivalent UK authorities insisted on human evidence (i.e. epidemiological studies) before making such a judgement (see Gillespie et al. 1979). Such cases demonstrate that the specific relations between institutions and particular forms of scientific argumentation can be extremely important for the resolution of risk conflicts – a level of analysis to which broader sociological discussion (for example, at the level of 'science and modernity') cannot aspire.

Whilst a conventional sociological approach to science might view these empirical points as interesting but peripheral, from the SSK perspective such scientific differences are fundamental to the construction of environmental concerns. It is precisely on the basis of these assessments that conclusions are drawn, in this example, concerning the risk posed by a particular chemical. Equally, the SSK approach typically avoids generalized statements about the 'scientific worldview' or 'scientific rationality' but instead offers a much more textured and detailed account of specific scientific and social processes. Accordingly, SSK avoids both a 'scientific triumphalist' and an 'antiscientific' account.

Thirdly, and very importantly, SSK has adopted a methodological approach that typically *emphasizes the particular contexts and situations within which 'facts' are constructed and defended.* Very often, this methodology involves 'following the actors' (Law and Callon 1988) – in other words, the careful observation of how scientific and other sorts of evidence are accumulated and organized by different groups of individuals and institutions. In the case of nuclear power, this might involve a detailed analysis of the construction of risk assessments. What scientific and professional judgements are involved? How are uncertainties negotiated within the process? Which occupational and disciplinary groups are included or excluded? As one aspect of this analysis, the opinions of scientists themselves would be consulted. Certainly, it seems reasonable that those who work directly on the technical evaluation of risk may have worthwhile views on the subjects raised here.

This sociological style, of course, contrasts strikingly with more conventional approaches to social theory, which typically view particular case-studies as illustrative of a wider framework (as examples to be selectively plundered) rather than as key sites in themselves. We have already presented Beck as operating just such an approach. More generally, social theory has a tendency to work at a distance from the assessments and opinions of those being analysed.

At this point also, we begin to see that SSK does not simply extend sociological analysis into areas that are conventionally (i.e. in both policy and sociological terms) seen as scientific and, therefore, as no-go areas for the discipline. The perspective introduced in this chapter suggests an approach to *how* we conduct sociological analysis and, indeed, a fresh understanding of the character of social relations. Through its emphasis on the hybridity of environmental issues and on the shifting relationship between what is defined as 'scientific' or 'social', SSK raises fundamental questions for the discipline – and especially in problematizing the social–natural distinction upon which sociology was founded.

Rather than viewing the social or the natural as fixed points within environmental discussion, each of these becomes the subject of argument and negotiation. We cannot unproblematically separate the social from the natural elements within the BSE crisis or nuclear power debates, because neither of these elements is unchanging or self-evident. Instead, the social–natural relationship is varyingly constructed (or, more accurately, co-constructed) by various parties (including, of course, sociologists). In this way too, SSK moves us beyond the familiar argument over whether environmental problems are *either* social *or* natural.

SSK implies the need to work in an explicitly cross-disciplinary manner (especially across natural and social science boundaries), but also for sociologists to challenge their own operating assumptions even as they challenge those of other social actors. What makes sociological analysis especially valid compared to other forms of analysis and discussion? What indeed does 'validity' entail once one suspends judgement as to the absolute truth of any statement? Certainly, it follows directly from the arguments of this chapter that sociology cannot grant itself uniquely privileged status amongst the environmental hybrids.

As a very final point in this chapter, it can be noted that for scientists, governments, industries and campaigning groups alike this perspective can raise a series of uncomfortable questions about science and its application to environmental discussions and concerns. In particular, science becomes a legitimate area for public debate and questioning rather than simply a trump card for the resolution of environmental disputes. Furthermore, the notion of science as social process raises important institutional questions about the current operation of scientific arguments within environmental debate. If social and professional assumptions are unavoidable within scientific activities in this area, should policy processes be adjusted so as to make this explicit? Going further, might this fresh perspective on science not also imply the need for radical changes in how environmental decisions are taken at, for example, the national level?

The SSK perspective may appear empirical and case-specific in orientation. Nevertheless, and largely because of this methodological approach to 'science in context', it also has wide conceptual implications in terms of the discipline of sociology and the institutional processes through which environmental problems are identified and acted upon. As we will emphasize in the latter half of this book, environmental knowledge represents an essential element within the emerging relationship between sociology and the environment – but also for the larger development of sociology itself.

4

Risks in Context: The Local Construction of Environmental Issues

All dead. The crabs were dead. So it cannot be doing nothing any good if it's killing them. And the boat – er the, the paint used to peel off the boats . . .

> Jarrow resident and recreational fisherman
> discussing pollution in the River Tyne

[P]eople themselves become small, private alternative experts in risks of modernization.

> Beck 1992, p. 61

This chapter marks a shift in our approach to sociology and the environment. Rather than beginning with a particular institutional or sociological framework, we start to explore the enactment of environmental concerns within particular social settings and contextualized practices. Here, we focus on one often-neglected group within environmental discussions: the wider publics.

The chapter begins with a discussion of the sociological implications of chapters 1, 2 and 3 before introducing two cases of the public construction of environmental issues and problems. The chapter emphasizes the inter-relationship between risk understandings and cultural world-views, the complexity of local responses, and the possible gap between official environmental discourses (for example, of sustainable development) and the heterogeneous, hybrid and embedded understandings presented by discrete publics. In so doing, this chapter also outlines a conceptual and empirical approach, which (taking particular inspiration from the SSK framework for society, nature and knowledge) moves beyond the social–natural duality.

Developing from the framing of social and environmental issues within the sustainability problematique, we have subsequently been introduced to a distinctively sociological level of analysis through concepts of the risk society and the sociology of scientific knowledge. In so doing, certain important themes have become apparent:

1. The notion that environmental threats are not simply imposed upon societies but are in some way *socially constructed*. As the discussion has developed, it has become increasingly difficult to maintain any notion of the environment as simply an external force that 'impacts' upon the social structure. Instead, in all three of the previous chapters we have observed the varying construction (or 'framing') of environmental problems.
2. Linked to this, the idea that *the boundary between the social and the natural is not fixed but shifting*. The previous chapters have noted that terms such as 'social' and 'natural' do not refer to predetermined entities but rather have a changing discursive and rhetorical role to play. Beck, for example, argues that there is no longer a meaningful distinction to be drawn here.
3. The concept that *environmental knowledge is complex, problematic and characterized by uncertainties and ambivalences*. This point has so far been made with special reference to scientific forms of understanding, but can reasonably be applied more generally (including, of course, to sociological knowledges). For reasons linked to the previous point, all attempts to separate 'environmental knowledge' from issues of social life and existence seem to be built upon questionable foundations.
4. An argument that suggests that *environmental issues raise fundamental problems for social institutions*. We have begun to indicate the difficulties for existing institutions in coming to terms with a set of questions that appear to be becoming more slippery and amorphous over time. In that way, environmental issues do not just represent business as usual for existing social institutions such as government departments and industry. Instead, they offer a substantial challenge to their operating assumptions and practices.
5. The suggestion that *environmental issues in turn raise even wider issues* for our sense of social progress and for the developing social structure. Beck, but also Latour, indicates that our current sense of crisis is intimately connected to problems of the modernistic world-view (even if these two theorists disagree as to whether we are edging beyond modernity or instead have never been modern).

6. The implication that these points raise a *challenge to the discipline of sociology* if it is to engage with environmental matters. In chapters 2 and 3 specific issues have arisen, including the difficulties (for Beck) of a modernistic sociology responding to a late modern crisis and (as raised by SSK) the problem of maintaining a fixed boundary between the social and the natural. What happens to the disciplinary identity of sociology when the realm of the social can no longer be ring-fenced?

These points can be established both generally and with regard to a variety of case-studies. If we further develop the example of BSE from chapter 3, these thematic landmarks emerge as follows:

1. The *social construction* of mad cow disease as a problem. BSE is closely linked to specific social practices (especially factory farming) so that the disease cannot be presented as an external threat, but seems more properly to be the outcome of human activities. At the same time, the problem is socially constructed in the sense that we rely upon the institutions of science and, to some degree, government for its identification.

2. The manner in which a *shifting boundary* can be discerned between the social and the natural within debate over this issue. As we have already discussed, cows are varyingly constructed as either 'natural' (as seen from the city-dweller's point of view) or 'social' (since their very existence depends upon human intervention).

3. The clear difficulties of *knowing* the problem. The long-running dispute over the possibilities of disease-transfer between species (and especially from cows to people) illustrates especially clearly that knowledge can be contested and subject to major indeterminacies.

4. The major *policy difficulties* encountered especially by the UK government in coming to terms with the questions raised. Issues such as BSE can create large institutional uncertainties. Should governments attempt to reassure the public or openly discuss the underlying issues in all their complexity and indeterminacy? Should it be left to the experts or should a more democratic approach be taken? What should be the relationship between government and the affected industry (to protect farmers or to adopt an explicitly consumerist perspective?)? In such a situation, the *institutional framing* of the issues becomes extremely important, since subsequent discussions tend to operate within a set problem definition. Should this be seen as a matter of animal rights or a

small matter of agricultural practice? Does it represent a fundamental change in government–consumer relations or yet another
argument over Europeanization? Influence over this 'pre-framing'
accordingly represents a major form of institutional power.

5. The controversy over BSE also challenges the modernistic *vision
    of 'progress'*. Whilst certain parties might attempt to present them
    as merely technical difficulties, the wider issues seem inescapable.
    Has factory farming actually unleashed major health problems?
    Have we engaged in practices that can persuasively be described
    as 'unnatural' (e.g. feeding animal offal to other animals)? Has our
    food production system become out of control?

6. Taken together, these points raise the possibility that sociology
    might need to view these issues not as simply localized and
    specific but as *more widely consequential*. Cases such as BSE
    are troublesome not only in health and institutional terms but
    also for existing forms of sociological analysis (especially due to
    their hybrid character, which defies disciplinary classification).
    What kind of sociology is needed to analyse cases such as these?
    Already we can see that sociology cannot restrict itself to the
    social element without imposing a very arbitrary distinction
    between the social and the natural elements of the issue.

In chapters 4, 5 and 6 we will develop these points and observations
through the closer exploration of three topics: the *wider publics* for
environmental matters, questions of *decision-making and governance*,
and *technological change*. Each of these represents a suitable focal
point for the social scientific exploration of contemporary risks and
environmental concerns. As such, analysis will allow a more grounded
and empirical approach to environmental knowledge, the social and
the natural, and their enactment and embodiment within institutional
practices. In so doing, we will also enrich our understanding of the relationship between risk, sociology and social practice. We start in this
chapter with a citizen-oriented perspective.

Making Sense of Environmental Concerns

Throughout these discussions, public groups and citizen concerns
have played only a shadowy (or perhaps ghostly) role – often invoked
but rarely observed in the cold light of day. Of course, the Brundtland agenda anticipates significant scope for the world's population
within 'a political system that secures effective citizen participation

in decision making' (WCED 1987, p. 65). Equally, Beck has much to say about emerging forms of sub-politics and the kinds of 'pragmatic alliance' created by groups of citizens in the face of risk concerns. Both place public evaluations and actions at the very core of environmental change.

However, neither approach necessarily gives us any direct insight into the ways in which people actively interpret (or 'make sense of') environmental issues within the conditions of everyday life. Instead, both Beck and Brundtland accord great significance to public groups and their role in environmental matters but do not consider in any detail the possible complexity of public environmental understandings. In the discussion so far it seems to have been taken for granted that citizens simply 'respond' once environmental issues make their presence known. In that respect, both Beck and Brundtland are operating within a crude realist assumption of environmental problems as existing apart from human interpretations and constructions.

We have also suggested in the case of Beck that this generalized treatment of public groups links closely with his theoretical presentation of modernity. Such a sweeping portrayal of any period in history depends upon a necessarily homogeneous treatment of the 'citizens of the risk society'. The clear danger of such an approach is that it fails to recognize significant social *differences* as well as similarities within public reconstructions of environmental matters. Equally, it tells us relatively little about the manner in which environmental issues are given priority (or otherwise) by citizens within the conditions of everyday life. Rather than assuming the centrality of risk to our modern existence, it may be more appropriate (and sociologically revealing) to consider this as an important topic for sociological investigation. This more empirical and analytically flexible approach will form the basis of this chapter. In so doing, we will draw explicitly upon the SSK perspective outlined in chapter 3 in terms of the symmetrical and sceptical treatment of claims to environmental knowledge.

Accordingly, we now consider the kinds of environmental understanding and environmental awareness constructed by lay groups (in other words, by the bulk of the population). In particular, we consider what it might mean to approach the relationship between environmental matters and citizen groups not in the terms of international commissions or generalized social theory but from the viewpoint of citizens themselves.

Rather than simply treating public response to environmental issues as if it was a matter of (environmental) cause producing a

(public) effect, it is necessary for us to explore the relationship between public groups and environmental matters in a more
thorough and open fashion. As part of this, it is important to
consider the linkage between environmental and other, non-
environmental concerns within everyday life. We have so far been
dangerously close to suggesting that risk is the *only* issue that
matters to most people. Equally, and given the enormous range
of issues that can claim to be environmental in character (from
collecting waste paper to saving whales), it seems central to a sociological understanding of the environment that it should consider
how people select *which* (if any) environmental issues to be concerned
about.

This chapter will therefore illustrate and discuss the various ways
in which people select, interpret and act upon environmental concerns within the particular contexts of everyday life. Rather than presenting the problems as simply 'given' (or as if they somehow speak
for themselves), it is sociologically important to explore their active
construction within specific social settings. Thus, the conventional
notion of 'environmental response' seems to assume agreement as
to the nature of the problems to which responses are being made.
Instead, we will consider the differential construction of 'problems'
and the relationship between these constructions and the wider conditions of everyday life. Equally, the very notion of 'response' accords
an essentially *reactive* role to the publics: we will consider here the
more *active* interpretation of environmental concerns by two publics
in particular.

This citizen-based approach has potentially radical implications
for environmental policy as well as for sociology. At least at first
approximation, it is far easier for policy-makers and other groups
(including industry and environmentalists) to assume that the public
is simply ignorant in environmental matters. Surely if members of
the public don't support our environmental campaign or recognize
our environmental achievements, it must be due either to their lack
of understanding or our inadequate communication of the facts? The
deficit approach to the public suggests that further information and
careful persuasion is all that is required to 'win public groups over'
to one's own point of view (see Irwin and Wynne 1996). Typically
also, the deficit approach suggests that public groups are merely
blank sheets of paper upon which various environmental messages
can be written.

This chapter will suggest that, while such an assumption may be
tempting to various organizations (not least because it avoids more
fundamental questions about environmental matters and institutional

practices), it offers a highly inadequate (and, consequently, impractical) basis for grasping the more complex ways in which different publics actively interpret environmental issues. The deficit approach assumes simple public ignorance, whereas one of the major themes of this chapter will concern the 'knowledgeability' of different publics (even if such knowledges can be rather different from those provided by official institutions). As will be apparent within both the cases discussed here, public groups can be expected to bring more than blank sheets of paper to environmental debate: memories of previous incidents, moral judgements and forms of local knowledge can all play a part in local understandings of environmental issues and in the very constitution of those 'issues'.

One important element within this new perspective relates to what we can term 'environmental knowledge': the kinds of evidence and expertise upon which people draw when seeking to interpret and understand environmental problems. So far in *Sociology and the Environment*, the main form of environmental knowledge discussed has been *scientific* knowledge – though we have noted the variations and, sometimes, contradictions involved in this diverse body of institutions and intellectual practices. Once one adopts a contextualized approach to the local understanding of environmental concerns, an even wider variety of knowledge claims and forms of evidence come into play: from those provided by 'official' institutions (perhaps government or industry) to (as suggested in this chapter's opening quotation) more public assessments of the state of local crabs and the condition of fishing boats. On that basis, 'situated knowledge' (or 'lay epidemiology') becomes an important theme.

At the same time, we will suggest that knowledge is not readily separable from wider questions of cultural understanding and everyday experience. Knowledge should not be taken to imply a static or fixed category (a body of facts) but rather a *process* of sense-making within particular social and personal contexts (what we can term 'knowledging'[1]). Here, we will adopt one of the basic principles of the sociology of scientific knowledge (SSK) – the methodological imperative to 'follow the actors' – in order to adopt a citizen-oriented perspective on these issues and perspectives. We will, especially, explore the social dynamics involved in the local construction of environmental concern.

Two cases will provide a route into this sociological perspective. As offered here, these cases represent admittedly partial explorations of the local construction of environmental beliefs and concerns. They have been selected as a means of illustrating and opening up issues rather than providing a definitive sociological account.[2] The first is drawn from the work of Couch, Kroll-Smith and Kindler and considers a former coal-mining town in north-eastern USA. The second is also based in the north-east – but this time a former shipbuilding town in north-eastern England.

The Centralia Mine Fire[3]

Centralia is a small community located in Pennsylvania among the northern ranges of the Appalachian mountains. It was settled in the 1850s and 1860s by Irish immigrants and subsequently by other European peoples. By the end of the nineteenth century, coal-mining was the main industry and the population numbered over two thousand. However, and in line with the story of industrial decline and change that will be discussed in the case of Jarrow, by 1960 very little coal-mining was still taking place. The town's population had declined, little new industry was attracted to the area and the largely working-class population included a high percentage of elderly people, many of whom had lived in the area all their lives. As described by Couch (1996), those who remained often exhibited a rather fatalistic and suspicious outlook on the world outside their community – and especially towards large corporations and government institutions.

Within this particular social and cultural setting, the story of one environmental problem has unfolded since the early 1960s. Importantly, Couch has described this not as a 'natural disaster' but essentially as a problem for the community. In that way, the mine fire in question has represented a form of *social devastation*: 'Intense intracommunity conflict has taken place, conflict which ripped apart the bonds of communality and civility and tore at the very basis of the social fabric that binds people together' (ibid., p. 60). The problem at the heart of the Centralia story relates to a fire, which has spread uncontrolledly through abandoned mine shafts and tunnels under the town. The fire was first discovered in 1962 and all attempts to deal with it have so far ended in failure – causing concerns about health and safety across the community. In 1981, a 12-year-old boy narrowly escaped death as the ground opened up beneath his feet. Shortly afterwards, an elderly man was overcome by carbon monoxide in his home and again was almost killed. A voluntary relocation scheme began in 1984 and, by the early 1990s, the state authorities were contemplating the seizure of properties in order to compel the removal of the relatively small number of remaining residents.

What then can we say about the local construction of this environmental issue? One central finding is that, even within a single community, local constructions of environmental problems can vary immensely. It is apparent from research carried out by Couch and Kroll-Smith (1985) and Kroll-Smith and Couch (1993) that the community was heavily divided over the severity of the situation – an evaluation partly linked to the varying sense of vulnerability to the hazard. For example, while one group viewed it as a dangerous and imminent threat requiring swift action, another saw it as altogether more remote and unthreatening. Couch (1996) also presents the 'disaster subculture' of the area (linked to its mining history) as encouraging a kind of stoicism – such problems must be borne with equanimity. Equally, many of the residents felt a strong commitment to the area. They did not wish to contemplate even the possibility of moving.

As events developed in the 1980s, these varying constructions began to polarize. One group of residents established 'Concerned Citizens Against the Centralia Mine Fire', which urged government to do whatever was necessary – even if that meant their relocation. However, many fellow citizens reacted strongly against this campaign – viewing it as an attempt to force government purchase of their homes: 'To these people, the spectre of relocation was more frightening than the fire' (ibid., p. 65).

The consequence of these different interpretations of the issue was a period of intense community conflict: 'Town meetings ended in shouting or fist fights. Telephone threats were made, car tyres slashed, and at least one fire-bombing occurred. Many neighbours – and even some family members – no longer spoke to one another' (ibid., pp. 65–6).

In this situation, one group's sense of appropriate action simply served to antagonize and divide the community – leading to intra-community conflict on a major scale. Different interpretations of the extent and scale of the problem constituted 'fertile soil for intense community conflict' (ibid., p. 69). These splits became wider as new organizations established themselves. For example, the Homeowners' Association (which hoped to assist residents in getting a fair settlement price) was opposed by the Citizens to Save Our Borough (whose goal was to maintain Centralia as a viable community).

Of course, these developments frustrated state and federal officials, who could not simply tap into a single community agenda but were obliged to deal with competing factions. Meanwhile, and as will be found in the Jarrow case, the only thing that served to unite residents was their antagonism towards the government – which was universally viewed as failing the community. This sceptical approach also applied to the kinds of expert knowledge that outsiders brought to the area. Couch observes that government agents were often 'shocked that their well-trained mining engineers were not believed or treated with much respect by local residents, most of whom had no college education' (ibid., p. 80). However, and as Couch goes on to observe in a comment highly relevant to the discussion of 'situated knowledges', 'a person with knowledge of the local mining culture would not have been surprised – many townspeople had worked in the mines under the town and firmly believed that their first-hand knowledge was worth much more than that of any "book-trained" engineer' (ibid.).

Here we see that the kinds of knowledge and expertise drawn upon by local people may be close to the 'alternative expertise' referred to by Beck at the very beginning of this chapter. In a direct parallel to Centralia, one study into a former mining community in England (again in the north-east and not too far from the Jarrow area to which we will shortly turn) observed the manner in which ex-mineworkers represented an important resource when a colliery site was proposed for conversion to a toxic waste dump (Hooper 1986). In that case also, the general knowledge of outside experts was matched by the more specific and detailed (although less 'scientific') understandings of those who had spent a large part of their working lives in that setting.

More generally, researchers such as Couch, Kroll-Smith and Kindler emphasize the importance of local context for the construction of environmental issues – even if this local context serves to divide as well as bind communities. As they express this, the Centralia case emphasizes that '[d]ifferent people and groups interpret the situation differently over time' (Couch et al. 2000). Seen from that perspective, the very definition of environmental problems becomes an important topic for sociological investigation – especially since interpretative differences lead to different forms of environmental action. Linked to this point, whilst government agencies defined the issues as primarily *technological* in character, for these authors they are largely *social*.

Finally, it is worth considering the role of sociological analysis within such complex and dynamic social contexts. Couch, Kroll-Smith and Kindler have discussed both the methodological and the theoretical implications of working within settings where sociologists cannot simply stand apart from the context being studied but must inevitably play a part within it. Thus, in order to gain sufficient access to the case, the researchers needed to become a highly visible presence – and resource – within the community. Certainly, they could not just observe, they were also participants.

In the Centralia case, Couch et al. found themselves unable to maintain a traditionally objective role, since, for example, in order to gain access to one of the group's meetings, one of them had to agree to act as a volunteer consultant to that group – thereby ensuring that competing groups would inevitably restrict access to their own meetings. As Couch et al. (2000) suggest, in getting access to the research data, they themselves became part of the data. This process meant that they were obliged to offer their own views and interpretations from an early stage in the investigation. In that way, sociological thinking fed into the social processes as they developed.

As a result, the researchers' concept of 'chronic technical disaster' (Couch and Kroll-Smith 1985) entered the everyday language of Centralia and became one way in which the citizens in question began to comprehend their own situation. The boundaries between researcher and researched became blurred, and, instead, each became linked within the common task of trying to make sense of a challenging social situation. In other words, the sociologist and the citizen became indistinguishable – not least because sociologists are also citizens and citizens employ the language of sociologists. Of course, the same point could be made about scientists – who are also citizens and members of the lay public. In all these cases, social roles are not fixed but actively adopted and differentially interpreted.

The Jarrow Study[4]

The second example in this chapter relates to another community that has experienced industrial growth followed by economic decline and which also possesses a strong sense of its separation from the outside world. Jarrow sits on the southern bank of the River Tyne in the North-East of England. Coal-mining became a major industry in the area at the start of the nineteenth century. The chemical industry and, especially, shipbuilding followed. On that basis, the town grew from a population of 3,500 in 1851, when Charles Palmer opened his world-renowned shipworks, to 7,000 by 1861 and, eventually, 35,000 in 1921 (see Wilkinson 1939, pp. 71–2).

The closure of the shipyards in 1936 led to a famous moment in British labour history – the Jarrow March – when a band of the unemployed (unemployment in the 1930s reached 74 per cent in this area) trooped the 300 miles or so to London in order to register their protest. Since 1945, the local economy has regenerated somewhat, but Jarrow has always been vulnerable to economic change. Certainly, unemployment is still a major issue in the locality. The 50th anniversary of the Jarrow March was marked by another march of the unemployed – but this time with significantly less media and public attention.

Jarrow is, then, a place with a strong sense of its own cultural heritage and industrial history. This has certainly not encouraged local people to be risk-averse. In coal-mining and shipbuilding, for example, work has traditionally been seen as hard, dangerous and often bad for one's health. However, the loss of local jobs and the changing character of the area has meant that risks now present themselves in new ways – at home rather than at work, to children rather than (mainly) men, as bad smells and river pollution rather than industrial deafness or localized exposure (for example, to welding fumes or coal dust).

The study described in this section[5] focuses on Jarrow people living close to (indeed in some cases just across the road from) one chemical works near the centre of the town. The works in question is one of the larger industrial enterprises in South Tyneside and began operation in the mid-1950s. Since the early 1980s, chlorine has been stored and used at the site. Consequently, a number of regulations have been applied concerning major industrial hazards, and an area extending out to about 400 metres from the site boundary is subject to special land-use planning controls. Nearly two thousand people live in this area and these residents became the focus of sociological investigation.

In the late 1980s, there was public protest about smells from the site. Local controversy has also been stirred over proposals for further development within the existing site. In general, however, the regulatory authorities class it as a 'fairly quiet' site where no major incidents have been recorded.

Discussions with local residents presented – as we will see – a rather different picture and, especially when prompted, offered a more critical and sceptical account of the site's operation. However, it is basic to this chapter's whole argument that risk and environmental concerns need to be taken firmly *in context*. Local people generally expressed greater spontaneous concern over crime, unemployment, rowdy youths, lack of leisure facilities and the quality of housing. In an area that experiences a range of social problems associated with poverty and high unemployment, it seems hardly surprising that such concerns should be vocally expressed. More importantly, we begin to see something of the wider context to life in this area and can start to interpret the part played by environmental concerns within this broader picture. Certainly, we are a long way at this point from the general international agenda, which claims to speak for environmental matters as if all the citizens on the planet saw their futures as being 'in common'. However, we are an equally long way from sweeping sociological talk of late modernity.

Before moving into this discussion, it should be briefly explained *how* sociological research was conducted in Jarrow. Of course, there are a number of possible ways in which public understandings of the environment might be explored: from formal questionnaire surveys (inquiring, for example, about experiences of, concerns about, and attitudes towards local pollution issues) to participant observation (which would typically involve living in the area for a considerable number of months and keeping a detailed record of conversations and events). Certainly, the selection of research method should be seen as inseparable from matters of theoretical perspective and research strategy. Sociological method is not just a neutral tool for research but also an embodiment of theoretical choices and epistemological assumptions concerning what counts as appropriate evidence. The methodological approach adopted in this Jarrow research operated on the principle that it is important to maintain an open rather than closed (or predetermined) approach to public understandings. The study was concerned with the processes through which such understandings are formulated, expressed and amended (or maintained). In this, the research was explicitly drawing upon the SSK tradition discussed in chapter 3.

This tradition when applied to environmental matters implies a sensitivity to the contextual and cultural understandings of different groups and to the different ways in which environmental issues are framed. Equally, and in sharp contrast to certain psychological approaches – which typically assume that people carry round fixed and well-defined attitudes, which can then be aggregated and measured – this sociological perspective suggests that environmental understandings may be better seen as *context-related, dynamic, discursively formed and open to negotiation and change*. In terms of method, therefore, approaches that constrain public responses (or attempt to accommodate them within the researchers' own framework) are likely to be less satisfactory than those that are flexible in terms of the different – and varying – assessments of participants.

For the Jarrow study, focus group discussions were selected as the main research method.[6] Whilst not being as open or flexible as participant observation (since the setting is inevitably artificial and researchers must, at least to some degree, structure discussions), this offers access to a number of local people whilst remaining responsive to the views and assessments expressed. In this case, the discussions followed as relaxed and group-led a format as possible so that participants appeared relatively at ease in the often heated and lively discussions that ensued. The use of focus groups also meant that, as in the Centralia case, it was impossible for the researchers to stay at a distance from the matters under consideration (especially by the second of the two meetings for each focus group, when an informal atmosphere had been established).

What then emerged from the Jarrow discussions? Perhaps the most striking aspect of this research concerned the close (indeed, inseparable) relationship between the views of environment and pollution expressed by local people and the wider sense of what it meant to live in Jarrow. Throughout this project, it was clear that environmental matters did not stand apart from the larger dimensions of everyday life. Instead, concerns about local pollution were woven into other forms of discourse concerning, for example, the expressed lack of faith in local and national politicians or the manner in which Jarrow was seen to be persistently overlooked by those who lived outside the area. In that way, and in a manner similar to that described in the Centralia study, issues of pollution were not viewed primarily as a scientific or technical matter but rather as a reflection of local social relations. Put simply, pollution was one visible symptom of a larger sense of powerlessness and relative neglect. This provoked both local resentment and a sense of fatalism. Cultural understandings and ways of viewing the world do not simply influence environmental assessments but represent the *whole framework* within which these are developed and articulated. As the anthropologist Mary Douglas has expressed it: 'the view of the universe and a particular kind of society holding this view are closely interdependent. They are a single system. Neither can exist without the other' (1980, p. 289).

This contextual observation relates strongly to the public understanding of the chemical plant at the centre of this study. From a local viewpoint, the plant was considered remote and disconnected from those who lived so close to its perimeter fence. Unlike the shipyards that had once crowded along the River Tyne, the industrial site was seen to contribute little by way of jobs to nearby residents. This observation would often be expressed through the contrast between the streams of workers who could once be seen walking through the streets of Jarrow, and the current situation where there was very little visible sign of life other than the occasional car pulling into or out of the works. Of course, this also meant that much would be read into such external signs as did emerge: bad smells, plumes of smoke, large container vehicles rumbling through the neighbourhood – all would typically be interpreted as a threat to the local community and its quality of life.

This changing economic relationship increased the sense of resentment among many of those interviewed: why should we be exposed to any level of risk when we gain little from the company's operation? It is important not to over-generalize such evaluations. There were those, for example, who defended the company and its role in supporting local schools and community groups. Such voices, however, tended to be drowned by others who argued, in a manner that the company would find both ironic and disturbing, that the company must have something to hide – otherwise why would it give money away? The majority of respondents expressed a sceptical and critical world-view when considering what were seen to be 'outside' organizations. Thus, the North American ownership of the company in question only raised further doubts: if the site is so safe, why come over to the North of England?

However, it must be emphasized that there is nothing fixed (or fixedly causal) about the relationship between the company and local residents. In that sense, it is important to recognize that the company–community relationship is, in principle, open to a number of local constructions. These might hypothetically include the models of a 'captive community' (desperate for whatever jobs are available and therefore disinclined to criticism) or the 'deficit'-based interpretation of an ignorant and uninformed public (who might be expected to have no particular views, since residents are largely unaware of the toxic risks from the plant). Other local constructions of the environmental consequences of the plant are certainly possible.

The ways in which local people 'make sense' of pollution is subject to individual variation and, also, to disagreement and debate. The point is not to present such cultural understandings as fixed or one-dimensional. Equally, from this chapter's perspective, there is nothing inevitable or predetermined in the ways in which local people discuss these matters. Instead, it is more appropriate to see local understandings as *dynamically and discursively formed within a given context*. As examples of this process of active 'sense-making', we can pick out three characteristic forms of discourse in Jarrow: the importance of local memory, the usage of evidence and expertise, and the expression of moral judgements.

Memory, Situated Expertise and Morality

One of the more striking aspects of the Jarrow focus groups is that local people often possess vivid memories of previous events – memories that can be presented as collective rather than individual in character since they extend back before some of the respondents were even born (although even collective memories would inevitably be given personal variations and spins). The local fondness for telling certain anecdotes and stories – often going right back to the 1936 Jarrow March and encompassing many of the changes that have occurred since in terms of jobs, housing and local facilities – built up in focus-group discussions to represent a rich backcloth to the specific environmental matters at the focus of our attention. This pattern of local memory also suggested that there was a strong temporal and historical dimension to hazard-awareness. Any environmentally driven initiative taken today by the company, any pollution incident, any publicity campaign will be 'read' in terms of previous actions (and, especially, when there is seen to be a contradiction between stated policies and previous events).

As noted previously, the Jarrow site has been relatively quiet and very few even medium-sized incidents have actually occurred. The company has also stressed on various occasions that no loss of life outside the site (i.e. in the Jarrow community) has ever taken place as a consequence of activities on-site. For many local people, such a confident claim invited a critical response. For example, one regularly repeated tale concerned an event in the early 1960s, when three men were killed during their work at the site. The point of the story is that one of these men was blown off-site and through the roof of a nearby house – thus effectively representing a fatality in the community. The event would sometimes be recalled in a serious and conventionally respectful manner – especially since the man in question was known (at least by family association) to many of the participants. Inevitably, in a culture where jokes are an important part of everyday talk, various amusing and occasionally ribald versions of the story also existed – usually featuring the scene inside the house when an unexpected visitor arrived. In addition to capturing the potency of local memory, we gain some insight into Jarrow culture and its mixture of serious-mindedness and mutual respect, sharp humour and fondness for story-telling. Of course, official statements from the company did not participate in this discourse but would generally operate within a more scientific mode when discussing such matters.

It is easy to trivialize such local stories and jokes, to see them as a distraction from the 'real' business of encouraging environmental action or as a manifestation of public ignorance and indifference. This, however, is to miss the point. Shared accounts serve to bind this community together. Memories such as this 'perform' community and give it substance through forms of discourse that reinforce a particular sense of self-identity. Such stories help build a sense of 'us', which would be contrasted with a generalized 'them' who did not understand local people or their way of life. For the management of the plant, this incident was largely forgotten. For local people, who led the researchers to the (long-repaired) roof in question, this was an event whose physical reality (rather like the town-hall clock in our introductory chapter) had not faded over time.

Stories of this kind reinforce a self-image of a community under threat from the outside world. In particular, this tale starkly juxtaposes the company and local residents. It gives voice also to local concerns and anxieties. Of course, we can imagine that the vivid nature of such accounts will make them highly resistant to change. Certainly, the story is unlikely to fade, no matter how many public reassurances and glossy publications are provided by the company. Equally, we can see in such stories a self-identity, which emphasizes a sense of social powerlessness. Closely linked to this social recycling of previous events and attitudes, there are also times when particular residents are granted expert status – albeit in a provisional fashion. Such status is generally not awarded on the basis of formal or scientific credentials (very few residents would qualify in this regard). However, and as was noted in the Centralia case-study, it is more typically granted to those who are seen to have particular experience or practical involvement in a relevant area. In the case of Centralia, this particularly related to those with 'first-hand' mining experience. In Jarrow, special authority within environmental discussions might be granted to those who had worked at, or had recent dealings with, the company in question or who had other relevant practical experience (for example, of working with explosive or hazardous materials elsewhere).

Thus, one local resident (quoted at the beginning of this chapter) was widely recognized for his expertise in fishing and all matters related to the nearby river. On various issues concerning water pollution, the condition of fish and the possible linkage with industrial outflow he was granted due respect and allowed to speak (at least for a minute or so!) without interruption. In this, and especially when combined with the assessments of other local people with fishing experience or simply experience of observing the river over an often considerable period of time, we can identify the 'alternative expertise' discussed by Beck.

The existence of such forms of 'situated knowledge' indeed represents an important local resource – and one that draws upon a very different basis for authority than the forms of expertise provided by official institutions such as industry and government. Such knowledges are typically rooted in the community itself rather than being imposed from the outside. This means, for example, that 'local experts' will be taken seriously but will also be subjected to criticism and contestation if they are seen to be moving beyond their area of expertise or (as would be ruthlessly exposed within Jarrow's egalitarian culture) are perceived to be at risk of becoming self-important or pompous. As McKechnie (1996) observed in a study of local expertise on the Isle of Man, 'expert status' is conditional and bounded.

The key point about local expertise in the Jarrow case, however, may be that, compared to more official sources of information and expertise, it operates upon the basis of particular assumptions concerning what should count as 'valid knowledge'. The language of science emphasizes generalization, 'facts' and the need for objectivity. The contextual knowledges developed in this case explicitly give weight to local factors, personal views and subjectivities, and mix together different kinds of evidence (for example, fish deaths and human ailments, bad smells from the plant and the charitable activities of the company). In this, of course, locally generated expertises reflect the wider characteristics and culture of the contexts in which they arise and are maintained.[7]

In the case of Jarrow residents, such forms of evidence and expertise would often become incorporated within wider moral statements concerning the environment and the quality of local life. As Douglas and Wildavsky have noted more generally: 'pollution beliefs uphold conceptual categories dividing the moral from the immoral and so sustain the vision of the good society' (1983, p. 37). The 'good society' for Jarrow residents was often defined as the opposite of their everyday conditions. Feeling themselves powerless and ignored, criticisms of current environmental practices were inseparable from a wider sense that there was something morally wrong with a situation where residents were expected to suffer risks without (as far as they could tell) any tangible benefits. This moral judgement inevitably coloured all assessments of environmental matters. It represented a key aspect of the self-identity of many of the people living in this locality. It also provided a substantial link between environmental topics and the whole range of local concerns voiced by residents – including housing, education, employment, crime and vandalism. Here again, the environment did not stand alone but was constructed in terms of a larger cultural understanding of local life. Typically, this cultural understanding emphasized a sense of powerlessness and neglect. The experience of risk and environmental harm was readily accommodated within this world-view.

Considered from the perspective of official institutions, such contextual expertises and moral statements could be seen as an irrelevance to the key issues at hand. Environmental protection is typically framed, for example, by regulatory authorities as a 'best judgement' informed by scientific evidence, rational analysis and a negotiation between industrialists and regulators. For local people, this could easily appear to be a collusive relationship that fails to incorporate their understandings and opinions. However, it is an important part of the argument in this book that – whether acknowledged or not – both official and public understandings incorporate social judgements and cultural commitments.

We are presented, therefore, with a situation where environmental understandings appear inseparable from larger matters of local culture and contextually generated assessments, opinions and forms of expertise. Environmental problems may sometimes be presented as external to the social world, but the Jarrow study suggests the extent to which environmental concerns are a projection of the social onto the world around us. As Beck puts this: 'natural destruction and large-scale technological hazards can and must be apprehended and deciphered as mystified modes of self-encounter, twisted outwards and reified' (1995b, pp. 158–9).

Discussion: Things that go Bump in the Night?

Earlier in this chapter we suggested that public concerns have often made a 'ghostly' appearance within environmental discussions – the subject of numerous exhortations (especially towards increased public participation) and various constructions but relatively little sociological analysis. By the end of the chapter, we seem to have reached a point where risks and pollutants have instead assumed a ghostly status – especially as people in Jarrow try to interpret the safety of the area on the basis of various, apparently mysterious, clues and external manifestations (and, sometimes literally, things that go bump in the night).

As we have seen, such important matters as the *causes* of risk and pollution or the extent to which pollution issues are viewed as *matters of concern* cannot simply be established in scientific or technical terms. Instead, we have offered a more fundamental role for sociological analysis in identifying and interpreting risk and pollution issues. Rather than seeing problems as simply given, we have viewed 'sense-making' as a process of *active construction within particular contexts and settings*.

From one point of view, the kinds of account offered by local people in Centralia and Jarrow can be seen as reflecting an information shortage (or 'deficit'). If only residents had access to more complete and authoritative information, then they would not need to bring together such partial information and clues – they could simply deal with the 'real' situation. On that basis, the stories, irreverent jokes and assertions discussed here represent further evidence of residents' ignorance about what is really going on. Of course, this formulation also grants privileged status to the experts (whether scientific, industrial, governmental or, indeed, sociological) who might be expected to understand best what the situation really is.

In contradiction to this formulation, there are a number of arguments to be made – and not least the point established in chapter 3 that no single authoritative account of complex pollution issues is likely to exist. Instead, we are dealing with more hybrid and indeterminate phenomena. In this chapter, we have stressed the extent to which pollution beliefs – including those of regulatory institutions and scientists (see Wynne 1989) – reflect wider cultural understandings of the world. Thus, industrialists may see risks as complex but ultimately controllable, whilst more critical publics may operate on the assumption that 'whatever can go wrong, will go wrong'.

In Jarrow, new information (e.g. provided by the company) is not simply absorbed but may instead be dismissed (since people feel they have 'heard it all before') or read in a sceptical fashion. Knowledge claims, including those of local experts, will be seen as provisional and open to challenge. Equally, such claims will be interpreted against a background of previous experience and assessments. On that basis, public understandings of risk and the environment represent the changing outcomes of a dynamic and active process – and not simply a blank sheet of paper or a straightforward agglomeration of individual attitudes to pollution matters.

In this chapter, we have especially emphasized:

1. The close relationship between risk understandings and what have been described as *cultural world-views*. In particular, we have drawn attention to the manner in which risk concerns are likely to reflect (and also focus) established ways of viewing the world in which one lives (and within which risks are seen to arise). We have stressed the extent to which making sense of these issues may not simply be a matter of individual cognition but may also draw upon *shared* experiences and processes. In the Jarrow focus groups, individuals would regularly alter opinions and arguments as the discussion progressed – suggesting a degree of flexibility and sensitivity to the views and assessments of others. It must be stressed, therefore, *that these world-views are developed even as they are expressed with regard to specific topics – we should not suggest that social and cultural factors are fixed or predetermined.*

2. The *complexity of local responses*. As the Centralia case especially suggested, even within one community there are likely to be differing assessments of pollution and environmental issues. There is always a danger with the kind of rapid summary provided in this chapter that local responses become reified or presented in simple adversarial terms (for example, of the company versus the community or of lay groups versus experts). More generally, the sociological approach adopted here attempts a receptivity to competing and contradictory perspectives even within one locality.

3. The *possible gap* between official talk of sustainable development and public involvement, and the more complex responses of different publics. Again, the point here is not to present such a gap as inevitable or unchanging; relations between different groups of actors should more properly be viewed as situated and operating within particular social settings. In principle, there seems no necessary or structural reason why improved communication could not be developed in the Jarrow setting.[8] However, the discussion does suggest some of the difficulties that may be encountered.

4. The distinct role for *sociological analysis* in this area. As we have seen, such an analysis opens up the ways in which envi-

ronmental issues are formulated within everyday discourse. The point (so far as this is possible) is not to prejudge how environmental problems are formulated or, indeed, what gets formulated as a problem. In one illustration of this in Jarrow, for regulatory authorities the key problem was one of large-scale toxic release, whereas for many residents smell, childhood asthma and river pollution were the major concerns. Equally, the company was inclined to emphasize the technical challenges of local environmental planning and emergency response. Meanwhile, residents often formulated the issue in terms of morality and their own feelings of powerlessness.

Of course, we have only considered two cases – and just one of these in any depth. The main purpose of this chapter has been to open up an area for sociological inquiry and analysis rather than to reach broad generalizations about how a range of publics is likely to deal with the variety of environmental issues now being discussed worldwide.

If this discussion has hinted at the complexity to be found even within a single geographical area and a single source of hazard, one can imagine the greater complexity that would be encountered as one moves across different locations and hazard constructions. Equally, the material presented here could usefully be supplemented by a treatment of other forms of culture and contextual understanding. It would be particularly useful to consider the role of gender or ethnicity in such understandings.

Certainly, the suggestion in the Jarrow study was that the relationship of women to environmental concerns was especially interesting – with female members of the focus groups generally presenting higher levels of anxiety than their male counterparts (in terms of age and occupational status). This level of concern would frequently be expressed in terms of worries over the welfare of children – suggesting that the self-identity of women may have important consequences for environmental awareness. Again, however, we need to be wary of the suggestion that there is a fixed relationship between gender and risk-awareness. Instead, a more open and contextually sensitive approach is required.

Put like this, public environmental understandings appear as an important research area, which is still at an early stage of sociological consideration. In saying this, it should be stressed that this is not an area in which only sociologists have something to offer – for example, geographical and anthropological work in this area has already made a substantial contribution.[9] This suggests that the development of sociological research does not preclude (but rather encourages) the parallel development of cross-disciplinary links.

The specifically sociological challenge with which we are left, however, concerns the relationship between such empirical and contextual treatment and the more sweeping form of social theory that we have especially associated with Beck. The picture presented in this chapter of local publics as active and resourceful in the face of environmental and other concerns does not in itself contradict Beck's theoretical formulation of the conditions of late modernity. We have, for example, referred to his analysis at more than one point within this discussion.

However, the particular sociological approach adopted here has stressed the need for flexible and context-specific approaches to environmental issues and understandings. At the same time, it must be observed that the two cases in this chapter suggest that issues of social class and social powerlessness (at least at the level of self-identity) continue to play an important role with regard to risk-awareness. Overall, we have emphasized the significance of a sociological perspective that is open to competing environmental constructions rather than merely seeking to test out the larger formulations of social theory. A similar perspective will be adopted in chapter 5 as we turn to the study of institutional practices and their relationship to environmental concerns.

5

Institutional Judgements and Contested Decisions: The Governance of Environmental Problems

Who has made the decision that sets in motion these chains of poisonings, this ever-widening wave of death that spreads out, like ripples when a pebble is dropped into a still pond? . . . Who has decided – who has the *right* to decide – for the countless legions of people who were not consulted?

Carson 1991, p. 121

The technocracy of hazard and its advocates must fry in the purgatory of their false safety pledges.

Beck 1995b, p. 11

The governance of environmental problems has become a matter of significant practical and institutional concern – as cases such as mad cow disease and the regulation of genetically modified foods suggest. Restricted notions of 'sound science' and 'independent expert advice' have come under challenge and the uncertainties of environmental decision-making are now widely recognized. This chapter draws upon the case of pesticide regulation to explore institutional constructions of environmental problems and the relationship between society, nature and knowledge in this area. Rather than describing environmental decision-making as a straightforward technical issue, processes of scientific and institutional review are presented in terms of the dynamic negotiation of hybrid issues. In so doing, the possible contribution of environmental sociology to effective and democratic environmental decision-making is opened up for preliminary discussion.

In chapter 4, we considered the kinds of environmental understanding possessed by what are conventionally defined as 'non-expert' or 'lay' groups. Such understandings were portrayed as being, on the one hand, highly complex and dynamic and, on the other, closely linked to the contexts of their generation and maintenance. Rather than simply representing the 'environmental publics' as passive in the face of various issues and problems, the chapter portrayed the *active*, but also potentially diverse, construction of knowledge and meaning within a wider framework of cultural world-views and experiences – a process we have termed 'knowledging' (Irwin et al. 1999). However, the point is not to reify or romanticize such understandings but rather to analyse them in an appropriately open and flexible manner. Certainly, the two main examples in the previous chapter should not be taken to imply that *all* local publics will behave similarly nor that they will define the issues and problems in similar terms.[1]

It also follows from the analysis throughout this book that public, and other, groups do not simply *respond* to environmental problems. Instead, it is more appropriate to consider different groups as defining, framing, contextualizing and, in that sense, *generating* such problems.[2] Put in that way, the approach taken in chapter 4 fits with Hannigan's broad description of 'social constructionism':[3] 'A social constructionist approach . . . recognises the extent to which environmental problems and solutions are end-products of a dynamic social process of definition, negotiation and legitimation both in public and private settings' (1995, p. 31). Whilst the conventional notion of 'public response' presents environmental problems as a straightforward 'input' that is then differentially perceived and interpreted, the sociological approach being advocated here views the very definition of an environmental problem as an important topic for analysis. Looking across at a factory chimney, an anxious resident might observe a threatening cloud of pollution, whilst a company engineer sees a harmless emission of steam. Either way, the diagnosis is the *outcome* of a process of definition based on previous experience and established expectations.

The treatment so far of public understandings leads us to the question of how similar (or different) a sociological approach we should adopt as we move to a second context for environmental discussions: formal institutional structures of decision-making and regulation. Can we observe similar processes of environmental framing and problem definition within official settings and more institutionalized patterns of social action?

There seems little doubt about the significance of institutional approaches to environmental concerns. One important justification for this focus is provided by Douglas and Wildavsky: 'A real-life risk portfolio is not a selection made by private ratiocination. In real life the social process slides the decision making and the prior editing of choices onto social institutions' (1982, p. 85). Rather than simply being a matter of individual awareness (or 'ratiocination'), environmental assessments and decisions involve a wide range of institutions (including governmental and industrial bodies) on an almost daily basis. Should a new highway or housing estate be built in open countryside? Should a particular chemical be banned? What level of pollution should be permitted from an industrial site? In each case, institutional judgement must be based upon a sometimes complex array of social and technical factors in situations that can be both uncertain and open to multiple interpretations.

How institutions choose (or feel themselves obliged) to operate in the face of what can prove to be difficult policy issues reveals much about the contemporary interpretation of environmental problems. As Douglas and Wildavsky imply, the operation of institutions in this area is not simply a 'technical' or 'routine' matter but is more broadly symptomatic of how the 'social process' deals with these concerns. At the same time, such a focus inevitably raises questions about the capability of contemporary institutions to cope flexibly and effectively with environmental issues – and of the possible role of sociology within institutional practice. On that basis, we now consider *institutional understandings*: how have different governmental institutions sought to 'make sense' of environmental matters?

Within environmental debate, a conventional distinction is drawn between 'institutional' and 'public' forms of discourse and understanding. Whilst the notion that public groups can be knowledgeable about environmental matters is still seen as controversial,[4] one important legitimation for institutional decision-makers is that they are capable of acting in a balanced, logical and technically informed manner. The involvement of experts is especially important in supporting this social legitimation. As Jasanoff has commented: 'The proposition that science-based decisions should be reviewed by independent experts strikes us today as hardly more controversial than the proposition that there is no completely risk-free technology' (1990, p. 1). At this point, we can see that the institutional issues discussed in this chapter link very closely to chapter 3's treatment of scientific knowledge. As we noted then, environmental decisions are often defended on scientific grounds. Certainly, one characteristic rationale for environmental decisions is that the facts should decide. However, this can place scientific expertise under great public and political pressures. On the one hand, environmental problems increase the public and institutional demands on science. On the other, they encourage public discussion and criticism of science – especially when it is seen to fail in the mission it has been set:

> In the age of large-scale hazards, scientific advances have perforce led science into a marriage of hatred with the public. . . . The hazards exacerbate the dependence of everyday life on science, but they simultaneously open the scientific monopoly on truth to public discussion, down to the details of production of the results. (Beck 1995b, p. 161)

This chapter will, accordingly, pay particular attention to the relationship between scientific advice and institutional decisions. It will be very apparent that institutions do not simply follow broad and established principles, but must instead tread a sensitive path between scientific evidence, social pressures and commercial anxieties. To those outside this institutional nexus (including, for example, many public groups), governmental bodies can appear all-powerful. From the perspective of those within, institutions are obliged to reach decisions in an area where there may be few fixed navigational points or unambiguous sources of evidence.

Jasanoff portrays the institutional dilemma for the US Environmental Protection Agency (EPA) in its early efforts to control pesticides: 'If the agency curbed the use of pesticides it was perceived as caving in to naive romanticism and misplaced back-to-nature demagoguery. If it permitted continued use of suspected chemicals, it was seen as captive to powerful agribusiness interests' (1990, p. 123). She continues: 'To project scientific self-confidence under these circumstances was difficult at best, and neither EPA nor its scientific advisers proved entirely equal to the task' (ibid.). These policy dilemmas are generally exacerbated by the difficulties of establishing scientific proof of environmental or human harm. As we will find in the aldrin/dieldrin case, the situation is far more complex than simply 'letting the facts decide'. Equally, we will witness the generally unacknowledged flexibility, interpretation and negotiation at the core of institutional decisions. This view represents a sharp contrast to the sociological argument that such institutions simply embody the logic of modernity.

It will be suggested that the adoption by institutions of a scientific approach does not necessarily resolve the issue but instead raises a whole series of further questions concerning the constitution of sufficient evidence. At what point is the evidence judged to be clear? What burden of proof should be applied? Such situations stretch the conventional process of scientific peer review (based on the supposedly unbiased analysis of new evidence by experts) to the limit. We can suggest at this point that the processes of scientific and institutional review are neither fixed nor objective. Instead, they constitute *a dynamic negotiation of hybrid environmental problems*.

It will also be necessary to bear in mind the sociology of scientific knowledge's portrayal of science as itself a social process. It follows from previous discussion that the boundary between the social and the natural is not simply given but must be actively negotiated within particular institutional settings. Environmental hazards of the kind discussed in this chapter intermix technical and social, ethical and political, human and ecological concerns. Once again, we will find that what are often presented as objective statements about the natural world will inevitably embody social and institutional judgements. However, we will also see that regulatory institutions characteristically present a *technical* rationale for their decisions. Governmental and other institutions, therefore, do not simply receive (or respond to) scientific advice but play an important role in defining *what counts as 'good science' within particular decision-making contexts* – an active, and sometimes contested, process that will be emphasized within this chapter's case-studies. In such situations, institutions must somehow attempt to achieve closure of discussion even whilst competing evaluations threaten to re-open the underlying issues and debates.

It follows directly from this preliminary discussion that in exploring institutional interpretations of environmental problems, we are also exploring a set of assumptions that lie at the heart of contemporary treatments of environmental concern. Given the social significance that is granted to, especially, governmental institutions in controlling various forms of environmental threat, it is important for us to consider *how* such institutions operate and on *what* basis. Viewed in this way, apparently obscure discussions over the safety or environmental impact of, for example, a specific chemical become more widely suggestive of the contemporary institutional treatment of the environment.

As this chapter will suggest, there has been no shortage of regulatory controversy over such matters since the late 1960s. More than just being a matter of the *quantity* of problematic decisions being taken over chemical safety, these issues have raised a series of fundamental challenges for decision-makers and regulatory institutions. In 1962 Rachel Carson, one of the most important spokespeople for the 'new wave' of ecological concern, diagnosed the situation in terms that foreshadowed Beck by some 25 years:

> As the tide of chemicals born of the Industrial Age has arisen to engulf our environment, a drastic change has come about in the nature of the most serious public health problems. Only yesterday mankind lived in fear of the scourges of smallpox, cholera and plague. . . . Today we are concerned with a different kind of hazard that lurks in our environment – a hazard we ourselves have introduced into our world as our modern way of life has evolved. (Carson 1991, p. 168)

As Jasanoff notes, Rachel Carson's *Silent Spring* 'not only launched a new social movement but helped locate pesticides at the very heart of environmental politics' (1990, p. 123). In this, Carson was also offering an early statement of the contemporary sense of environmental threat as a direct (and pervasive) consequence of social change and our 'modern' form of existence. If Carson was to be taken seriously, what manner of action should be taken? Who should decide about these controls? What kinds of institution would be needed to cope with this new generation of environmental problems?

Partly in deference to Carson, but also because this represents one of the more widely discussed forms of human and environmental threat, we will examine these questions with particular regard to the assessment of pesticide hazards in the United States, Britain and the European Union. If pesticides represent a good example of the kinds of hazard 'we ourselves have introduced into our world', what measures have 'we' (through our institutions) taken to deal with them?

Deciding About the Environment

Aldrin/dieldrin

Aldrin and dieldrin assumed an especially prominent position within Rachel Carson's critical onslaught on pesticides. Based upon the evidence available at that time, Carson established her general case:

These insecticides are not selective poisons; they do not single out the one species of which we desire to be rid. Each of them is used for the simple reason that it is a deadly poison. It therefore poisons all life with which it comes into contact: the cat beloved of some family, the farmer's cattle, the rabbit in the field, and the horned lark out of the sky. (1991, p. 99)

By the 1970s, aldrin/dieldrin (A/D) had been widely employed in agriculture. By that time also, serious concern was being expressed not only about their impact on animals but also on human beings – and, especially, in terms of their carcinogenic (cancer-causing) potential.

In this section, we will draw upon Gillespie, Eva and Johnston's classic study of carcinogenic risk-assessment in the United States and Britain in order to examine the operation of institutional and decision-making processes.[5]

In 1974, the US EPA declared that A/D posed an unacceptable carcinogenic hazard and that usage should therefore be suspended. In the same year, and in response to the EPA's decision, the British Advisory Committee on Pesticides and Other Toxic Chemicals (operating within the framework of the Pesticides Safety Precautions Scheme, PSPS) reviewed A/D only to conclude that no policy action was needed. Gillespie and his colleagues present us with this institutional and scientific puzzle: how was it decided that A/D[6] are carcinogenic in one country but not in another? How could a chemical cause cancer in the United States but not in Britain?

It is quite clear, then, that the experts and decision-makers in PSPS and EPA reviewed the same experimental evidence of A/D's possible carcinogenicity and came to contradictory conclusions. Furthermore, although each group of experts and decision-makers was aware of A/D's status in the other decision-making forum, this did not change their conclusion. We therefore have a genuine paradox to explain. (1982, p. 306)

As these authors note, the case of A/D dispels any lingering notion that such institutional decisions are straightforward or unproblematic – or, put differently, *that nature can speak to society in an uncontested and univocal fashion*. Equally, the fact that the equivalent decision-making structures in two countries could conclude so differently tells us something about the *institutional variation* that is possible within such processes. This is an important sociological point, since more sweeping talk of 'late-modern institutions' tends to emphasize structural similarities rather than more subtle, and subtly negotiated, differences of this kind. As with 'public' constructions of environmental threat, the temptation to adopt a homogeneous treatment of institutional structures can be extremely strong (especially as a kind of sociological shorthand). However, a more detailed sociological treatment suggests the heterogeneity and dynamism of these social arrangements – a treatment that, as we will discuss, has both empirical and theoretical implications.

In discussion of this institutional paradox, Gillespie et al. consider a number of potentially important explanatory factors (1982, p. 330):

'The uncertainty inherent in the relevant scientific field'
As considered in chapter 3, scientific evidence relating to environmental matters is characteristically uncertain and, therefore, particularly susceptible to deconstruction,[7] contradiction and competing interpretations of the evidence. This was certainly true for the evidence relating to A/D. However, Gillespie et al. observe that such uncertainty cannot in itself explain the central paradox since it was common to both the US and British evidence. Instead, the question becomes one of the *differential interpretation* of such uncertainty.

'The application of different scientific standards, motivated by different scientific and social commitments'
Here, Gillespie et al. identify substantial differences between the two decision-making processes and their operational assumptions. In the United States, witnesses for the EPA convinced the relevant hearing that animal evidence based on the mouse was sufficient and that there was no need for them to establish a specific mechanism for cancer causation. Equally, it was acknowledged that it would be 'ethically unjustifiable' to await scientific evidence of human harm. On this basis, the EPA was able to defeat the Shell lawyers and scientists who set criteria for carcinogenicity that required the development of tumours in more than one species and also more convincing human data.

Moving to the British context, no public record of the equivalent discussions is available (a common characteristic of UK institutions[8]). However, Gillespie et al. conclude from such evidence as is available that British decision-makers were much closer to the general position adopted by Shell. Mouse-based evidence alone was seen to be both ambiguous and insufficient. Meanwhile, the epidemiological (i.e. human-based) evidence did not indicate a cancer link. Gillespie et al. on this basis characterize the US decision as 'health protective' in orientation, whilst the British was 'agriculturally-oriented' (1982, p. 317). It is important for us to note that both these 'orientations' combine 'social' and 'scientific' factors rather than separating neatly into one element or another.

'The bureaucratic politics of the agencies with responsibility for regulating pesticides'
Special emphasis here is placed on the *location and institutional mission* of each regulatory authority. PSPS operates within the Ministry of Agriculture, Fisheries and Food (MAFF), which is closely involved in agricultural production and efficiency. EPA is a body solely responsible for environmental protection. Whilst PSPS advisers, for example, are formally 'independent' of such agricultural connections, Gillespie et al. emphasize the 'tradition of close cooperation' between these advisers and industry (a point also discussed with regard to 'regulatory science' in chapter 3), so that 'they were highly receptive to an argument which they had helped develop, and which was congruent with their social and scientific commitments' (ibid., p. 319).

'The way in which standards are defined in particular systems of regulations'
Here, Gillespie et al. deal with the institutional interpretation and definition of such apparently fixed categories as 'carcinogen' and 'burden of proof'. Their particular empirical point is to examine the national frameworks within which the evidence was sifted and evaluated. Thus, the US legal system played an important role in granting key decision-making authority to two non-scientists. In contrast, British decision-makers placed greater emphasis on the traditional requirements of scientific causality and placed the balance of doubt in favour of pesticide usage. In each case, the definitional process was considerably more flexible and interpretive in character than might be visible to an institutional outsider.

Rather than just being a matter of *applying* scientific or institutional principles then, the particular contexts of their *active interpretation* became extremely important. As with public understandings, it cannot simply be assumed that institutional understandings 'respond' to scientific input. Instead, the two systems discussed by Gillespie and colleagues actively constructed the risks of A/D in strikingly different ways.

'A series of contextual factors'
Discussion here centres on 'cultural and economic factors' as they are seen to operate in the two national settings. Such factors include the greater concern over environmental issues in the USA (at least in the early 1970s), the comparative national awareness of carcinogenic risk, Britain's weaker economic position, the different scientific traditions of the two countries and the differing styles of government. On this final point, Gillespie et al. emphasize what has become a standard conclusion of comparative analyses:

> In Britain, consensus is generally achieved by restricting both access to, and information of, the decision-making process, whilst allowing maximum flexibility for negotiation amongst the most directly involved parties. This contrasts with the American pluralist tradition in which great importance is attached to the clash of conflicting ideas and the evolution of policy through adversarial processes. (1982, p. 328)

The case of A/D suggests many of the features that have figured within other policy analyses involving the USA and the UK.[9] However, the intention in this discussion has not been to demarcate specific 'national regulatory styles' or to get drawn into a discussion of the safety of one category of pesticides. Instead, I have employed the accounts of Gillespie et al. (1982) as a means of demonstrating the significance of institutional understandings and, closely linked to this, of the wider contexts within which these operate.

As this section has suggested, environmental decisions are neither structurally fixed nor narrowly dependent on technical advice. We have instead considered a more subtle set of social, institutional and scientific negotiations as being at work. One important implication of this case-study is that national institutions do not simply operate in a uniform or standardized fashion but are capable of framing environmental issues in very different ways.

Crucially, we have seen that social and cultural factors play an important part within ostensibly technical regulatory processes. There is no culture-free framework within which scientific and institutional judgements can be reached. What this case especially suggests is that the significance of these factors can easily be downplayed by institutions anxious to emphasize their objectivity, capacity for control and technical competence. One advantage of the sociological approach taken here is that it encourages a critical discussion of these unacknowledged social assumptions and institutional orientations. This point will become even clearer in the next two examples of environmental decision-making.

2,4,5-T

As a second example of institutional processes at work, we can now consider the case of another controversial pesticide, 2,4,5-T. More detailed accounts of this case-study are available elsewhere.[10] Here, we will focus on certain key aspects of the institutional discussion of this chemical in Britain. In particular, I want to draw upon Wynne's important sociological argument (briefly introduced within chapter 3's BSE case-study) concerning the 'naïve sociology' that lies at the core of technical and institutional analyses of risk. As Wynne puts this with regard to 2,4,5-T: 'The point of general importance shown by this case is that different parties . . . defined different actual risk systems . . . because they built upon different models of the social practices creating or controlling the risks' (1989, p. 37).

The case of 2,4,5-T was highly contentious in Britain during the late 1970s. The official British body, the Advisory Committee on Pesticides (ACP), which also featured in the A/D case, was in dispute with the trade union representing British farmworkers. Whilst the farmworkers were pressing for a ban on the chemical in Britain (in line with an international campaign that had already been successful elsewhere), the ACP concluded after numerous reviews of the issue that there was no real evidence of harm *so long as 2,4,5-T was used 'in the recommended way and for the recommended purposes'*.

Of course, such disputes are often presented as a conflict between 'ignorant' lay people and 'rational' experts (Irwin 1995). However, and in line with the previous chapter's discussion of the more complex risk and environmental understandings generated by different public groups, it is also possible to portray the farmworkers as highly knowledgeable within the conditions of their everyday work and existence. Drawing upon the experiences of its members, the farmworkers' union compiled a dossier of unsafe agricultural practices and of the consequences of exposure to the pesticide for human health. According to the union (and others), such consequences included cancer, miscarriage and birth deformity as a direct result of 2,4,5-T.

Given the weight of such evidence, and given steps already taken in various other countries to ban this chemical, what possible justification could there be for the British authorities to continue to permit its use? Each side in this dispute presented what it considered to be clear technical evidence in support of its position. However, each side also constructed the technical evidence in its own particular fashion.

As in the previous case, one important institutional consideration concerns the burden of proof that is to be applied. Faced with uncertain evidence, at what point is it appropriate to make a regulatory judgement? As this was expressed in chapter 3, to what extent can absence of evidence be assumed to constitute evidence of absence? For the farmworkers, the evidence was sufficiently suggestive to justify a ban. Their case was that, even though individual case-studies and scientific reports might be open to question, there was nevertheless a consistent pattern running through the evidence as a whole. In a situation where so much doubt had been raised, surely the only sensible move was to ban the pesticide?

The ACP meanwhile found it impossible to justify a decision to ban on the basis of only partial data. Where was the conclusive human evidence? Might not the kinds of health effect identified by the farmworkers be a consequence of exposure to other chemicals or indeed random occurrence across the population? Where, in other words, was the convincing scientific demonstration of cause and effect? For the ACP, to ban on the basis of such limited evidence was not scientifically justifiable. At the same time, and as the concept of 'naïve sociology' serves to emphasize, there were also differences in the social assumptions upon which the two sets of judgements were being built. The farmworkers based their call for a ban on an assumption that the world of pesticide usage was inherently messy and uncontrollable. In a situation where strict controls could not reasonably be exercised – especially given the varied and disorganized conditions within which individual farmworkers must operate – a ban was a reasonable precautionary move. Put differently, the farmworkers built their case upon a particular model of the 'real world' of pesticide usage and reached a conclusion that followed quite logically from this.

The ACP, by contrast, pinned its requirement for the 'recommended way' and 'recommended purposes' upon the assumption that pesticide administration could indeed be strictly controlled. The farmworkers' experience was of highly informal conditions of operation where it was possible that those spraying the pesticide might not even know what chemical they were using and where, even if they did know, they might find themselves unable to follow officially designated precautions (especially when working away from washing and changing facilities). The ACP members, meanwhile, were operating on the basis of their own experience of 'good laboratory practice':

> The scientists' implicit assumptions were of idealised worlds of herbicide production and use; and the validity and credibility of their 'objective' risk analysis was committed to this naïve sociology embedded in their technical analysis. Conversely the workers . . . had real empirical experience, indeed expertise, that was directly relevant to an objective risk analysis. (Wynne 1989, p. 37)

Whilst it may be tempting to conclude in such a situation that the advisory committee was *deliberately* attempting to stifle farmworkers' concerns in order to protect some social or economic interest (a conclusion that was certainly reached by many of the trade-unionists involved), it is also possible to imagine more subtle forces at work. In this case, the institutional process operated according to a model of scepticism in the face of new evidence, which is well established within a conventional scientific setting: when in doubt, the most rational approach is to await further evidence. The farmworkers meanwhile felt that what they interpreted as a 'wait and see' (or, put more negatively, 'counting the bodies') policy was profoundly ill-suited to this particular situation on ethical as well as scientific grounds – but also based upon their direct experience of pesticide usage. Thus, the farmworkers approached the evidence from a very different perspective – one that might be characterized as a 'precautionary' approach.[11]

From the viewpoint of social groups who feel themselves excluded from these institutional discussions (as the farmworkers considered themselves to be in this case), scientific and institutional processes can be represented as a *barrier* to public demands – as Beck also suggests. However, the case of 2,4,5-T – and indeed the other cases discussed in this chapter – suggest a rather more complex pattern of social and technical factors in operation. For example, the farmworkers were also supported by certain scientists in their case.

Rather than simply being a matter of science resisting public demands, this case highlights the kinds of assumption that underpin technical evidence. We witness once again the delicate judgements that lie at the heart of institutional action in this area – judgements that encompass and interlink 'social' and 'scientific' matters. Especially important in this regard is the 'pre-framing' of the issues so that the underlying assumptions and working practices of the advisory committee had a profound effect on its overall judgement – but also allowed it to present this judgement as entirely 'rational' in character. Institutional control over the form and presentation of issues represents a crucial – but generally unrecognized – social influence over decision-making.

At the same time, the 2,4,5-T case suggests an important role for social scientific analysis in identifying and exploring these institutional framings and socio-technical assumptions. As Wynne concludes his discussion: 'Social scientists must lend their expertise in helping to fathom this new terrain, and to ensure its constructive mapping' (1989, p. 45). It follows that, rather than simply taking sides, there is a useful purpose to be gained by institutional analyses of this sort – and especially in opening up largely unchallenged (and unacknowledged) assumptions to critical scrutiny. After all, and as the participants in the 2,4,5-T dispute were only too aware, these individual cases have wider implications for the control of pesticides more generally and, indeed, for the social control of environmental and health hazards. At this point, a critical sociology can prove its practical value – and not least by facilitating wider debate about the social and cultural foundation for institutional action.

Constructing a Single Europe[12]

As this chapter has already considered, the institutional resolution of environmental issues even within one nation can represent the outcome of processes that are both socially and technically complex. In this third example, I want to consider these processes as they operate not simply at a national level but also within international systems of regulation. Whilst international regulatory systems may claim legitimacy on the grounds of their scientific rationale, the establishment of these systems perhaps paradoxically serves to re-emphasize the importance of local negotiations and institutional judgements. It will be argued that scientific statements inevitably embody cultural and institutional understandings concerning the practical development of environmental control.

On that basis, and again building upon the sociological perspective developed in this book, there is a potential tension between the 'universalistic' claims of international regulatory systems (which often draw explicitly upon the language of science as perhaps *the* most universalistic frame of understanding) and the kinds of social and cultural assumption that have been emphasized in the previous two cases. Whilst certain international regulators (notably at the European level) might view such assumptions as minor anomalies to be dismissed or overcome once fully developed regulatory systems have been established, this book's wider argument is that institutional and technical judgements are inevitably bound up with social and cultural assumptions. The sociological challenge is to consider how best we can analyse this relationship between the 'local' and the 'universal'. In practical terms, the challenge for environmental policy-making becomes one of building systems that do not simply enforce a reductionist or 'scientistic'[13] approach but instead acknowledge, and indeed build upon, such variations in cultural understanding.

One of the main arguments in favour of the international harmonization of regulatory standards has been *economic* in character. To take the case of agrochemicals, companies have found the existence of separate national regulatory systems to be a major impediment to free trade. From a commercial point of view, the international movement of goods is greatly assisted by a level playing field of regulatory requirements. The harmonization of such requirements offers the possibility of standardizing the review process so that approval by one (for example) European country leads to approval in others. At the same time, the 'Europeanization' of agrochemical regulation can serve to protect all European nations equally in terms of public and occupational health, wildlife and the environment.[14] Essential to such harmonization processes is the argument that *science is universal* in character. What counts as evidence in a Lisbon laboratory should also be true in San Francisco, Cork or Kuala Lumpur. The adoption of common scientific standards – backed up by what is known as 'Good Laboratory Practice' – provides a solid basis for international agreement. Once again, we see a broad scientific rationale being deployed as support for what is essentially an economic and welfare-based argument. However, and as I will suggest, different technical cultures approach scientific evidence in rather different ways – with important consequences for decision-making.

Looking more specifically at the control of pesticides across Europe, regulatory authorities certainly accept that the environmental review of pesticides needs to take account of some local and regional differences. However, these differences are considered to be natural in character. On that basis, ecological variations cannot be ignored across the nations of such a diverse area as the European Union. The Scandinavian nations, for example, possess a very different range of habitats from Italy or Portugal. Within each national setting, therefore, ecological factors need to be taken into account when assessing pesticide safety and environmental impact: might any local species be especially affected or will the conditions of usage cause particular problems? On the same logic, there is little point testing the environmental impact of a pesticide for use on (say) potatoes in a country where that crop is not grown. Some measure of local and regional differences must therefore be considered within any system of controls – but these differences are seen to relate exclusively to 'environmental' rather than social or cultural factors.

For these acknowledged reasons, the European Union's Plant Protection Directive (91/414/EEC) is designed as a two-tier approval system. Active ingredients – in other words, the specific chemicals responsible for pesticide action – are authorized at the European level. Specific agrochemical products, meanwhile, are approved at the level of member states. Within this system, data requirements and evaluation guidelines are common – subject to modification on the basis of the above forms of variation. Member states are then expected to recognize each other's approval of agrochemicals and to accept commonly agreed active ingredients.

Viewed from a sociological perspective, what issues arise for this system of international control and standardization? We can begin by considering the character of scientific evidence in this area and its relationship to the kinds of institutional assumption discussed so far. As I will suggest, the adoption of standardized systems raises questions not so much of *whether* social and cultural assumptions are incorporated but rather of *what form* these assumptions should take. Whilst 'standardization' offers the promise of a common set of operating principles, implicit cultural and institutional factors may work in the opposite direction. Equally, whilst ecological differences may be invoked as a distinguishing factor between national settings, the definition of such 'contextual variation' is, once again, a matter of institutional judgement. What appears to be an essentially technical set of arguments is inevitably bound up with a range of social and institutional reconstructions.

At this stage, we need to recall chapter 3's discussion of what was termed 'regulatory science' and the changing conditions of modern scientific practice. As was noted then, scientific research in the area of agrochemicals does not simply spring from an institutional vacuum. As we have observed on previous occasions, scientific evidence (like other forms of environmental construction) needs to be contextualized within the conditions of its development and application.

It becomes significant for the Europeanization of regulatory controls, therefore, that scientific research in this area is heavily dominated by industrially sponsored facilities. It also follows from this institutional location that technical questions about, for example, the safety of a pesticide are not easily separated from economic and commercial questions of the likely profitability of a specific product. In addition, this is an area of considerable technical complexity where testing may be far from straightforward. Whilst international regulation may operate on the principle that technical arguments are exportable across national settings, the particular scientific and institutional character of regulatory science can work against this. One major challenge for Europeanization – like other forms of standardization – concerns the manner in which these national policy cultures can be brought together.

In Britain, for example, a very well-established relationship of trust and mutual understanding has developed between the agrochemical industry, government regulators and the various individuals and institutions engaged in scientific research. This relationship has been further assisted by the movement of personnel between these roles. Test results are interpreted on the basis of discussion and shared learning across this network. According to the prevailing British ideology, scientific tests need to be conducted properly, but at the same time common sense and commercial awareness must be maintained. A mood of pragmatism thus prevails – albeit one founded on quite specific notions of who and what should be included within this pragmatic ideology. In that way, the adoption of a specific form of institutional practice and technical discourse serves to exclude groups that are not seen to comprehend the 'realities' of regulatory science – with environmentalist groups typically finding themselves placed in just that category.

According to one empirical study, however, British industrialists view German regulators very differently (see Rothstein et al. 1999). Whereas the British approach is seen to acknowledge contextual variability and 'learning by doing', this is contrasted with a more bureaucratic and formalized style in countries such as Germany. Whilst the German system is portrayed as complex and cautious, the UK system is seen to be practical and facilitatory. According to this characterization also, whilst British regulators are willing to listen to the opinions of industry and take these into account, their German equivalents generally prefer to decide for themselves and then inform industry of their verdict. Whilst UK regulators take pride in a case-by-case approach to the evidence, German officials are seen to engage in 'box-ticking' (i.e. adopting a mechanical approach to test results).

Already, therefore, we find both scientific and institutional reasons why the imposition of standardized systems may prove highly problematic. Equally, interviews with regulatory and industrial officials raised doubts about the technical competence of some member states to conduct and interpret notionally standard tests. On that basis, technical approval in certain countries may not carry the same international status as approval in others. At the same time, British industrialists considered that particular member states (for example, Germany, Denmark and The Netherlands) were generally inclined to take an unreasonably tough line on all pesticides. Such nations were characterized as seeking to limit the use of pesticides to the greatest possible degree.

Taking these factors together, we can identify some of the cultural and institutional factors that lead to problems for standardized regulatory systems. Whilst British participants will denigrate what are portrayed as unrealistic expectations and hypothetical scenarios, other nations will inevitably be suspicious of what they see as the closed and cosy relationship between regulators and the regulated in the UK. Certainly, the British regulatory culture emphasizes open and flexible discussion between a small number of recognized participants. Whilst for an insider this seems like an excellent system, outsiders – as in the case of 2,4,5-T – can find it all collusive and secretive. Significantly, however, this is not just another example of national political prejudices and cultural stereotypes (although these elements are undoubtedly present). Such characterizations are also likely to prove influential over ostensibly scientific decisions.

In this way, the attempted harmonization of regulatory requirements serves, paradoxically, to emphasize the differences between what we can term 'technical cultures'. In this situation also, we can judge that technical statements contain tacit social and cultural assumptions about, for example, the trustworthiness of certain institutions or the manner in which contextual variability should be taken into account. Although such statements claim to describe an external real world, they inevitably embody a sense of social and institutional order. Whilst ecological variation might be claimed as an objective statement about the natural world, technical judgements of nature depend upon social and institutional reconstructions.[15] In one example of these local constructions of difference, German attempts to study the stability of a pesticide through standardized wind-tunnel tests were ridiculed from a UK perspective as an inappropriate attempt to convert a matter of professional judgement into another form of 'box-ticking'. As one industrial regulatory affairs manager put it:

> Effectively you had to spray a load of dwarf French beans and then take them down a wind tunnel and then blast air at them, I mean it was so crazy, the whole concept, but it had never been discussed with industry. Unfortunately that data requirement has now sort of been copied into the European legislation so in a sense we are all caught up in that.[16]

Such small examples reveal the extent to which scientific judgements depend upon wider socio-technical cultures. What counts as 'crazy' or 'common sense' is constructed on the basis of wider institutional judgements of evidence, professional competence and regulatory effectiveness. Scientific judgements in these settings become inseparable from social and institutional judgements of what constitutes an appropriate control system – a point that takes us back to the 'naïve sociology' discussed in the 2,4,5-T case.

What this account also suggests is that contemporary institutions have not slavishly followed the same abstracted logic of (late) modernity. Instead, institutional approaches and technical cultures can be understood as more diverse and differentiated in character – especially as economic pressures towards standardization cause local and national differences to be (perhaps surprisingly) re-emphasized. Of course, this does not rule out the attempted imposition of 'scientistic' cultures as a means of ironing out cultural variation. However, it does suggest the continuing significance of the 'local' within systems that are ostensibly global in character.

Our argument in this more complex example has taken a number of forms. First, I have emphasized the *local negotiations and contextual variations* that lie at the heart of apparently universal systems of environmental control. What may appear as a standardized or global approach is actually dependent upon social and cultural assumptions that can vary considerably across contexts.

Secondly, I have highlighted *the role of science within these processes*. Whilst often presented as a universal form of rationality, we have seen that this is once again dependent upon a variety of often tacit judgements and a hybrid series of networks – including informal links between the regulated industry and the regulatory authorities.

Thirdly, we have suggested *the variability of institutional and scientific discussions*. Rather than simply enacting some predetermined logic or collective world-view, scientific and regulatory institutions are engaged in often complex negotiations over both the technical assessment of pesticides and the most appropriate mechanisms of control. As has been suggested, one essential – albeit frequently unacknowledged – element of these negotiations has been the operation of a range of social and cultural assumptions over, for example, the practical implementation of European regulatory processes and the trust that can be placed in different national authorities. Whilst European regulatory structures can appear remote from the social and cultural factors discussed in this book, this case suggest just how central these are, even within apparently universal systems.

Discussion

This chapter has raised a number of issues concerning institutional actions and environmental decision-making. Throughout the three cases, we have seen the active judgements, institutional reconstructions and interpretations at the heart of decision-making processes. As with the previous discussion of the 'environmental publics', we have especially emphasized the importance of contextual factors, including localized constructions and social assumptions. In line with the previous chapter's discussion of public groups, institutional judgements have been presented as the outcome of active processes of 'sense-making'. To use Hannigan's phrase once again, they are 'end-products of a dynamic social process of definition, negotiation and legitimation' (1995, p. 31).

In this chapter, operational assumptions concerning the status of various kinds of evidence have been especially significant. Institutions might seek to present the outside world with an unimpeachable justification for decisions over, for example, whether a specific pesticide is a carcinogen – and scientific argument is seen to be particularly powerful in this regard. The examples in this chapter, however, suggest that institutional judgements are inevitably based on a more delicate balance of social, political and technical factors. As cases such as A/D suggest, the evidence is open to multiple interpretations and varying constructions. In sociological terms, the closure of discussion is the outcome of often complex social processes rather than simply a straightforward reflection of the 'evidence' (or indeed of 'nature'). As Jasanoff has suggested, such balancing acts can be difficult to defend when exposed to full public scrutiny. However, we saw in the case of 2,4,5-T that institutional decisions can also be resilient in the face of external challenges. In this situation, the institutional role of scientific evidence takes on special significance. While science is conventionally presented as standing apart from political, social and economic factors, this chapter has revealed the judgements and working assumptions upon which scientific evidence is based.

At the same time, the material presented in this chapter argues against the crude notion that science simply stands in opposition to environmental concerns. The polarization of, on the one hand, science and institutions and, on the other, public and environmental pressures is inadequate for a number of reasons. First, we have seen that scientific argumentation is typically employed by every side within environmental disputes – including trade-union and 'public interest' groups. Secondly, the selection of risks for institutional review is often generated by non-scientific as well as scientific groups. Thirdly, and most importantly for our current discussion, the operation of science cannot be separated from social and cultural assumptions. The kinds of 'naïve sociology' discussed by Brian Wynne remind us that, whether acknowledged or not, scientific assessments are inevitably built upon social and institutional assumptions. *'Science' cannot then be counterposed to 'Society', since this is to ignore the social construction of both these categories.*

The study of institutional actions in this area emphasizes once again the hybridity of environmental issues and also the active processes through which social and institutional actors 'make sense' of such concerns. As we have seen, decisions over the definition of carcinogenicity or 'sufficient evidence' are the dynamic outcomes of institutional boundary-setting. Environmental threats (and nature more broadly) do not simply present themselves to institutions. Institutions must instead judge, negotiate and define the character and scale of such threats. As the third example in particular suggested, this opens up questions of the relationship between the local and universal conditions of scientific and environmental construction.

This chapter has also suggested a distinctive role for sociologists within these complex social processes. Wynne presents this role as working to improve the quality of public debate and, hence, of environmental decision-making. It may be that it is not the business of sociologists to make authoritative moral or prescriptive statements. After all, the judgements of sociologists are as open to deconstruction as those of any scientific, public or institutional group (as critical readers of this book may be all too aware). However, this is not to deny the practical significance of sociological analysis – indeed, the interesting sociological contribution only begins once a more self-critical and open stance is adopted.

Thus, a simple realist account, which emphasized the partiality of the usage of scientific evidence within policy disputes, is likely to raise a relatively limited set of questions since so much of the technical ground is assumed to be given. The sociological approach adopted here suggests a more thoroughgoing interrogation of institutional assumptions – and an awareness that greater scientific input is unlikely in itself to overcome institutional difficulties. Equally, the abandonment of the belief that science is capable of generating absolute solutions to environmental problems should not cause despair (or a rejection of scientific input to decision-making) but rather encourage new thinking over how best to deal with environmental concerns. It also follows from this analysis that the natural world cannot be separated from the social and institutional world of environmental decision-making and governance. Instead, we have observed the centrality of social and cultural assumptions to the definition of environmental problems and responses.

Ultimately, the sociological treatment advocated in this book stresses that environmental decisions are, at their core, a matter of social choice. Rather than limiting or undermining environmental discussion, a sociological approach should shed light on current institutional and technical assumptions. As Wynne suggests, this task of opening up decision-making processes to wider scrutiny may in itself serve a valuable democratic and scientific purpose – for instance, by holding up unacknowledged assumptions to critical scrutiny. Equally, an acceptance of the human judgements at the centre of environmental action should serve to stimulate fresh forms of engagement and activity on the part of various institutional and extra-institutional groups.

Thus, a recognition of the socio-technical uncertainties and contested judgements at the heart of environmental governance does not necessarily lead to inaction or, to borrow one familiar criticism of constructivism, environmental quietism. Instead, an awareness of the local negotiations within decision-making might lead to more open and accountable forms of decision-making, where closure depends upon more than precommitments and a narrow form of technical argumentation. Equally, sociological exploration of this kind reinforces the importance of the 'precautionary principle'. When nature cannot offer uncontested truths, the most cautious response might be to act more readily on suggestive rather than definitive evidence.

Presented in this way, the sociological approach adopted in this book can improve our disciplinary understanding but also make a critical contribution to environmental decision-making. Sociological analysis of the kind advocated here does not represent a turning away from matters of environmental policy and action. Instead, it can suggest new forms of engagement and activity, which challenge existing intellectual and epistemological assumptions – including those of sociology itself.[17]

6

Kamikazes and Chromosomes: Sociological Perspectives on Technology

An understanding has crept in, according to which modernity is reduced to the frame of reference of technology and nature in the manner of perpetrator and victim. The social, cultural and political risks of modernization remain hidden by this very approach, and from this way of thinking (which is also that of the political environmental movement).

Beck 1992, pp. 24–5

In the dominant paradigm, technology is seen as being above society both in its structure and evolution, in its offering technological fixes, and in its technological determinism. . . . Its course is viewed as self-determined. In periods of rapid technological transformation, it is assumed that society and people must adjust to change, instead of technological change adjusting to the social values of equity, sustainability and participation.

Shiva 1995, p. 193

One important enactment and embodiment of relations between society, nature and knowledge comes in the form of technology. Rather than presenting technology as an asocial process (as a matter best left to scientists and engineers) or viewing technologies as having predetermined social and environmental impacts, chapter 6 argues that technologies give tangible form to material and social relations. Building upon a discussion of two technologies – nuclear power and biotechnology – the negotiated boundaries between society, nature and knowledge are explored. As the first case in this chapter suggests, technologies are not simply 'given' but are varyingly constructed, experienced, worried over and enjoyed. Seen in this light, the contextual study of technology emerges as a major site for exploring relations between the social and the natural.

So far in this book we have considered the relationship between sociology and the environment both in the most general terms (for example, through the discussion of sustainable development and debates around the risk society) and with regard to particular issues and empirical cases (local publics dealing with environmental hazards, institutional judgements over pesticide risks). We have also paid attention to the argument that scientific expertise in this area seems inevitably to embody cultural assumptions and implicit sociological judgements – of the kind labelled 'naïve sociology' in chapter 5. In that way, the previous chapters have moved beyond the usual idea that sociology should be concerned only with the manifestly 'social' aspects of the environment and have instead begun to develop a considerably broader sociological agenda based upon an awareness of the hybridity of environmental problems and concerns.

Nevertheless, in discussion so far we have not directly considered one of the most recurrent themes within environmental debate: the power and consequences of technology. Whether viewed as a negative or positive force, technological change is central to environmental action. As this chapter will suggest, the study of technology has been a difficult area for sociology: technologies are typically represented within environmental discussion as if they are *asocial* in character. Sociologists have characteristically been more willing to discuss topics that are conventionally defined as 'social' or 'political' change (such as environmental group membership or green campaigning) than to consider technological change as a suitable case for analysis. This conventional portrayal tends to place dramatic restrictions on sociological understanding. In this chapter, we will not consider technology, nature and society as fixed, static or separate from one another. Instead, and in keeping with discussion in the previous two chapters, we will explore their overlapping and dynamic construction within environmental debate and action.

One perspective on this relationship is provided by the quotation from Beck at the beginning of this chapter. For Beck, technology is conventionally viewed as being the very opposite of the natural. Thus, technologies are often represented as an intrusion on the natural world. They symbolize humanity's destructive powers. Hence also the environmentalist call for us all to 'get back to nature' (as if nature was a paradise untouched by both humanity – at least until our arrival – and the technologies it has developed).

Sitting alongside this opposition of the natural and the technological, however, there is another conventional separation: between the technological and the social. The very notion of, for example, technologies possessing certain social *impacts* suggests that the technological and the social are somehow separable. As we will discuss in this chapter, the concept of social (or environmental) impact may be highly misleading – and sociologically unproductive. Certainly, the assumption that technologies are distinct from social relations may have helped create a situation where technology has become a no-go area for most sociologists. If technology and sociology are so easily separable then it follows that technological change is a matter best left to scientists and engineers – with sociologists perhaps tinkering around the edges of technological change, dealing with what are often represented as the 'soft' issues of social and organizational response. Equally, such a presentation suggests that technology can be left alone within environmental debate; it is the 'given' to which humans and nature must then respond.

In this chapter, I will argue that technology is a vital area for sociological analysis in general and for environmental sociology in particular. I will suggest that sociological understanding can help us explore the character of technological development and the relationship between this and contemporary environmental debate. Whilst a single chapter can only scratch the surface of these topics, I want to emphasize the sociological and environmental significance of technological change – and also the potential scope for sociological analysis in this area. In order to achieve this, I will focus on two technologies – nuclear power and biotechnology.

These points will be developed as the chapter progresses. For now, let us firstly consider the role of technology within environmental discussions. Following this, we can deal with one prevalent approach to technological development – an approach that I will simply (in line with the quotation from Shiva at the start of this chapter) characterize as 'technological determinism'. Having dealt with those two preliminary points, we can begin to explore ways of considering the relationship between technology and the environment in more sociological terms.

To begin at the beginning, then, why should technology be considered so important in a book dedicated to the relationship between sociology and the environment? The most obvious response to this question is simply to note the centrality of technology to environmental debates. Whether technology is presented as the cause of environmental 'bads' (depending on one's environmental perspective, new road building programmes, nuclear power, genetically manipulated crops) or as the provider of environmental 'goods' ('green' vehicles, alternative energy systems, cleaner products and industrial processes), it remains pivotal to the discussion.

According to one very simple argument, *technology is far too significant an influence over contemporary environmental debate for sociologists to ignore*. As a slight variation on this, technology has become *a central element within the construction and definition of alternative environmental futures*. Whether the future is seen to contain windmills, electric vehicles and eco-villages or centralized power systems, faster automobiles and bigger cities, all these visions hinge on technology and the manner in which it will shape our lives – as science fiction writers and advertisements for various consumer products so often suggest. Accordingly, and as Beck and other social scientists have pointed out, key technological decisions being taken right now in corporate boardrooms are likely to make a major difference to our lives over what can be a considerable period of time – and, given international technological development, a considerable proportion of the globe.

At one extreme, decisions to develop a civil nuclear energy programme taken in the 1950s still have consequences today (and will have consequences for many years to come). At a less obvious level, even the decision to modify an apparently small-scale technology such as the ink cartridge for a printer can prove to be of great significance – especially when one considers the potential sales and international spread of such a pervasive technology. The point is that technological decisions can have ramifications over years and even decades (or, in the case of nuclear power, centuries). Meanwhile, many sociologists seem to miss the significance of such technological decisions – assuming perhaps that they are of only technical interest. At the same time, and as we will discuss, the notion that 'consequences' represent an inherent characteristic of technologies serves to restrict sociological analysis.

A third point concerns *the observable relationship between technologies and social life* – and we should emphasize here the environmental relevance of contemporary patterns of living and working. Once we move beyond the immediate environmental significance of an individual technology, we begin to see the wider importance of what we can term 'social and technological networks'. The motor car as a specific technology may have certain material characteristics. However, the car (and its environmental consequences) cannot be considered outside the social and cultural setting within which it is now placed (and in whose development it has played an integral part): freeways and out-of-town shopping malls, suburban life and daily commuting, reliance on private means of transport, the economic infrastructure linked to the automobile (from auto manufacturers through to local gas stations). Whilst the conventional notion of the automobile's environmental impact simply focuses on the technology itself, and therefore suggests that its replacement will solve technologically created 'problems', a sociological approach immediately suggests the more complex relations between technologies, patterns of social life and definitions of environmental harm.

The point here is that technological change becomes inseparable from social and cultural change. The environmental consequences of a technology can only be understood *within* particular social, environmental and technological settings. After all, the automobile was originally seen as considerably cleaner than its predecessor, the horse-drawn carriage (automobiles generally possessing less anti-social toiletry habits).

It can also be noted that any change towards greener technologies and lifestyles is bound up with the possibilities for new social and institutional relations. Thus, the technology of the personal motor vehicle has become so embedded in our whole culture and way of life that it is now difficult to imagine a means of replacing it (and hard for many of us as individuals to function without one). Any viable alternative to the motor car cannot simply take the same place in the larger network. Instead, new cultural and social networks may be required, which, for example, build upon a mix of public and private transport systems and perhaps also draw in other technological systems such as information technology. In these ways, the social, environmental and technological characteristics of the automobile must be seen as intertwined. Whilst an engineer might present lean-burn engines, catalytic converters or recyclable materials as an environmental solution, it is clear that such solutions depend upon a much wider array of factors. These include individual transport behaviour and city planning, perceptions of personal safety and the operation of public transport services, political decisions over resources and cultural attitudes to the automobile. Technologies play a part in this wider picture but cannot stand aloof from social, political and economic factors.

This discussion of the relationship between sociology, technology and the environment is given further relevance by the often-portrayed linkage between *technology and the character of modernity*. According to theorists such as Giddens, technologies play a central role within everyday life – not least in raising a confusing array of possibilities and choices. At the same time, they represent a form of alienation in that individuals do not feel capable of controlling these technologies: 'The technological changes which impinge upon people's lives are the result of the intrusion of abstract systems, whose character they may influence but do not determine' (Giddens 1994b, p. 75). Consequently, one central question for contemporary politics concerns the possibilities for social control over technological systems so as to open up underlying social choices to wider participation and influence. More generally, experiences of technology are inseparable from those of 'being modern' – experiences that combine pleasure and suffering, a sense of progress and the possibility of environmental destruction. Both in terms of its social and environmental consequences, and its relationship to everyday experience, technology seems, therefore, to represent a key topic for sociological analysis. Certainly, within discussions of the risk society, technology plays an absolutely central role.

Nevertheless, one characteristic means of interpreting these social–technological–environmental relations is to present technological change as the primary factor. It has proven particularly difficult within environmental discussion to resist the, decidedly non-sociological, idea that technology has a life of its own: in other words, that it shapes society, irresistibly sweeping aside traditional social practices and establishing new ways of living and working. From this conventional perspective, *technology is largely independent of the social*. It has social and environmental impacts and may depend upon social institutions for funding and support. However, within this view, technologies ultimately follow their own technical trajectories. They are open to use or abuse but in themselves are socially neutral. At the same time, the environmental consequences of technology are inherent in the technology itself.

According to this *technological determinist* perspective, the latest developments in, for example, computer technology (or, more broadly, information technology) represent a vision of the future – or at least the broad framework within which our lives will be shaped. New working practices, new patterns of employment (and unemployment), new sets of social relations will all follow. Just as the first Industrial Revolution is presented as transforming society through its unleashing of new technological forces, the technologies of the future will shape both human life and the natural environment. From this perspective too, the development of civilization is a story of technological change – from primitive tools to weapons of mass destruction and from the invention of the wheel to telecommunications.[1] Such technologies may be utilized in different ways but they cannot easily be resisted, nor can they be 'disinvented'. From the perspective of this book, sociological analysis of technology has been hindered by such conventional assumptions and, in particular, by the regular presentation of technological change as being separable from social change. Rather than promoting the notion of technology as an independent force, sociologists of technology have more recently considered *technologies as the outcome of processes of social construction.*[2]

For a constructivist account, the processes through which technologies are shaped, implemented and assessed are ultimately *social* in character. In that way, the study of technologies is simultaneously the study of human relations. Put differently, *technologies embody and give tangible form to social relations.* As will be argued in this chapter, such a view of technology has major consequences for our understanding of the relationship between technology and environmental change. Technology can no longer simply be presented as having environmental impacts: instead, technology and the environment are bound together through *social processes and social practices.*

Of course, the suggestion that technology development should be open to thoroughgoing sociological analysis is not without its difficulties. What exactly have specific technologies – whether the computer keyboard on which I am now typing or the train I am hoping soon to catch – to do with social and personal relations? Opponents of constructivism are inexhaustibly fond of pointing out that social relations do not keep jumbo jets in the air.

In response, and as even the most conventional of accounts will acknowledge, it can be argued that technologies depend upon institutions of various kinds for their creation and survival (the company that manufactured my PC and software package, the confusing range of bodies that run the UK rail network). Nevertheless, critics of constructivism argue, microprocessors and trains don't follow the rules of social life – they function according to technical principles (or else, don't function at all).

The analytical challenge to sociology is therefore to demonstrate that patterns of social relations are significant even within what appear to be robust and highly technical systems. To use the now clichéd phrase, sociology needs to demonstrate that it can get inside the 'black box' of technology. Instead of simply treating technologies as if they sprang fully formed into the world, it becomes important to consider the social basis of technological systems – and the social and environmental assumptions embedded within particular technologies. Rather than accepting that technologies work, the challenge is to explain what that work involves and, in more practical terms, how technologies might work differently. At this point we begin to see the large sociological challenge posed by technology.

These sociological discussions over technology are very relevant to the environmental area. To take the example of nuclear power, it is not at all difficult to present this as a force external to people's lives – as an alien presence on the cultural and environmental landscape. The technology came to prominence in the 1940s and has proceeded to create significant environmental consequences (and stimulated various social movements into action). As the title of one book dealing with the UK Sellafield nuclear power plant puts it, local people are 'living in the shadow' of the technology (McSorley 1990). The powerfully argued dichotomy is between 'human suffering' and the 'might of technological creation'. In the same way that the people of Jarrow (discussed in chapter 4) struggle to 'make sense' of a nearby chemical works, those who live close to Sellafield must read the signs from this technology in a climate often characterized by doubt and suspicion.

The sense of technology as an alien presence can be reinforced in a number of ways: the presentation of physically threatening consequences (especially in terms of scale and pervasiveness), the language of science used to justify such forms of progress, the possible social dislocation between those who develop the technology and those who live nearby or operate it. Of course, technologies can also be represented as beneficial: bringing jobs and prosperity to localities, meeting social needs, improving the quality of modern life. Regardless of its positive or negative portrayal, however, the notion remains that technology stands apart from everyday social life. One might add that such a view is also reflected through our educational systems – engineering and sociology are generally presented as distinct rather than (as I would suggest) overlapping disciplines.[3]

The SCOT (social construction of technology[4]) account of nuclear technology emphasizes instead the social, cultural and institutional relations that lie at the heart of this body of expertise and practice. Nuclear technology did not simply spring into life. It was the product of a very specific set of institutions and a coordinated programme of activities. Equally, views of this technology are differentially constructed so that it is simultaneously hailed as a major environmental threat and as a way of combating other environmental threats (notably, the greenhouse effect). From a constructivist perspective, nuclear technology represents a heterogeneous area of social practices – including medical as well as military uses. From this perspective also, the technologies do not simply impact on society. Instead, they are actively interpreted and 'made sense of' within different contexts.

None of this denies the environmental significance of nuclear accidents or releases of low-level radiation. However, it does suggest that significance cannot simply be taken for granted. Instead, it is itself the outcome of social constructions and multiple interpretations. As a brief example of this, the 1986 nuclear accident at Chernobyl can be presented both as a powerful symbol of the threat posed by nuclear power and as a demonstration of the greater inherent safety of Western European and US reactors. *'Consequences'* *do not simply represent an unmediated truth: they are constructed* *in particular settings and according to different value systems and* *beliefs.*

Already from this preliminary discussion, we can see that the relationship between technology, modern life and the environment has assumed fundamental importance for sociological understanding. The question that now arises is how to open up this topic to sociological analysis – and, especially, how to move beyond a simple description of technology's environmental possibilities in order to establish an appropriate sociological framework. In particular, the challenge is to present technological change *neither* as a reflection of technological determinism *nor* as a simple source of environmental use/abuse. Instead, the adoption of a sociological perspective requires a thoroughgoing analysis within which categorizations into the 'social' and the 'technological' are not fixed in advance but are instead open to sceptical and empirical analysis. In this chapter, we will examine the relationship between technology, social relations and environmental concerns in greater depth. Starting with nuclear power, the aim is to consider how it might be possible to move beyond the notion that technology simply has social and environmental *impacts* and towards a sociological analysis of technological and environmental change.

As in previous chapters, we will tackle these questions through particular examples – starting with nuclear power. Throughout the following sections, the intention is to challenge the conventional view that technology, nature and society are separable in this context.

Rather than 'black-boxing' technology (or society), we will identify underlying social and material processes.

Nuclear Landscapes, Rentiers and Kamikazes

Nuclear power plays a central role within Beck's discussion. Certainly, the Chernobyl accident brought added significance to his themes. The threat of nuclear destruction represents an abiding symbol of the risk society. Most especially, nuclear power suggests the far-reaching and indeed inescapable character of the new generation of risks coupled with the difficulties of scientific interpretation and institutional management. Whilst technological optimists tell us that the precautions are virtually foolproof and the probability of failure exceedingly low, concerned groups have found themselves battling against both the technology and the institutions that develop and defend it.[5] Put in these terms, nuclear power appears the very embodiment of modernity or perhaps, given all the contradictions, of 'troubled modernity'. Such a portrayal certainly presents a vivid picture of both modernity and its discontents. It also leads us into an account of nuclear technology not simply as the embodiment of a particular form of rationality but also as a set of institutional forms that are global as well as national in their sphere of operation.

Whilst this general account of nuclear technology may appear stimulating and suggestive, it also suffers from a number of sociological difficulties. In particular, there is a distinct danger that this disembodied and over-generalized treatment of nuclear power will simply reflect a new sociological variation on technological determinism. In Beck's analysis, nuclear technology is presented as an emblem of modernistic progress rather than as the outcome of specific sets of social practices and socio-technical assumptions. As a result, there is a danger that the technology itself is simply 'black-boxed' – in other words, presented as a fixed and inevitable outcome rather than as a diverse and differentially constructed set of socio-technical activities.

In order to establish this point, Beck's structural account of the relationship between technology and modernity can be contrasted with Françoise Zonabend's ethnographic analysis of one 'nuclear community' – those who live and work at Cap la Hague in Normandy, France. Whilst Beck's account emphasizes a very general and sweeping portrayal of nuclear technology and its risks, Zonabend deals with one nuclear site in closer anthropological detail. Equally, rather than focusing directly on the technology itself (as if it can simply be taken out of context and 'black-boxed'), Zonabend considers the manner in which nuclear technology is reinterpreted and reconstructed in one setting:

> In this invisible, impalpable, inaudible world the human imagination does its usual job of restoring to that world the kind of materiality and humanity that will enable man to comprehend and move within it. Through the medium of symbolic thought, the perils of nuclear energy are slotted into what societies know and have always known. (1993, p. 110)

Rather than taking the technology as the fixed point, and then gauging social responses to this (an approach that would once again reflect a determinist viewpoint), Zonabend focuses on the settings within which workers and local inhabitants make sense of the technology. In order to achieve this, her account draws upon a series of interviews, discussions and observations with both the community close to the nuclear plant and workers on site. Viewed from these perspectives on life in la Hague – what Zonabend terms here 'Hagar experience' – modernity seems a considerably less rigid concept than theorists such as Beck suggest:

> If we define modernity as the distinguishing characteristic of technological societies avid for change and innovation and prone to ceaseless self-questioning, it looks in the light of this Hagar experience as if one of the questions we should be asking ourselves very concretely is how well-founded such a tradition is. Modernity has not swept tradition away. The fact is, tradition has a surprising way of re-emerging where we least expect it. (Zonabend 1993, p. 125)

For the purposes of this chapter I intend to highlight the manner in which workers at the nuclear plant in question do not simply respond to a 'given' technology and its risks but instead actively redefine and reconstruct its meaning and significance. As Zonabend puts this: 'In place of the official scientific presentation of work in a nuclear environment they substitute their own language, their own interpretation, their own way of seeing it and "having their being" within it. In short, they refashion an industrial world to suit themselves' (ibid., p. 104). Central to this account is the workers' own interpretation of the risks of nuclear technology. Formal training courses attempt to convey the simplicity and safety of operations –

and often use a mix of scientific and domestic language to reinforce this ('The reactor is like a pressure cooker', 'The plant's as simple as a dairy, except that you're dealing with radioactive products'). Moreover, Zonabend considers the important role of language in the kinds of distinction that workers themselves develop within the plant – between those who work in different areas, their different grades, and employees or contract workers. Fear plays its part in workers' discourse also – helping to create a gulf between those who work 'on-limits' and those who rarely enter the main radioactive zones. Here, I want to focus on two particular aspects of these discourses as described by Zonabend: the distinction between 'irradiation' and 'contamination', and the division of workers into 'rentiers' and 'kamikazes'.

Zonabend notes the important distinction made by workers between *contamination* from invisible dust particles and *irradiation* caused by rays given off by nuclear substances. Whilst the two forms of radiation exposure have similar biological effects, they are seen very differently by workers:

> Irradiation, caused by the rays emitted by a nuclear substance, is seen in a positive light. Here images of 'cleanness' come high on the list; ideas of 'strength' and 'power' loom large. By contrast, the contamination that arises from contact with radioactive dust particles is thought of in negative terms and associated with an impression of 'filth', allied to the notion of 'decay'. (ibid., p. 107)

These different attributed meanings have large consequences for workers' reactions to radiation risks. Irradiation, as measured, for example, by one's radiation badge, is a relatively private experience and workers may attempt to conceal it completely. Contamination, on the other hand, triggers immediate alarms and is often a much more public event – leading to ostracism sometimes even by one's own partner. Irradiation is both clean and fleeting. Contamination penetrates 'flesh and blood' and is seen to be dirty, to be a source of shame and ostracism. As Zonabend's discussion emphasizes, technological consequences are not simply self-evident and fixed. Instead, they are actively interpreted within specific social and discursive settings: 'Playing on these notions of clean and dirty, strength and decay, and order and disorder, workers at the plant have recreated a world of coherence, a world of their own on which they can then seek to get a purchase in order to prove their power and ability to brave and surmount the perils of *le nucléaire*' (ibid., p. 111).

These discursive distinctions also link to the separation of workers into the 'kamikaze' and the 'rentier'. Zonabend suggests that the workers divide themselves into either 'rentiers', who are cautious and will make sure every possible precaution has been taken before commencing a task, or 'kamikazes', for whom speed and efficiency are more pressing than safety. Kamikazes will generally prefer direct confrontations with irradiation – and will often engage in acts of (generally) male bravado (such as bypassing elaborate procedures in order to 'get the job done'). Rentiers typically work to control contamination – often developing their own tricks of the trade to deal with delicate situations and counter-intuitive strategies to minimize risk (for example, tackling certain operations with bare hands rather than protective gloves, since this is seen to encourage greater care and so reduce the risks of contamination). Both groups, however, can be seen as asserting their own form of control. The development of alternative rules and tacitly learnt ploys represents a small victory for the worker: 'Apparently tamed or circumvented in this way, the dangers of nuclear energy become malleable, manageable. A person may then play with that energy in a positive way and on his own account, as we have . . . seen, like a sort of white magic that will ward off the perils surrounding him' (ibid., p. 115).

Just as in chapter 4, where groups of local residents were portrayed as actively constructing their relationship with various categories of hazard through memories, jokes and stories, the workers in this case-study do not simply take the situation for granted but create their own forms of discourse and understanding. Whether motivated by boredom, anxiety, the attribution of blame or the need to portray themselves in heroic light (like their predecessors in the mines), the workers (and residents) in this case-study have developed a whole repertoire of strategies, forms of speech and social practices. As Zonabend also observes:

> Given this space where all is mechanisation and automation, men surreptitiously reintroduce tactics, practices and a language borrowed from elsewhere. They find a thousand and one ways of, so to speak, prevaricating with an order that has been imposed on them from outside, the object being to make the anxiety bound up with this work more bearable, to place their own stamp on technical procedures that have been devised without consulting those concerned. (ibid., p. 124)

From the sociological perspective of this book, Zonabend's account opens up a sense of the fragmented and contradictory experience of modernity – and certainly argues against the notion that workers simply comply with imposed forms of control and discipline (what we might view as the dead hand of modernity). In that sense, social theorists may indeed have overstated the power of modernity to assert a unitary form of order and discipline. As chapter 4 also implied, social groups and individuals can be highly resourceful in their interpretation of particular problems and sources of anxiety.

In specific terms of technology, however, Zonabend's study opens the possibility that not just social problems and concerns but also technologies may be open to reconstruction – and often in very ingenious and imaginative ways. Thus, we can begin *to consider nuclear technology not as simply 'given' but as varyingly constructed, experienced, worried over and, indeed, enjoyed.* Certain workers may see the plant as exciting, dangerous and risky (at least those with kamikaze tendencies) while others attempt to avoid risk and adopt a more controlled and cautious sense of the technology. Meanwhile, management employs a mix of scientific and oddly domestic forms of language. It seems quite clear that rather than simply representing a single black box, the technology in question is open to a diversity of understandings and treatments. Equally, this example suggests the inseparability of the technology from the social context within which it is experienced. In Zonabend's study, traditional forms of understanding and practice not only serve as the basis of the technology's interpretation but also blur the relationship between the social and the technological. Within contexts of everyday experience, these factors are not readily separable. The determinist notion that technology has impacts or effects 'in itself' is strongly challenged by such evidence.

It follows also that technologies are not experienced in some immediate (or unmediated) fashion. Instead, the relationship between people and technological systems is differentially constructed and consumed. In this case, certain residents in the nearby villages may indeed view the plant as an alien presence and adopt an implicitly determinist model of the technology's development. Meanwhile, workers may view their relationship with the plant in explicitly human and social terms – the technology is under their control and manipulation. In that way, patterns of everyday life and culture serve as the basis for different relations between the social and the technological.

In sociological terms, competing risk constructions and assessments of the socio-technical systems within which people live and work become important topics for analysis – and especially since they open up new perspectives on the contemporary nature of social life and on relations between people and technologies. Rather than separating these factors from afar, the challenge is to examine the dynamic, cross-cutting and mutually dependent interactions involved. It is in such specific and messy situations that the conditions of modern life and environmental concern are being forged.

However, these matters of social interaction within technological systems are not simply of sociological and theoretical significance. Early in 2000, the UK Nuclear Installations Inspectorate (NII) published a damning report on procedures at the Sellafield nuclear plant. The suggestion was that crucial safety checks on mixed uranium-plutonium fuels had not been conducted but, instead, data had been falsified by process workers. The report identified a lack of 'proper safety culture' at the site where workers had been 'deliberately falsifying records to avoid doing a tedious task'.[6] Such a case highlights the disparity between the external presentation of technological systems as operating according to technically precise and highly controlled procedures, and the everyday reality of institutional and procedural practice. The modernistic vision of control – but also the sociological distinction between technology, society and nature – is contradicted by such everyday processes.

In the next section of this chapter, we continue to explore the social reconstruction of technology through a second example: the case of biotechnology and genetically modified organisms (GMOs). In this case, we will see that the technology is variably constructed both as the very embodiment of sustainability and as a major social and environmental threat. Once again, we will suggest that technologies – and the risk and environmental claims made on their behalf – are not readily separable from the kinds of social, contextual and cultural factor considered here.

For the purposes of this discussion, biotechnology can be defined simply as 'the industrial harnessing of life forms and processes' (Hobbelink 1995, p. 226). However, such a definition itself embodies substantial ambiguities about what is actually being included – not least since 'industrial harnessing' is as old as agriculture itself. From the very start, 'biotechnology' must be recognized not as a fixed entity but as a social – and variable – construction. This point is further emphasized by the evolving terminology in this field, with many companies now appearing to prefer the term 'life sciences' to describe their activities, since 'biotechnology' (or 'genetic engineering') has increasingly acquired negative connotations.

Sustainable Technology?

We start this discussion with the 1997 *Environment and Bioethics Report* of a major health-care and industrial enzyme company with headquarters in Denmark. As the head of Novo Nordisk rather understatedly notes in the report: 'Sustainable development continues to be a complex challenge' (Novo Nordisk 1997, p. 2). As he also establishes – in terms that should by now be familiar to readers: 'Despite problems of semantics the concept of sustainable development has an important advantage in that it recognizes the interdependence of the economic, environmental and social spheres' (ibid.). In his view, however, sustainable development is precisely about *development*:

> [T]his means that industry can gain without the environment having to lose and vice versa. We believe that Novo Nordisk can make an important contribution to a sustainable future through the products we make and the technologies and processes we employ. And we do believe that we can be part of the solution – not the problem. (ibid.)

Immediately, therefore, we can identify a particular construction of the relationship between technology, the environment and the wider public. For Novo Nordisk this is about providing 'sustainable biological solutions to industrial problems', engaging stakeholders and conducting business as 'socially and environmentally responsible neighbours'. Gene technologies fit perfectly within these aims, since they are seen to offer a number of benefits. Amongst these, the following seem especially relevant:

- they improve the efficiency of industrial production;
- they reduce the environmental impact of production (fewer resources are needed per unit produced);
- they eliminate the risk of toxic or unwanted by-products;
- they avoid the problem of finding healthy human and animal donors (for example, of blood, pancreas and pituitary glands).

On this basis, the company in question eagerly employs the language of sustainability as support for its activities. Moving outside this single company, biotechnology has been presented as being sustainable in other ways too. As applied to agriculture, for example, it will increase food production in an environmentally friendly fashion. Herbicide tolerant crops can be developed in order to allow more effective use of pesticides. Biological pesticides and pest-resistant crops can also lead to the reduced usage of chemicals and a more sustainable approach to crop production. Whether in the area of pharmaceuticals and industrial processes or agriculture and pesticides, biotechnology is being heralded as a positive environmental step.

From the viewpoint of those seeking to develop biotechnology, the benefits are clear. One major problem, however, comes in the form of public concerns and resistances to the technology. Accordingly, public perceptions of the technology are routinely portrayed as an obstacle to progress.[7] Novo Nordisk puts this problem in relatively progressive terms – even if the notion of 'improving' public acceptance implies a strong value-judgement: 'In order to improve public acceptance of modern biotechnology, we must be able to document sound performance in environmental safety, ensure high ethical standards, engage in stakeholder dialogue and commit ourselves to sustainable development' (1997, p. 24). But the company also notes that there are groups in society that view these technologies as 'unnatural, immoral or dangerous'. A 1998 publication from the European Commission Innovation Programme puts the matter of external opposition rather more bluntly. As one article puts it: 'What prevents Europe from reaping the economic and employment rewards of its own inventiveness?' Amongst the 'principal obstacles' faced by biotechnology in Europe are: 'problems of public perception, involving concern over ethical and health issues'.[8]

What seems interesting about these formulations – whether seeking to 'improve public acceptance' or identify 'problems of public perception' – is the manner in which the relationship between technology and the wider public is being constructed. According to this representation, the technology has major benefits – and not least in environmental terms. The challenge is to persuade the wider public to appreciate these benefits. Otherwise, a major technological opportunity will be lost. As the EC publication presents this: 'public mistrust of biotechnology ... constitutes a real constraint on the commercialisation of its products.' In answer to the question 'Does biotechnology raise special ethical issues?', the EC report rather loadedly states: 'Some people believe it does. Others see no difference between today's techniques and traditional methods of genetic manipulation – and believe that costs and risks should be weighed rationally against the huge benefits' (ibid., p. 19). Such a statement aligns rational thought and support for the technology. After all, say the developers, biotechnology is not new, since people have engaged in 'the industrial harnessing of life forms and processes' for generations – such 'harnessing' is fundamental to the production of, for example, beer and wine, cheese and yoghurt, various animal breeds and plant varieties. It seems reasonable to conclude that public opposition to new biotechnologies can only be based on either ignorance or irrationality.

According to this social perspective, biotechnology represents a rational development of a familiar form of technology. Scientific testing of new products can minimize (or eliminate) risk. The main challenge is to overcome the obstacles of public criticism and caution. The technology has developed, now resistances need to be overcome. Although phrased in different ways, this linear and determinist model leads to the idea that society represents an obstacle to technological progress.

For critics of biotechnology, this presentation of the technology as safe and controlled is utterly inappropriate. For such opponents, the environmental and health consequences of GMOs could be catastrophic. Might they disturb the ecological balance? What about the long-term effects on human health and wildlife? A whole series of moral and ethical arguments is also put forward against the technology: is it appropriate to tamper with nature on this scale? Much criticism has also been made of the increased power and control such technologies give to industry – for example, with the patenting of life forms.

Those concerned with the international implications of this technology – especially for developing countries – have been particularly critical of the influence the technology will give to a small number of Western industrialists. As Vandana Shiva puts this with regard to the agricultural implications of biotechnology: 'The "improvement" of the seed is not a neutral economic process. It is, more importantly, a political process that shifts control over biological diversity from local peasants to transnational corporations and changes biological systems from complete systems reproducing themselves into raw material' (1995, p. 199). Feminist critics have also been vocal in presenting biotechnology as a new form of patriarchal control over life. What were once natural processes have been overtaken by science and technology working to dominate both women and nature. Biotechnology, and linked to this the whole area of new genetics and reproductive technologies, is a threat to women's control over their own bodies and over the natural world in which they live. Biotechnology represents a masculine colonization of life itself.[9]

For biotechnology critics, the problem is certainly not one of surmounting public obstacles to technological innovation, but instead concerns the inappropriate development of technology. In that sense, companies such as Novo Nordisk – despite their rhetoric to the contrary – are very much part of a problem now facing both society and the natural environment. In a noteworthy congruence, however, technology is still presented as external to both social groups and nature – the key difference is that now the impact of the technology is seen as negative rather than positive. Critics see themselves as offering reasonable resistance to a technology that can undermine both society and nature. Thus, technological determinist models are being employed by both proponents and critics of the technology in question.

In making this point about the usage of determinist models by both 'sides' in the controversy over biotechnology, GMOs and genetic engineering, it is important to note that there are also those who attempt to transcend the current – and rather restricted – terms of the debate. As the critic and activist, Jeremy Rifkin, has presented the issues:

> From an intellectual point of view, I really think that the shift into the age of genetic science is the greatest opportunity in history. It should force us all, this generation and the next generation, to ask all the big questions. What is the value of a human being? Does life have intrinsic or just utility value? What is our obligation to future generations? What is our sense of responsibility to the creatures with which we co-exist? It really does force us, if we are willing and open to have the debate, to rethink our humanity and the meaning of existence. (1998, p. 37)

We can also observe the contradictions that exist around the definition of sustainability within these discussions. Whilst one side presents genetically engineered enzyme products as the very epitome of sustainable development, other voices denounce such approaches as displaying the same arrogant and science-centred outlook that has led to environmental crisis. Accordingly, the definition of 'sustainability' becomes highly contested and also variable depending upon the social perspective being employed. *Whilst each side is inclined to present sustainability as an inherent characteristic of the technology itself, we can see that this is a matter of social judgement and construction.* As we can also identify, the reconciliation of these contradictory assessments of sustainability may be very difficult to achieve – and for reasons that may be less to do with the technology itself than its social and cultural significance for different groups.

On the basis of the discussion so far, we can discern within this debate a wider set of concerns over how we should interpret the contemporary relationship between the social, the natural and the technological. In so doing, we should bear in mind the previous section's emphasis on different contextual interpretations and enactments of technology. As Ingunn Moser has put this during a discussion of biotechnology:

> [T]o speak of science and technology 'in themselves' or 'as such' is an abstraction, a construction or fiction. . . . Science and technology are always realized in concrete social, cultural, historical and ecological contexts. Both the meanings and uses of knowledge are always contextual, they are never found outside time and space, social relations and structures, cultural hopes and fears. (1995, p. 12)

One starting point for this sociological analysis hinges on the usage of 'nature and the natural' within this discussion. As has already been suggested, critics of biotechnology portray the technology as tampering with nature. For certain feminists, this represents a masculinist attempt at control. For critics of science and technology, the whole enterprise is based on arrogance and hubris – with inevitably dire consequences. Meanwhile, defenders of the industry see it merely as an incremental development. Surely progress has always been made in this way? Nature from this perspective is a resource that can be developed and 'harnessed'. Technology is indeed providing new solutions that will improve all our lives.

In all the heat generated by these discussions, it is possible to identify very different social constructions not only of the technology in question but also, and inextricably linked to this, of the natural world. We encounter images of 'harnessing' nature and of what the European Commission publication describes as 'the speed with which nature can be persuaded to serve human ends'. Equally, we are confronted by accounts of nature as a world of purity, which can only be contaminated and corrupted by technological intervention. From this perspective, 'harnessing' represents an inappropriate form of control: nature is only diminished and corrupted by such a relationship.

Thus, and whilst both the promise and the threat of biotechnology are expressed in very specific and tangible forms, the concept of nature that lies at the core of these expressions appears to be open to redefinition from different cultural and political perspectives. Rather than being the fixed point around which environmental debate then hinges, nature is open to reconstruction and to differential construction. As Donna Haraway has argued: '[N]ature is not a physical place to which one can go, nor a treasure to fence in or bank, nor an essence to be saved or violated. Nature is not hidden and so does not need to be unveiled. Nature is not a text to be read in the codes of mathematics and biomedicine' (1995, p. 70). Instead, nature operates within the biotechnology debate as a social projection and a focus for underlying doubts and concerns. Can industry be trusted to operate in as responsible and equitable a fashion as companies such as Novo Nordisk claim? Will further industrial development lead to an improved quality of life or will it simply increase the gap between rich and poor? Does the future represent a threat or a promise? As Haraway suggests: 'Nature is . . . a *topos*, a place, in the sense of a rhetorician's place for consideration of common themes; nature is, strictly, a commonplace' (ibid.). From this perspective, nature is not a domain separate from social life but a 'figure, construction, artifact, movement, displacement. Nature cannot pre-exist its construction, its articulation in heterogeneous social encounters' (ibid., p. 71). In an area such as biotechnology this process of construction is inevitably loaded and also polarized, as different groups seek to impose their own interpretation and place their own boundaries around the natural world. As Levidow has observed, the biotechnological reconstruction of nature takes a number of forms. The industry characteristically sees immense benefit in its 'reprogrammed nature' and in its taming of 'wild nature': '[I]ts environment-friendly products will overcome the limits of chemical-intensive agriculture, keep agriculture secure from environmental threats, and fulfil nature's cornucopian potential' (1995, p. 177).

Critics, meanwhile, adopt a very different myth of nature, which emphasizes the fragility of the natural world and the *dis*order that biotechnology will generate. 'Tamed nature' from this perspective represents a form of abuse and corruption. In such reconstructions, we can identify the manner in which nature (or, as presented in the Introduction, 'social nature') has become a 'focal point for a nexus of political–economic relations, social identities, cultural orderings, and political aspirations' (Castree and Braun 1998, p. 5).

In a situation where no one nature can be identified and agreed upon, the relationship between plural (and contested) natures and social relations becomes highly significant. Equally, the ability to frame debate within certain assumptions about the natural world becomes a key form of political influence. Meanwhile, moves to open up biotechnology policy to public debate that simply reproduce the deficit assumption that public opposition must be a consequence of public ignorance significantly fail to challenge such underlying assumptions. At this point, we can identify a distinctive role for sociological analysis. Rather than seeking to defend a fixed notion of the natural within environmental debate, it becomes necessary to *explore the social origins, contestations and selective reconstructions of the natural within environmental discussion.*

It is also necessary to emphasize that not just nature but also technology is open to differential construction: biotechnology is a matter of patriarchal power, it is a rational extension of technical principles. As with nature, technology can be reconstructed in various ways: as solution and problem, as sustainable or as catastrophic.

We thus find ourselves in a situation where it is inappropriate to consider biotechnology as a unitary technology. Instead, this appears as the outcome of different, contextually generated meanings. Models of technological determinism as employed by various sides in this debate present technology as fixed and external to both nature and society. Examined from a sociological perspective, technology appears considerably more malleable – to the extent that the sinister technology represented by critics seems unrecognizable from the perspective of industrial organizations. More generally, this presentation alerts us to the social and cultural dynamics of environmental debate. Biotechnology can be presented as simply a matter of specific agricultural techniques, medical applications and industrial innovations. However, from a sociological perspective, it is inevitably bound up with a variety of alternative constructions, value systems and cultural understandings, which influence the very definition of the technology itself. In this way also, ecological issues merge with larger questions of social justice, political influence and democracy.

The presentation of this controversy as a matter of only technological interest therefore misses its sociological significance. Meanwhile, we can imagine that the development of a sociological perspective on these questions could also help to illuminate current disagreements. Certainly, determinist models of technological development appear inadequate both at the level of description and as a guide to future action.

Technological Determinism Revisited

This chapter began with two basic points: the significance of technology within environmental discussion and the suggestion

that determinist notions represent a substantial barrier to sociological understanding. In discussion throughout this chapter, a
number of more substantial points have been built upon these simple
foundations:

- that the boundary between the social, the technological and the
  natural is neither static nor fixed but is open to contextual negotiation and reconstruction;
- that human meanings are invested in technology and nature
  so that both can be viewed as social and cultural projections;
- that technologies do not simply possess intrinsic or self-evident
  impacts and consequences (whether social or environmental) but
  that they are instead socially negotiated in different ways;
- that sustainability may be presented as an intrinsic and fixed characteristic (as also in terminology such as 'clean technology') but
  that this attribution is also a matter of social judgement and may
  be open to political contestation;
- that the prevalent reliance upon technological determinism within
  environmental discussion serves to conceal such social, cultural
  and material processes.

Accordingly, and although we may have started discussion with the
apparently common-sensical notion that technology represented
the non-human and society the human, we have seen that this
human/non-human distinction is impossible to maintain in a consistent fashion. Of course, the same point can be made about the conventional notion that nature is synonymous with the non-human.
Once again, this boundary is permeable to the point of collapse.
Rather than seeking to capture some essence of what it means to be
technological, social or natural, we have observed the contextual generation of such attributions. Put differently, rather than attempting
to ring-fence these categories, we have begun to expose them *to
critical reflection and empirical exploration within the particular
contexts of their generation and maintenance.*
    At this point, it must be acknowledged that this approach to
the relationship between technology and environmental concerns
represents not an end-point but a start to further inquiry. Grint
and Woolgar have expressed this in particularly provocative
fashion:

> The emergence of the 'truth' is sometimes represented as the outcome
> of a transparent reading of a text. In practice, however, the social con-

stitution of truth is more akin to a labour of Sisyphus than Odysseus' quest: there is no 'homecoming' awaiting the completion of the tasks, there is only another task; there is no single final truth, only different interpretations that construct, rather than reflect, the phenomenon. (1997, p. 33)

As hardly needs pointing out, this is potentially an uncomfortable conclusion. How can we possibly tackle apparently pressing environmental problems on such a basis? In opening up social and ecological issues in this way, and especially in acknowledging the existence of contested natures,[10] we are not turning away from the reality of environmental problems, but are instead capturing a richer and more diverse sense of that reality.

Crucially, our treatment allows a re-engagement with issues of alternative social and environmental futures, institutional choice and democratic control. Once techniques such as biotechnology are recognized as dependent on social reconstructions, we open up fresh possibilities for wider debate and the exercise of environmental citizenship. Rather than presenting public groups as an obstacle to technological development, the publics become an important resource within decision-making processes. Whilst notions of technological determinism constrain such possibilities, a sociological approach allows us to debate the social roots of technological and environmental change. As Vandana Shiva puts this in discussion of genetically modified crops: 'The seed has become the site and symbol of freedom in the age of manipulation and monopoly of its diversity. . . . The seed . . . embodies diversity and the freedom to stay alive. . . . In the seed, cultural diversity converges with biological diversity. Ecological issues combine with social justice, peace, and democracy' (1998, p. 126). Conventional models of technological determinism evade such contested debates. As we can identify also, sociological analysis has an important contribution to make within this larger framework of public policy and citizen engagement. However, this contribution needs to build upon the dynamic relationship between society, nature and knowledge rather than squeezing it back into separate over-abstracted pigeon holes.

We could continue to explore other substantive topics and examples. Certainly, the possibilities for further inquiry are substantial. However, we have for now reached the stage where taking stock is required. What general conclusions – for both the discipline and environmental practice – can be drawn from these empirical and conceptual excursions through contemporary environmental practice? More particularly, and given the claims that have been made for a fresh sociological perspective in this and the previous chapters, what lessons can be drawn for the relationship between society, nature and knowledge?

7

Society, Nature, Knowledge: Co-constructing the Social and the Natural

We must find another relationship to nature beside reification, possession, appropriation and nostalgia. No longer able to sustain the fictions of being either subjects or objects, all the partners in the potent conversations that constitute nature must find a new ground for making meanings together.

Haraway 1995, p. 70

Real *things* are independent of us, but what it *means* to be real depends on us . . . in order to understand what it means to be real, we have to look at how things present themselves as real *in the context of human life*.

Polt 1999, p. 82[1]

We now consider the implications of the previous chapters for the sociological analysis of the environment and for environmental practice. Beginning with a review of the realist–constructivist debate within environmental sociology and a clarification of the constructivist perspective in particular, we look to the future through the concept of co-construction. As I suggest, such a perspective encourages us not only to frame environmental matters differently but also to take a critical look at the construction of the 'social' within the discipline (even if the 'social construction of the social' sounds an improbable catch phrase). We then move on to consider the practical significance of sociological inquiry for environmental policy-making and action.

Sociology and the Environment *concludes with a plea for theoretical pluralism and open-mindedness. Rather than imposing a single intellectual framework, we should stay alert to the new sociological possibilities in this emerging area of scholarship, research and practice.*

This book began with the general argument that sociology can no longer afford to disregard the natural environment. In making such an uncontroversial point, it was also stressed that this sociological disregard is not a mere oversight (if such were possible) but has been built upon a particular dualism between science and social science. According to the conventional viewpoint, science deals with nature and sociology with society. As we have suggested, an acceptance of this division of intellectual labour either leads to a weak and subordinated position for the discipline (dealing with the 'soft' side of environmental problems) or a sociological dismissal of the natural (as if only 'social' issues deserved attention). Either way, the crude social/natural separation is analytically flawed and practically unhelpful.

However, and as we saw in the Introduction, the increasing acceptance by sociologists of the need to engage with environmental issues has led to the incorporation of this same dualism within the discipline itself – and hence the entrenched battle between realists and constructivists. Simply put, whilst one group maintains the ultimately real (or natural) character of environmental problems and concerns, another emphasizes the centrality of human constructions and social interpretations. Whilst realists trade on the objectivity of environmental problems, constructivists are accused of social reductionism (i.e. of eliminating anything other than social causes from their analyses). Either way, the same social–natural duality remains in operation but is now embedded within the discipline itself.

From a realist perspective, it is essential to recognize that the natural ultimately exists apart from social constructions and cultural projections. For constructivists, there are broadly two kinds of response to this reassertion of a social–natural distinction. The majority form of 'mild' constructivism acknowledges that there is indeed a distinct realm of the natural but argues that this is not necessarily relevant to the social selection and treatment of environmental problems. Meanwhile, a smaller number of radical or 'strong' constructivists argue that, since truth is the outcome of (rather than input to) social negotiations and processes, there is little to be gained (and a lot to be lost) by assuming that nature is a predetermined category. The realist response to strong constructivist claims is to suggest that such an approach has overwhelming analytical flaws (since it cannot distinguish between the social and the natural) and offers no basis for practical action.

In this final chapter, I want to review the realist–constructivist debate briefly before clarifying the perspective advocated in this book: a perspective that has aimed to move beyond the social/natural dichotomy (*either* environmental problems are real *or* they're constructed). Rather than getting bogged down in a philosophically unresolvable and sociologically distracting debate, we have attempted instead to address the more complex, dynamic and hybrid character of environmental issues and concerns. Equally, and rather than attempting to reduce the issues and processes at work to a crude two-dimensional model, the previous chapters have tried to enrich the sociological understanding of social–environmental relations. Within such an approach, it is especially important to explore the non-discrete character of environmental problems and issues. The environment does not sit apart from everyday reality but is encountered, constructed and shaped by a range of social and institutional processes.

In presenting this concluding review, I will focus on two key questions:

1. How should we conceptualize the relationship between sociology and the environment (and, more specifically, between the social and the natural)?
2. What does this mean for the relationship between sociology and environmental practice?

Basic background to this debate was presented in the Introduction and it might be helpful to re-read the relevant section ('Elements of an Environmental Sociology') before continuing here.

Constructive Realists and Real Constructivists: The Social–Natural Debate in Environmental Sociology

... the by now rather dull debate between 'realists' and 'constructivists'. (Macnaghten and Urry 1998, p. 2)

It would be misleading to conclude on the constructivist–realist debate without placing it in a wider intellectual context – although how this context is defined depends very much on the particular stance one adopts. Right now, so-called 'relativism' is under attack from a number of directions and especially for what is presented as its intellectual pretensions and practical irrelevance. Furthermore, whilst many of the constructivist perspectives presented in this book would characteristically distance themselves from (or at least treat very cautiously) the language of postmodernism, this has not prevented various critics of constructivism from making that connection in a decidedly negative fashion.

In one illustration of these contested connections, Hannigan (1995) deals very circumspectly with the possible linkage between his version of constructionism and arguments over the postmodern. He notes that there may be various 'echoes' of postmodernism in his analysis of environmental problems. Thus, constructivism typically suggests a deconstruction of fixed analytical categories (such as science and truth) and a suspicion of 'grand narrative'. Certainly, a congruity can be identified between the constructivist perspectives offered in previous chapters of this book and Zygmunt Bauman's (1992) account of a postmodern world where old certainties have faded and unsettling uncertainties have taken their place.

However, Hannigan rightly observes that 'most environmental researchers who have considered the matter have shied away from adopting a postmodernist perspective' (1995, p. 181). Thus, the SSK perspective indicates that scientific knowledge still retains substantial significance within contemporary social life. At the same time, the examples in previous chapters of the public reconstruction of environmental knowledges are not suggestive of a widespread loss of social identity. Furthermore, Beck's influential account of the risk society is explicitly designed to draw on certain elements of postmodern discourse whilst offering a criticism of what he regards as its broad and ill-focused perspective.[2] Latour (1992) too has objected to talk of postmodernity on the grounds that 'we have never been modern' in the first place. At a methodological level, SSK's commitment to 'following the actors' is very different from the more sweeping and less empirical style of postmodern philosophy.

Despite these important points of contrast, for realist critics constructivism has been seen to suffer from many of the same faults as have been attributed to postmodernism. John Barry (1999, pp. 171–5) presents the social constructionist approach of Hannigan as closely linked to the 'postmodern engagement with the environment'. In line with my argument in previous chapters, Barry notes:

> While most social constructionist approaches, such as postmodernism, would not go so far as to deny the reality of environmental problems, the important point they raise is that in analysing environmental issues one must be aware of the different actors, claims, types of knowledge, communication and cultural contexts in which these problems are articulated, contested, presented and re-presented. (ibid., p. 171)

However, Barry also argues that such 'postmodern analysis' is incapable of dealing with the 'political economy' of environmental destruction. Equally, it can engage neither with environmental politics nor with the material dimensions of environmental problems. Such charges are characteristic of a realist critique of social constructivism.

A better known (or perhaps more infamous) attack on the claimed 'cognitive' or 'epistemic' relativism of constructivists such as Bruno Latour has been presented by Alan Sokal and his collaborator Jean Bricmont. Sokal, a professor of physics, set out to undermine postmodernism[3] in very direct fashion. Sokal submitted to a leading US cultural studies journal a paper entitled 'Transgressing boundaries: towards a transformative hermeneutics of quantum gravity'. He wrote the paper as a parody of the postmodern treatment of science: full of intentional absurdities and non sequiturs, deliberately asserting an extreme form of cognitive relativism, proclaiming that 'physical "reality", no less than social "reality" is at bottom a social and linguistic construct' (Sokal and Bricmont 1998, p. 2). Sokal's moment of triumph came when the paper was published in 1996 by editors who were unaware of its subversive and satirical intent. Sokal then announced his successful hoax: 'For the editors of *Social Text*, it was hard to imagine a more radical way of shooting themselves in the foot' (ibid.).

The 'Sokal affair' attracted substantial attention and was further fuelled by the publication in the late 1990s of a book by Sokal and Bricmont, which extended the line of attack so as to include writers such as Jean Baudrillard, Jacques Lacan, Julia Kristeva and Bruno Latour. 'Postmodern' authors were accused of abusing scientific concepts and terminology (either by using scientific ideas totally outside their proper context or 'throwing around scientific jargon') and/or of espousing 'epistemic relativism' (the idea that modern science is 'nothing more' than a myth, a narration or a social construction). Tarred with the same brush as a diverse body of Sokal-branded postmodernists, social constructivism was put very much on the defensive.

In the scholarly setting of sociological arguments over the environment, realist critics of social constructivism have been rather more specific in their targeting. Realists have acknowledged an inevitable element of social construction in all knowledge claims since, as Dickens suggests, 'No knowledge has fallen out of the sky with a label attached pronouncing "absolute truth"' (1996, p. 71). However, it has been axiomatic for realists to maintain that 'the fact that knowledge is socially constituted does not entail that knowledge is *only* socially constituted' (ibid., p. 72). Whilst acknowledging an unavoidable element of overlap, the fundamental argument is that the social and natural worlds are ultimately distinct from one another. It follows that, whilst 'mild' constructivism is of some (albeit limited) value, more radical claims (of the kind deemed 'postmodern' in character) should be dismissed as no more than sociological reductionism.

In a useful review of this debate, Burningham and Cooper observe that the critique 'is not simply that social constructionism is incorrect in denying independent agency to the natural world, but also that the position is dangerous and morally or ethically wrong' (1999, p. 300). Certainly, one prevalent criticism of constructivism has been that it represents a disengagement from pressing environmental problems: an indulgence in sociological pyrotechnics whilst the rainforest burns.[4] In response to these charges, Burningham and Cooper suggest that most forms of constructivism acknowledge the existence of the natural world, and argue, very importantly, that even strong constructivism can engage usefully with environmental and ethical problems.

The starting-point for this defence of a constructivist perspective is a closer consideration of the more specific arguments being made by constructivist sociologists. Just as sophisticated realists such as Dickens acknowledge the relevance of some element of social construction in our interpretation of nature, most environmental constructivists do not correspond to the demonizing presented by Sokal or the sterility and over-abstraction alleged by realist critics such as Martell and Dunlap.

Instead, and as we have argued here, an SSK perspective specifically draws attention to the more detailed and nuanced treatment of risk and environmental issues within specific contexts. In the attacks on constructivists for their alleged sociological reductionism and lack of environmental concern, this more specific and context-sensitive analysis is usually overlooked. Instead, the realist onslaught tends to be played out at an abstract and categorical level and in terms of headlines rather than empirical studies. One immediate defence of the constructivist position is therefore that it brings *more* rather than less 'reality' to the issues (and especially in terms of social and cultural processes). Jasanoff puts this point as follows in a wider discussion of the constructivist perspective within science and technology studies (STS);

> It is, of course, profoundly misleading to identify the idea of decon-struction that has developed in STS scholarship with relativism or a denial of reality. On the contrary, the constructivist strain in STS represents, quite possibly, the most dedicated attempt to grasp the nature of reality that is currently underway in any of the social sciences. (1999, p. 66)

As Burningham and Cooper observe, most constructivist accounts in this area deliberately distance themselves from epistemic relativism and environmental quietism. Thus, it is actually rather hard to find constructivist accounts that fail to acknowledge the importance of natural and material factors. To take two quotations from authors in the constructivist and discursive tradition:

> [T]o show that a social problem has been socially constructed is not to undermine or debunk it; both valid and invalid social problem claims have to be constructed. The detachment required for social science should not become an excuse for cynical inaction. (Yearley 1991, p. 186)

> [J]ust because something is socially interpreted does not mean it is unreal. Pollution does cause illness, species do become extinct. . . . But people can make very different things of these phenomena. (Dryzek 1997, p. 10)

Although, as we have seen, Barry may have no hesitation in placing Hannigan within the 'postmodern' category, Hannigan's own position is self-consciously distanced from relativism: 'I am not by any means attracted to an extreme constructionist position which insists that the global ensemble of problems is purely a creation of the media (or science or ecological activists) with little basis in objective conditions' (Hannigan 1995, p. 3). Closer consideration therefore suggests that the attack on what we might term 'unrestrained and unprincipled' constructivism is largely wide of the mark within environmental sociology. Perhaps because of the general intellectual climate as demonstrated by the Sokal affair, but also a genuine desire to engage with environmental problems, there appears instead to be considerable caution about even appearing to deny the importance of natural causes.

The apparent animosity directed towards constructivism appears something of an over-reaction given the moderate claims generally put forward.[5] At the same time, and very importantly, the realist–constructivist divide seems more bridgeable than it is often presented – especially when we move beyond the cruder definition of both realism and constructivism.

As we can see from the above quotations, the argument being made by constructivists is *not* that the natural environment is a mirage or fantasy but rather that our only way of interpreting (or 'knowing') this environment is through human and social processes. Rather than making an ontological judgement (about how the world is), constructivism is characteristically stressing the unavoidable problems of epistemology (in coming to know about the world). Presented in this way, it may be that this entrenched battle over 'realism versus constructivism' has become rather pointless and, indeed, dull. The challenge instead, as I will argue, is to draw creatively on a broad range of sociological insights – whatever their theoretical provenance. Rather than seeking to reach a non-attainable level of theoretical purity, our objective should be to enhance understanding of the relationship between environmental issues and sociology. In this, the seminar room sniping may have become a distraction rather than a stimulus.

However, and building again upon Burningham and Cooper, this is not to concede that the minority form of 'radical constructivism' is necessarily deficient in analytical terms or incapable of environmental engagement. As Burningham and Cooper observe, even 'strong' arguments about the social construction of environmental reality may be based less on a denial of the natural world than on analytical scepticism and the methodological imperative to maintain an agnosticism in the face of competing knowledge claims. Rather than denying the existence of 'nature' (or indeed of reality[6]), they argue that 'radical' constructivists such as Woolgar can be considered as once again drawing our attention to the fundamental difficulties of 'knowing' the world in which we live (a point that has been central in earlier chapters): 'The strict constructionist position, then, can be summarised as a radical scepticism about ontological claims, and not as an ontological claim about the non-existence of (in this case environmental) reality' (1999, p. 309). Thus, and to take a vivid example from outside the environmental field, Grint and Woolgar have asked the stark question: what's social about being shot (1997, pp. 140–68)? Taking up the challenge to present a constructivist account of Russian roulette, they rather bluntly characterize the realist stance as 'a bullet is a bullet and no amount of wishful thinking will wish it away' (ibid., p. 153). It is not too hard to imagine a similarly direct assertion being made about global warming or pesticide-related cancers.

In response to the realist challenge, Grint and Woolgar energetically pursue the social constructions and epistemological assumptions involved in reaching the conclusion that someone has been shot by a particular firearm. From the social shaping of the revolver in question to the logical complexities of linking cause and effect, the argument is that social factors are fundamental. However, the point of this provocative treatment is not to deny the existence of a particular reality (in other words to reach an ontological judgement) but rather to argue that we cannot escape social reconstructions. As the previous chapters have repeatedly argued with regard to environmental problems, consequences do not simply present themselves to us in an unproblematic and 'objective' fashion. Or, as Grint and Woolgar put it: 'The sceptical perspective on technology . . . does not argue that technology (the bullet) is irrelevant, but it does argue that the process by which we come to know about its relevance is irredeemably social' (ibid., p. 164).

One immediate response to this reinterpretation of the realist–constructivist debate might be to acknowledge the sociological merits of such a position but to insist that such sophistication at the level of epistemology only leads to environmental quietism. Thus, it may be intellectually stimulating and entertaining to unravel the epistemological problems of 'knowing' the environment (or indeed that one has been shot), but it leaves us without any tools (or weapons) when dealing with environmental problems. Are we not at risk of turning pressing environmental problems into a language game and of building sociological careers on a wilful obfuscation of the world in which we live? Put differently, can we afford such analysis when the problems are so pressing?

There are a number of possible responses to this question of environmental engagement. One plausible argument is that it is not a necessary responsibility on the sociologist to get involved in this fashion. After all, we don't expect all botanists to campaign for the protection of meadows or every physicist to take a public stand on nuclear power. There is nothing ignoble about sociologists bringing their best analytical skills to bear and then handing over to other parties. Equally, an unwillingness to take sides in environmental controversies should not detract from the quality of analysis – and could indeed enhance this. It may also be that sociology is weakened by an over-enthusiasm to prove its value within the objective frameworks provided by scientific institutions rather than adopting a more critical perspective on the framing of environmental issues and problems. As a variant on this, it could be argued that the epistemological radicalism espoused by constructivism is in itself every bit as important as the more familiar political radicalism demanded by certain realists.

However, and assuming the importance of sociological engagement with the environment (as I have generally argued in the previous chapters), it is not necessarily the case that an acknowledgement of the social constructions at the heart of knowledge claims leads to environmental quietism or inactivity. Whilst certain forms of realism argue that the 'reality' of environmental problems is a precondition for action, the approach advocated in this book emphasizes the judgemental and institutional dimension to environmental engagement. Certainly, a constructivist perspective does not necessarily lead to a dismissal of environmental problems as mere symbols, representations and forms of talk (as is presumably implied by the pejorative usage of the 'postmodern' tag). Instead, to employ the phrase used by Burningham and Cooper, constructivists argue that social scientists should avoid playing the 'ontological trump card' (1999, p. 311):

> There is therefore no reason why a constructionist should not engage in political debate, or make political interventions: however, such an intervention will not justify itself in objectivist terms by making reference to, by suggesting non-mediated access to, or by claiming knowledge of an assumed incontestable reality. In other words . . . his or her epistemological privileges have been withdrawn. (ibid., p. 310)

Building on this point, it can be argued that, by avoiding inevitably contestable claims to 'know better' than one's opponents, constructivism opens up the ethical and political choices at the core of environmental engagement. *Rather than presenting sociology as bringing 'truth' to environmental disputes, the constructivist responsibility is to highlight value choices, challenge epistemological assumptions and avoid recourse to unjustifiable certainties.*

Accordingly, there is no reason why constructivism should be incapable of dealing with the political economy of environmental destruction, with environmental politics or with the material dimensions of environmental problems. On the contrary, and whilst constructivism is suspicious of rigidly attributed terms such as 'social interest', 'power' and 'materiality' – preferring again to see these as relationships and social processes rather than fixed categories – there is every reason why constructivism is well placed to explore such matters.

By refusing to accord 'truth' to any party to environmental disputes (including, of course, sociologists), we can be open and imaginative in our exploration of the social reconstructions and alliances at work within environmental politics. Crucially also, constructivist approaches encourage the challenging of existing political and cognitive framings of the environment rather than simply taking them at face value. This suggests that the critical analysis of what is presented as 'environmental reality' (for example, within debates over the best direction for sustainable development) is not a distraction but a practical necessity.

It is also reasonable to argue that there is no absolute requirement on constructivist sociology to maintain a neutral stance within environmental disputes. As the research discussed in chapter 4 implied, it can be entirely proper to take the position of the underdog (in that case, disenfranchised local publics) rather than claiming to analyse objective social conditions or, put more bluntly, adopting a 'God's eye view'. Whilst constructivism suggests the need to be explicit about the researcher's normative commitments, it certainly does not suggest non-engagement or non-commitment.

Co-constructing the Social and the Natural

The previous section was intended to defend constructivist claims against charges of intellectual inadequacy and practical irrelevance. I have argued that, in the wider intellectual climate of attacks on relativism, the more cautious constructivism presented by sociologists and discourse analysts such as Hannigan, Yearley and Dryzek is being inappropriately criticized.

I have also suggested that realist critics have generally neglected the detailed contextual treatments offered by constructivist sociologists – presumably since the critics interpret such research as illustrative of wider theory rather than (as in the SSK tradition) the very core of sociological analysis. To these points it might be added that certain forms of realist sociology may be inclined to take scientific arguments on trust rather than delving more intimately into the social construction of scientific knowledge. Meanwhile, radical constructivists' emphasis on analytical scepticism (on methodological agnosticism in the face of knowledge claims rather than predetermining what is a valid or truthful explanation) is often represented as ontological relativism and a dismissal of the material world.

Going further, I argued that constructivism could indeed be compatible with environmental engagement whilst characteristically emphasizing the conditional nature of knowledge claims. Such an approach has already been identified in chapter 5 with particular regard to the work of Brian Wynne and his argument that social scientists can play an important role in opening up implicit institutional assumptions about environmental decision-making to larger critical scrutiny.

Certainly, the constructivist tradition has been an important inspiration to the previous chapters. Whether exploring the local interpretation of environmental threats, institutional judgements over pesticide safety or the relationship between technology and environmental consequences, the intention has been to identify the cultural assessments and human choices at the heart of environmental action. In this way also, the aim has been to challenge the cruder realist assumptions within 'sustainability talk' and their suggestion that social concerns are secondary to the scientifically framed policy agenda. Instead, social and political matters now appear central to environmental action.

In building upon the emerging constructivist tradition, however, I have also drawn attention to some of the difficulties inherent in this realist–constructivist debate (or, more accurately, *non*-debate) and especially the fundamental constraint of continuing within a dualistic framework. Drawing upon previous chapters, I want to reinforce the point that the analytical challenge is to move *beyond* the natural–social dichotomy. As Demeritt has noted, both conventional realist and conventional constructivist approaches can suffer from the same fundamental limitation: 'Oddly, objectivists and relativists agree about one thing: representations must be explained either by nature or by society but the two transcendences can never be mixed together' (1996, p. 497). Very importantly, it has to be acknowledged that the previously identified tendency for constructivism to be caricatured as denying external reality and as 'quietist' is frequently matched by the constructivist portrayal of realism as simple-mindedly essentialist and scientistic. As we observed in the Introduction, more critical forms of realism are also committed to transcending the nature–society dualism – and, indeed, were pioneers of this argument within environmental sociology (as in the work of Riley E. Dunlap). Far from being unaware of the contested character of scientific understanding, writers such as Dunlap, Dickens and Benton have explicitly attempted to theorize the relationship between society, nature and knowledge – and in a manner that moves beyond this outdated dualism. Realism and constructivism, therefore, face the same sociological challenge – even if the consequent strategies to deal with this have varied substantially.

It may also be that constructivists have failed to distinguish consistently between epistemological anti-realism and ontological relativism. Instead, the tendency has been to push social causation to its logical extreme and then acknowledge that material factors may also be significant.[7] Meanwhile, realists have tended to play the 'ontological trump card' at a decidedly abstract level rather than engaging with the messier world of the laboratory, the advisory group or the field trial. Rather than emphasizing the significance of the natural world and then bringing in the social or vice versa, the apparent need – as suggested in the opening quotation of this chapter from Haraway – is to 'find another relationship to nature'. It is at this point that the notion of 'co-construction' may be of particular value.

Rather than maintaining that the social and the natural are separate entities, I have suggested in this book that these might be better seen as *actively generated co-constructions*. Co-construction as employed here captures the dual process of the social and the natural being varyingly constructed within environmentally related practices and particular contexts. To quote Demeritt again, 'nature and society are feats and co-constructions, not pre-existing tendencies that, in the final instance, can explain it all' (1996, p. 498). The concept of co-construction owes a major debt to social constructivism. However, it also avoids some of the perils of social reductionism inherent in constructivist analysis and takes us away from the sterility of dualistic logic. At the same time, the notion of co-construction forces us to re-evaluate not only the usage of natural arguments within environmental debates but also the shifting definition of the social.

Conducted at a broad theoretical level, the argument over whether a particular phenomenon (for example, the environmental consequences of genetically modified foods) is 'real' or 'constructed' appears unresolvable (and ultimately rather futile). Such a stark dichotomy misses the dynamism, richness and significance of this important case. Faced with competing knowledge claims, shifting political alliances, ethical ambiguities, divisions within the biotechnology industry, arguments between nations and ferocious disputes among environmentalists, the insistence that we must distinguish between social and natural factors takes on a sterile and almost theological character. Rather than engaging with the complex processes involved, over-emphasis on the social–natural duality represents a form of disengagement and retreat to the more comfortable world of established social theory and unchallenged natural science.

Accordingly, insistence on the division between the social and the natural becomes a barrier to adequate understanding: a fundamental division, which the realist–constructivist debate is simply reproducing. It can plausibly be argued, based on the evidence of the previous chapters, that the social and the natural can no longer be defined apart from one another. Instead, environmental and social problems draw upon the same nature–culture nexus and, as such, are co-constructed within environmental and sociological discussion.

As Latour (1992) has developed this analysis, rather than finding distinct entities (so that the world in which we live can be categorized into the social and the natural), we have encountered *hybrids*, which cross domains and interlink a diversity of phenomena. Hybrids do not fall into either of the competing categories of social or natural but instead weave together elements of both. No longer separable, humans and non-humans form networks within which it becomes impossible to tell where one ends and the other begins. Was the Chernobyl disaster caused by human or technological failure? Is GM food a social or an environmental problem? Is the destruction of the rainforests a social or natural disaster? In such contexts, the division of the human from the non-human and the social from the natural is a characteristic of contemporary thought that is falling apart under the weight of its own contradictions. Whilst we might attempt to tidy the world into discrete boxes, the current awareness of environmental problems and the difficulties of neatly classifying them remind us that reductionist thinking has severe limitations.

Rather than concerning ourselves with where to draw the line between the social and the natural (a task that is ultimately futile since the line is not fixed but shifting even within specific social and environmental contexts), we have viewed this very process of 'line-drawing' (including, for example, various groups claiming to 'speak for nature') as an important focus for sociological analysis. At the same time, rather than prejudging what is natural and what is social within environmental debate, the methodological challenge is to maintain (or at least attempt, since every analyst brings her own preferences, prejudices and blindspots) a sceptical perspective on environmental claims-making.

In chapter 3, we suggested that the mad cows at the centre of the BSE debate can be varyingly construed as social or natural, just as the BSE debate itself can be presented as a matter of science or of politics. Equally, various parties to the controversy have shifted categories within the cut and thrust of debate. The British government has frequently represented the mad cow issue as essentially scientific in character (the experts know best), but has at times represented it as a political battle between the UK and its European partners (the politicians and civil servants know best). On various occasions also, government sources have represented the issues as fundamentally economic in character (whatever we know, British farmers must be saved from extinction).

Sociology needs to be attentive to these multiple, changing and competing definitions rather than seeking to constrain a highly dynamic set of discussions within a set of predetermined boxes. Simply shouting 'it's really social' in the face of those who proclaim 'it's really natural' seems a less than productive basis for environmental sociology.

In chapter 4's discussion of the local construction of environmental threats, we witnessed shifting definitions of environmental issues and problems. It is quite clear in such cases that the environment does not simply impact upon social life, but instead that environmental constructions can serve as projections of wider socially generated concerns and problems. For example, in the Jarrow case, issues of cultural identity and social powerlessness provide a wider framework for a range of local issues.

Environmental problems do not sit apart from everyday life (as if they were discrete from other issues and concerns) but instead are accommodated within (and help shape) the social construction of local reality. Within such situations also, attempts to tell local people what is 'really' going on (whether from the viewpoints of science, sociology or official institutions) are likely to be viewed in a critical (or even dismissive) fashion – again in line with the local construction of everyday meaning.

The key point about such environmental constructions is that they should be seen *as fluid rather than fixed*. We should not replace the conventional notion of a 'given' environment with the view that social responses are likewise fixed or static. Instead, the discussion in chapter 4 suggests that environmental attitudes are not simply free-floating (as if waiting for the sociological researcher to come along and 'collect' them) but are *discursively formed within particular social settings and contexts*. The point is not to privilege the social over the natural (as if the former was somehow more real than the latter). Instead, a more open-minded approach is required to both of these categories and their mutually constituted character.

As has been suggested here, environmental *knowledge* is central to these hybrid negotiations. In particular, we have seen that scientific accounts do not possess an unmediated access to the environment but must themselves depend upon, often unacknowledged, assumptions and cultural interpretations. In chapter 5's discussion of pesticides, we considered the tension between attempts to impose a standardized scientific framework for evaluation (especially in the context of European harmonization) and the varying local and national contexts for regulatory science. We have been especially alert to the significance of *social and institutional practices* and the embedded (and embodied) character of environmental assumptions and beliefs. As in the 2,4,5-T and aldrin/dieldrin case-studies, institutions may claim to operate on the basis of objective and universal principles (especially for reasons of social legitimation) but inevitably depend upon cultural understandings and (to use Wynne's term once more) 'naïve sociology'. Thus, negotiations within regulatory science bring together the scientific and the political (how do we convince Brussels that this test failure is insignificant?) alongside the ecological and the economic (how commercially successful is this product likely to be?). In the modern conditions of scientific practice, and especially within fields of such social and technical uncertainty, social assumptions cannot be kept outside the laboratory door but instead form an integral part of scientific assessment.

In more policy-oriented terms, it was suggested that, rather than criticizing the contemporary character of regulatory science – as if with a little more effort a fully standardized and objective system can be reached – the point is to acknowledge the inevitability of contextual assessments but also consider, for example, how greater transparency might be introduced into institutional processes.

Thus, whilst a conventional scientific account might imply that contextual mediation and local negotiation represent unfortunate weaknesses in the system, which can be overcome with 'better science' or greater efforts at standardization, it becomes important to recognize the inevitability of environmental hybrids. Rather than seeking to iron out local and cultural differences within environmental policy-making, the challenge for both sociologists and policy-makers is to build creatively upon an awareness of difference as well as similarity.

The treatment of technology added a new dimension to the discussion of these local, institutional and technical practices. The adverse impact of modern technology is one of the recurrent themes of environmental discussion. I suggested that 'impacts' are not fixed or given but are instead the outcome of social negotiations. Does biotechnology represent a threat to nature or a means of enhancing nature's productivity? In chapter 6, we noted both the differential construction of technologies (as in Zonabend's study of a nuclear community) and, in opposition to technological determinism, the manner in which technology can serve as a 'commonplace' for competing views of our social futures. Both 'technology' and 'nature' were presented as malleable rather than fixed categories.

Our general approach – especially in chapter 4 – has also stressed that there is little point in attempting to calculate whether social and institutional understandings are 'real' or 'imagined'. A more appropriate sociological task is to consider the multiple experiences and constructions of environmental hazard – including, very importantly, the manner in which risk constructions interact with self-identities and wider social understandings. At this point, the relationship between social identity – including local cultural understandings, a sense of institutional and personal trust, the experience of power and powerlessness – and environmental concerns becomes central. However, what I want to emphasize here is that this encourages a fresh look at *social* as well as natural relations. Socially generated knowledges and understandings are not relegated – by comparison with the knowledges and understandings of science – to the level of (mere) perceptions, but represent an important means of interpreting (or making sense of) the world in which we live. Public fears and anxieties are not measured against 'natural' indicators but are seen as valid in themselves. Concepts such as social class and social power are not simply reified (or 'black-boxed') but are seen to be actively constituted and experienced within particular settings. Public fears over the environmental and social consequences of new technologies are not viewed as 'irrational' but instead are granted legitimate status.

These points are further reinforced by the differential and flexible manner in which, for example, the people of Jarrow can portray their own social setting. Whilst Jarrow residents will at times present themselves as culturally separate from even their immediate regional neighbours, they are also capable of constructing a common identity with socially disadvantaged groups elsewhere. The lines of self-identity and social construction are not set in stone but are continually redrawn within different contexts – and, inevitably, reflect the desire to present oneself in particular fashions (as oppressed or empowered, as the same or different, as anxious or playful, as secure or at risk). In these ways, the construction of the social can be as contextual, negotiated and dynamic as that of the natural.

In reconsidering and reconceptualizing the social, an argument is also being made for an empirically grounded sociology that does not simply trade in sweeping generalizations but also considers the complexities (and contextual specificities) of environmental understanding. In this we are indeed seeking to avoid, in Mills's (1973) famous terms, both 'abstracted empiricism' and 'grand theory'. Put more broadly, a changed understanding of the social–natural relationship challenges the conventional boundaries of sociological practice. The social can be considered as no more self-contained, fixed or given than the natural. Sociology enters a more exciting – and risky – territory, where existing categorizations – the social, the natural, the scientific, the technological, the human, the non-human – are seen to be fluid and contextually constituted rather than predetermined. On the one hand, this represents a threat to existing sociological categorizations. On the other, such a reconceptualization allows us to explore the diverse ways in which self-identities and risk experiences interact with and shape one another.

In final illustration of this, the Jarrow case-study raises questions of the relationship between environmental understanding and social powerlessness – especially in a community characterized by high levels of unemployment and relative social deprivation. It would be possible to apply an environmental realist approach to this case: do people worry about real or perceived risks? Equally, a social realist perspective could be adopted: how does environmental awareness relate to socio-economic status? The approach adopted here was instead to consider how residents' own sense of social exclusion related to risk awareness. How, for example, does a sense of one's lack of agency (the ability to change the conditions of one's life) affect response to everyday hazards? Does the construction of environmental problems stand apart from – or interlink with – the experience of other expressed concerns (such as crime, education or employment)? In approaching the issues in this manner, we can identify the discursive formation of categories and the close relationship between these formations and local experience.

Rather than representing a weakness, an acknowledgement of the constructedness of knowledge claims (including those of sociologists) leads to a reconsideration of sociological analysis at a profound level. My argument here is indeed an argument – and one that is open to challenge, criticism and disagreement from a variety of perspectives. The task of sociology is not to produce undying truths but rather to engage, provoke and reconstruct. In that way also, sociology should be seen as dynamic rather than static – as a changing formation rather than as a body of social facts. As Bauman has expressed a similar concept: 'I am rather inclined to see sociology today as an eddy on a fast-moving river, an eddy which retains its shape but changes its content all the time, an eddy which can retain its shape only in so far as there is a constant through-flow of water' (1992, p. 213). As the environmental arena in all its dynamism and speed of movement serves to emphasize, this realization should not lead to frustration or despair but rather to an acknowledgement of the constructed (and constructing) character of sociological investigation. This may well be one of the more valuable points that environmental sociology can draw from the 'postmodern' tradition. To quote Bauman again: '[S]ociology is a transient activity, confined to its time and place. It is part and parcel of the stage in the development of culture and it is no worse for this reason. I think that is precisely where it derives its value from' (ibid., p. 216).

Rather than undermining sociological analysis, an awareness of the co-construction of the social and the natural raises fresh possibilities for sociological analysis. At the same time, the call for an environmental sociology is also a challenge to sociologists to be alert to research emerging from different intellectual traditions. No longer is it possible for sociologists simply to hive off the social bits of the environmental discussion. Instead, a much broader and more challenging role is being created.

As demonstrated in previous chapters, this has taken us to the possibly carcinogenic effects of pesticides, the environmental impact of biotechnology and the operation of a nuclear power plant – areas that may look intimidatingly technical for many sociologists. One major implication of the analysis offered in this book is that a greater openness is required across disciplinary boundaries. This is not to deny the value of disciplinary concerns, but it does suggest the wider intellectual seas across which sociologists will need to navigate if they are serious in their wish to engage with environmental problems and concerns.

The environmental challenge to sociology is also a challenge for sociology to emerge from its self-imposed disciplinary exile and, especially, the social–natural duality that underpins this. In that sense, it is not a problem that environmental concerns and social experiences overlap and intertwine so extensively. Instead, this represents a major challenge for the discipline in advancing from the defensive academic posture it has assumed since its formative years.

Towards an Environmental(ist) Sociology

It follows from the discussion in this chapter that environmental sociology cannot simply ring-fence the social aspects of any environmental problem and then stay safely within recognized home territory. Instead, the challenge is for sociological analysis to explore matters of problem construction, underlying assumptions and the relationship between science, institutions and the policy process. In all this, the sociologist may appear a troubled (and troublesome) figure – more prepared to challenge existing social models and expectations than to state what should be done (how can sociologists claim moral or scientific authority?). Equally, sociology can seem marginal to environmental discussion: able to criticize but not to act, eager to deconstruct existing categories but not to engage or persuade, unhappy with the role of 'underlabourer' (Hannigan 1995, p. 13) but unwilling to adopt a position of intellectual leadership.

In opposition to this characterization, I want to suggest that the sociological approach outlined here can play an important role within environmental discussion. Furthermore, an awareness of the constructed nature of environmental claims opens up new possibilities for environmental action and policy-making. As part of this argument, I would like to emphasize that engagement with practical environmental concerns can be a vital learning experience for sociologists who generally have as much to learn as to offer. Sociologists certainly need to be alert to analyses that emerge from outside the institutional parameters of sociology, but which may nevertheless contain significant sociological insights. Over-concern with the social–natural duality represents a turning-away from such debates rather than a wholehearted and enthusiastic engagement.

Going further, a co-constructivist approach to environmental matters suggests a number of possibilities for practical intervention and contribution. One of the most important of these is the argument that the environment is not a self-contained and discrete entity but a topic and theme that overlap broadly with – and depend upon – social and institutional practices. Whilst 'environmental policy' is often represented as a special subject removed from other areas of governance and social activity, this book has suggested that environmental matters are embedded in a variety of processes and practices: from innovation strategy to local community action, from expert advisory committees to industrial manufacture.

The whole thrust of the co-construction concept is towards the recognition that environmental matters overlap and interconnect with a diversity of social practices. In that way also, it is possible to surmise that environmental change will be a product of a whole range of social practices and not simply of intentional environmental engagement. The international agenda of sustainability may not in the end be as important as smaller changes in social practice that cumulatively and undramatically change our world. Whilst it is relatively easy to focus on high-profile environmental decisions, the incremental shifts of industry, institutional politics and the wider publics may ultimately have greater socio-environmental impact.

To this basic point can be added a number of practical implications from the above discussion. First of all, and as Wynne argued in chapter 5, sociological accounts can be especially useful in opening up the (generally unacknowledged) social assumptions upon which environmental constructions often depend (including, of course, the constructions of scientists). In so doing, a more transparent basis for institutional actions can be established. Equally, sociological analysis is well placed to bring out underlying themes of uncertainty, indeterminacy and ambivalence within environmental assessment. Characteristically, policy processes tend to play down or deny such elements of decision-making.

Sociological accounts are also able to offer a symmetrical treatment of different environmental constructions and, in that sense, can provide a meeting point between competing definitions of environmental problems. For example, effective communication between oppositional groups and government institutions may be impossible so long as environmental issues are framed only in modernistic and scientific terms. In addition, and whilst policy-makers, as in the two case-studies discussed in chapter 4, tend to frame environmental issues within a technical discourse that constructs public responses and concerns as secondary to the facts, sociological explanation is able to explore the deeper-rooted questions of self-identity and local experience, which are linked to environmental concern. More generally, sociological analysis can serve a useful purpose in exploring and expressing the knowledges and expertises of lay groups. Whilst not advocating a form of sociological ventriloquism, a full awareness of competing forms of knowledge (including those generated by lay people as a consequence of living and working in hazardous environments) can make an important contribution to environmental debate.

Meanwhile, and although environmental debates frequently present 'technology' either as an alien presence or as an environmental saviour, the analysis in chapter 6 indicates the social constructedness of technological impacts. In so doing, sociological treatments can suggest (and lend significance to) possibilities for social debate that do not simply lead to a 'pro' or 'anti' dichotomy over technological change.

As Jasanoff has emphasized, not only sociology but also policy analysis has a tendency to take the boundaries between the 'scientific, the social and the technological worlds' as rigid and unalterable. This intellectual and institutional perspective can then lead to a 'premature narrowing in both the framing and solution of perceived problems' (1999, p. 67). Thus, technological fixes and institutional initiatives are imposed on complex socio-technical problems and cultural factors are disregarded in the search for rational solutions. Genetically modified foods are put forward as a sustainable response to pesticide risks and food shortages. European regulatory regimes claim to supersede national systems. International agreements offer new sustainable pathways. In each case, the neglect of the more complex and co-constructed character of the challenges at hand can generate unsatisfactory forms of practical response – as many current initiatives in sustainable development may unfortunately illustrate. Put negatively, inadequate sociological analysis leads directly to inadequate policy response. Put more positively, there is a substantial challenge here for sociologists to demonstrate their social value and make a real contribution to public policy.

There are ample possibilities for new forms of sociological engagement in environmental matters. As I write, new approaches to deliberative decision-making and inclusive democracy are being increasingly recognized as an important means of testing out the cultural assumptions embedded in policy-making and bringing the fullest range of knowledges and assessments to bear. The precautionary principle is being reassessed as both a technical and social judgement. Narrowly defined 'sound science' is no longer seen as a sufficient basis for decision-making but is under review in terms of the best relationship between science, the wider publics and policy-making. Civil servants and policy-makers are becoming ever more aware of the significance of public trust and credibility. In all of this, sociology has an important role to play in unravelling the connections between society, nature and knowledge and in creating critical and informed deliberation over alternative socio-technical paths.[8]

In the end, the practical role for sociology is not that of environmental arbitrator or judge. The challenge is to open up new possibilities for reflexive and democratic engagement and debate that do not reduce environmental concerns to narrow technical disputes or simple social–natural polarizations. At the same time, a sociological discussion of these issues reveals the intellectual paucity of most environmental discussions – and especially their dependence upon a narrow definition of environmental problems (generally as set by scientific institutions).

Returning to the sustainability agenda, which has proved so significant for environmental discussion since the late 1980s, sociological analysis seems uniquely placed to draw out the value choices, implicit assumptions and epistemological judgements upon which environmental debate seems to depend – but without suggesting that either values or knowledges can exist outside of social relationships and human experiences. Equally, these need to be seen as dynamic rather than static and as contextually generated rather than predetermined. In proposing a more satisfactory understanding of human and non-human relationships, sociology can also draw attention to the social and institutional questions that can be hidden behind scientific and policy constructions. Above all, sociology can recognize that lurking behind 'environmental' problems are a series of very human challenges and questions.

Once we step outside the conventional assumption that the social and the natural can exist independently of one another, fresh possibilities emerge for constructing new relations and more productive forms of dialogue and interaction. For the sociologist, this will mean engagement with a variety of human and non-human agents. In terms of the policy process, the need is for institutional forms that recognize the constructedness of environmental meaning and, in so doing, avoid the conventional pretence that the environment can simply speak for itself.

At this point, a variety of possible initiatives take on new significance: from local attempts to improve the quality of everyday life to discussions of how to draw into practical engagement those who see themselves as socially powerless. The diversity of environmental meanings suggests that there cannot be a single way forward from here. Instead, the sociological study of environmental problems indicates that environmental response is inseparable from larger questions of self-identity, sense of agency, reflexive awareness and trust in institutions. Put in that fashion, our study of environmental concerns has taken us from contemplation of a natural world 'out there' to the consideration of a set of human issues that exist very much within our existing institutions and everyday practices. In addressing environmental matters, we are unavoidably addressing the very constitution of society.

Conclusion

> [T]ruth from a pluralistic vantage point is not a search for the indisputable. Rather, it is more like a tolerance for difference that opens up possibilities and keeps them open. Its focus is not on whether a particular stance is true or false, but whether or not its particular terminology or vocabulary works to intelligibly frame the particular interests of the investigator. Stripped of its claims to universality, truth becomes a 'tool which helps us cope or make sense of the world'. (Kroll-Smith et al., 2000, p. 58)

At an early stage in this book's development, I discussed its structure with a very experienced colleague. The problem, as I explained it, was that there were so many interesting theoretical frameworks and empirical examples available that I couldn't impose any *order* on the material. Her nonchalant reply was 'why not do the usual thing?'. On being met with what was obviously a very blank look, she patiently explained that the 'usual thing' was to establish several competing frameworks, advocate one in particular, and then spend the rest of the book justifying that selection and ignoring (or dismissing) the others.

Pondering this well-intentioned (if rather cynical) advice afterwards, I guiltily realized that the 'usual' response to this academic manoeuvre was for reviewers to perform the same trick in reverse: observe the author's selection of a particular framework, and then either support this or (more likely) bemoan the failure to adopt an alternative/better-informed/richer approach of the sort generally favoured by the reviewer.

Now, just because something is 'usual' doesn't mean that it is wrong. Certainly, academic arguments need structure. Furthermore, it is only proper for competing perspectives to be respectfully reviewed and one's own preferences clearly argued. This at least stimulates engagement and debate – and so fuels the discipline's development. Indeed, such a structure can be discerned in *Sociology and the Environment*. In the latter half of this book, I have specifically advocated a theoretical and empirical perspective that draws on the sociology of scientific knowledge (SSK), science and technology studies (STS) and a broadly constructivist perspective. All of this represents a serious effort at responding to the question first asked in the Preface: what should be the relationship between the discipline of sociology and the study of environmental issues, problems and concerns? However, what I want to emphasize at this stage is that I do *not* want to conclude with the usual justification for 'my' choice.

Rather than pretending that only one sociological perspective still stands and that all the other theoretical bodies can now be dragged lifeless from the stage, I want to emphasize the importance of a pluralistic and open-minded approach to these questions. I recognize that I risk confusing those readers who might prefer at this stage to be given the 'solution' to social–natural relations. However, I would rather encourage further discussion and inquiry than attempt premature closure. At one level, this final plea for pluralism stems from my awareness that there are other sociological approaches and sociological topics than those presented here. Equally, there are alternative ways of dividing the field than the categorizations I have offered.[9] I take great heart from this, since it re-emphasizes the dynamism and diversity of environmental sociology.

This book is very much an invitation to go further than I have been able to do in one text. On that basis also, I do not find it all hard to identify future research sites and theoretical concerns. In fact, the possibilities stretch readily in front of me. In clear illustration of this, the book has said too little about gender, the developing world and concepts of environmental citizenship, environmental politics and environmental justice.

At a more profound level, however, I want to avoid the conclusion that sociological investigation is primarily about vanquishing the opposition or triumphantly brandishing the latest 'truth'. As I have already suggested, for example, whilst the rhetorical clash between realism and constructivism may have usefully served to highlight certain key issues, there is also an important sense in which it has represented a turning away from environmental engagement and sociological research (which I would define as both theoretical and empirical in character).

As I have argued, it may be that the issue of whether the environment is real or constructed is both unresolvable and ultimately irrelevant. Rather than seeking to establish the right line and then relax back into our sociological armchairs, we should critically scrutinize the merits of different approaches but then be prepared to move on in both theoretical and empirical terms. In making this point, I am also arguing that the merits of any framework cannot be judged solely in the abstract but instead stem largely from the new light they shed on the *doing* of sociological research. My case is for theories not simply to be assessed on the basis of their philosophical strengths but also, and very importantly, in terms of how they help us interpret, unravel and contextualize social and environmental problems. In that sense too, there may be more in common between critical realism and social constructivism than is keeping them apart. Equally, philosophical disagreement does not necessarily get in the way of stimulating and insightful research. Furthermore, no theoretical perspective can generate *all* the best ideas.

In adding my modest weight to a particular SSK and constructivist perspective, I am seeking to emphasize a set of sociological concepts and approaches that I believe has been neglected (and at times distorted) within environmental sociology. This is not to deny the importance of other approaches or to downplay the historical and current significance of critical and sophisticated discussions within the 'realist' tradition. From my viewpoint, there is no special merit in tying our conceptual hands behind our back when tackling such challenging and dynamic problems. To quote another sociologist whose work I would rather (critically) celebrate than sweep aside:

> I consider realism and constructivism to be neither an either–or option nor a mere matter of belief. We should not have to swear allegiance to any particular view or theoretical perspective. The decision whether to take a realist or a constructivist approach is for me a rather *pragmatic* one, a matter of choosing the appropriate means for a desired goal. (Beck 1999, p. 134; emphasis in orginal)

It is therefore entirely healthy for the discipline that it should be open to alternative perspectives – and that these perspectives should in turn be open to mutual criticism and debate. However, the prime challenge is to find imaginative and creative ways of transcending the social–natural dualism and considering the implications for the discipline and for practical engagement. Rather than narrowing the theoretical and empirical possibilities or backing one approach entirely, it seems more helpful to retain an open-minded and inclusive dialogue over such matters. This of course extends to developments emanating both within and outside the disciplinary boundaries of sociology.

In advocating a particular approach and demonstrating its capacities, it is vital that we also maintain an awareness of the theoretical and empirical opportunities within this exciting field. As I stated in the Preface, my aim has been to stimulate and provoke rather than to place this challenging subject in one tidy corner of the sociological edifice.

Far from standing at the end of a sociological journey, it seems instead that we are only at the beginning.

Notes

Preface

1. At that time, Newby was Chair of the UK Economic and Social Research Council (ESRC). The talk, given in February 1991, marked the occasion of the British Sociological Association's fortieth anniversary.
2. The Brundtland Report is discussed extensively in chapter 1.
3. For an early statement of this approach, see Catton and Dunlap 1978. For a more recent discussion, see Dunlap 1997. See also Buttel 1987; Erikson 1976.
4. Respectively, Yearley 1991; Redclift and Benton (eds) 1994; Dickens 1992; Eder 1996; Hannigan 1995; Bell 1998; Martell 1994.
5. See Macnaghten and Urry 1998.
6. Put very simply, realists emphasize the objective and independent reality of environmental problems. Constructivists, as we will discuss, emphasize the socially constructed character of environmental problems and argue that reality is actively manufactured in particular contexts through language and social interaction.

Introduction

1. Interestingly, this 'urban landscape of the mind' maintains its presence – fuelled, for example, by rumours about what has happened to the clock and whether or not it might make a glorious return.
2. In fact, it took an Act of Congress in 1864 to establish the Yosemite Valley as the USA's first region specifically set aside to protect wilder-

ness. For a fascinating journalistic account of the hold of 'wilderness' on the American imagination – and the tragic story of one young man's attempt to find this – see Krakauer 1996.

3. For a detailed discussion of this phenomenon within British sociology, see Studholme 1997.

4. This part of the discussion owes a major debt to Stehr and Grundmann 1996.

5. But see, for example, Barry 1999; Dickens 1992 and 1996.

6. For an introduction to this area, see Latour 1987; Mulkay 1991; Woolgar 1988.

7. Although natural scientists (notably Alan Sokal) have recently accused certain postmodernist thinkers of 'abusing' science by drawing upon scientific ideas and concepts (especially from quantum mechanics) in support of their more speculative arguments – and in so doing of misunderstanding and misrepresenting the science involved. On one reading, this may be a symptom of the excessive respect shown by social scientists to natural science rather than, as the scientific critics would have it, a devastating blow to the intellectual credibility of postmodernism and 'radical relativism'. See Sokal and Bricmont 1998.

8. For a discussion of rationalization, see, for example, Collins 1986, esp. ch. 4.

9. See Tönnies 1955 [1887].

10. Dickens 1992 and 1996; see also Dickens 1997.

11. See also Bramwell 1989.

12. See Benton 1991.

13. See the discussion of this in Barry 1999.

Chapter 1 Sustainability as Social Challenge

1. See Milton 1996.

2. See Sachs 1997, p. 71.

3. Brooks 1992 noted that at least 40 working definitions of sustainable development had appeared since 1987 (cited in Hajer 1995). Six years later, Dobson could note that 'something like 300 definitions' of sustainable development were now available (1998, p. 33).

4. Myers and Macnaghten present commonplaces as 'general and recurring arguments'. As they observe: 'Commonplaces are common both in the sense that they can be used in a wide range of arguments (for or against nuclear power) and that they can be assumed to be used by a wide range of people (road protesters, supermarkets and school-children)' (1998, p. 338).

5. But see, for example, Redclift 1992 and Sachs 1997; also Reid 1996.

6. Reid notes that credit for the term's invention has been accorded variously to organizations such as the International Institute for

Environment and Development and to several individuals (1996, p. xiii).

7. This is not to suggest that environmental concerns only emerged in the 1970s. See, for example, Worster 1977.
8. See, for example, Burke 1997.
9. Meadows et al. 1972, p. 24: quoted in Reid 1996, p. 31.
10. See Buckingham-Hatfield and Percy (eds) 1999; United Nations 1992.
11. By the 1997 New York meeting, very few countries remained on target to achieve this.
12. James Gustave, quoted in *New Statesman*, 20 June 1997, p. 16.
13. Her Majesty's Government 1990. See also, Her Majesty's Government 1994.
14. See, for example, Department of the Environment 1995.
15. *Independent*, 24 June 1997, p. 1.

Chapter 2 The Risk Society Thesis

1. At this stage, the work of a third important social theorist who has tackled the relationship between modernity and everyday life should also be mentioned (even if space does not allow a fuller treatment) – namely, Zygmunt Bauman. See, for example, Bauman 1991.
2. See Beck 1996, p. 38.
3. As Michael Bell puts this: 'One of the central driving forces of political conflict in poor countries originates very much from the feeling that "I am hungry"' (1998, p. 194).
4. K. U. Mayer, quoted in H. Nowotny, Reputation at risk. *The Times Higher Educational Supplement*, 20 November 1992, p. 17.

Chapter 3 Science and the Social Construction of Environmental Threat

1. There is a large literature in this area, which can only be touched upon in this chapter. For a good starting-point, see Collins and Pinch 1993; Mulkay 1991; Webster 1991; Woolgar 1988. For a useful review of the relationship between SSK and geography, see Demeritt 1996.
2. The allusion here is to one of the better-known books in the field: Latour 1987.
3. Further references on the sociological study of civil nuclear energy include: Macgill 1987; Welsh 1993 and 2000; Wynne 1982. See also Meehan 1984.

4. For further discussion of the BSE case, see Irwin 1997 and Ratzan 1998.
5. See also Lear 1997.
6. Universities Survey. *The Economist*, 4 October 1997, p. 16.
7. For further discussion of the regulation of chemical hazards, see Jasanoff 1990. See also chapter 5.

Chapter 4 Risks in Context

1. Credit for coining this term should go to Peter Simmons.
2. Other accounts that explore related issues include Brown 1992; Brown and Mikkelsen 1997; Burningham 1996; Couch and Kroll-Smith (eds) 1991; Edelstein 1988; Freudenburg and Pastor 1992; Gill and Picou 1991; Kasperson et al. 1992; Kroll-Smith and Hugh Floyd 1997; Moffatt et al. 1995; Phillimore and Moffatt 1994; Picou and Gill 1996; Picou et al. 1992; Wynne 1996.
3. The discussion in this section draws upon empirical and theoretical research conducted by Couch and Kroll-Smith. See Kroll-Smith and Couch 1990. See also Couch 1996; Couch and Kroll-Smith 1985 and 1991; Couch et al. 2000; Kroll-Smith and Couch 1993.
4. I would like to acknowledge the financial support of the Health and Safety Executive for the original research upon which this section is based. I also wish to thank my co-workers on the Jarrow study: Peter Simmons (Lancaster University), Gordon Walker (Staffordshire University) and Brian Wynne (Lancaster University). For a full account of the research project, see Walker et al. 1998.
5. See also Irwin et al. 1999.
6. To be more specific, six focus groups were recruited in Jarrow – involving a total of 37 people from the area. Each of these groups met twice. Focus group data were supplemented with a series of interviews involving key local informants (for example, at the company in question and with regulatory authorities).
7. Of course, a similar point could be made about scientific knowledge, which also represents a 'contextual' form of understanding.
8. See the discussion in Irwin 1995.
9. For a geographical contribution, see Burgess 1990. For anthropological work in the area, see, in addition to previous references, Douglas 1986. See also the discussion of Zonabend in chapter 6.

Chapter 5 Institutional Judgements and Contested Decisions

1. A point made especially clearly within the wider project of which the Jarrow case-study is just one part. Other case-studies of similar hazard

sites demonstrate very different forms of local understanding and evaluation.

2. Despite some familiar criticisms of constructivism, this form of sociological explanation does not imply that such problems are merely a figment of the (individual or collective) imagination.

3. Hannigan's usage of 'constructionism' of course raises the question of how this should be distinguished from my favoured term 'constructivism'. However, and as noted in the Introduction, I have taken these as synonymous.

4. A point discussed at some length in Irwin 1995.

5. For this chapter, I have relied upon the version of this paper published as Gillespie et al. 1982. In chapter 3, a reference is given to the original 1979 paper in *Social Studies of Science*.

6. As Gillespie et al. note: 'Aldrin rapidly degrades to Dieldrin in plants and animals, so when we discuss the hazards of A/D we are really talking about the hazards associated with Dieldrin' (1982, p. 305).

7. Such deconstruction as the scientific evidence falls apart under critical public scrutiny is a particular concern for Jasanoff. See Jasanoff 1990.

8. For a discussion of this point with regard to pharmaceuticals, see Abraham 1995.

9. For examples of this literature, see Brickman et al. 1985; Irwin 1985; Vogel 1986.

10. For treatment of this case, see Cook and Kaufman 1982; Irwin 1995. See also Irwin 1989.

11. For a wider discussion of the 'precautionary principle', see O'Riordan and Cameron (eds) 1994.

12. The research discussed in this section draws upon a research award from the Economic and Social Research Council (award number L323253019). I am very pleased to acknowledge the contribution of my co-workers on this project: Elaine Mc Carthy, Henry Rothstein and Steve Yearley. For an account of the original research project, see Irwin et al. 1997b.

13. By 'scientism' in this context, I mean the presentation of social, cultural and ethical judgements as if they were merely technical in character. For a related discussion, see Habermas 1978, pp. 62–80.

14. For an empirically based discussion of some of the points in this section, see Irwin et al. 1997a.

15. See also Waterton and Wynne 1996.

16. Interview data from regulatory science project, 1996.

17. See also Irwin 1997.

Chapter 6 Kamikazes and Chromosomes

1. For the classic statement of this approach, see Bronowski 1973.

2. See Bijker 1995; Bijker et al. (eds) 1987; Grint and Woolgar 1997.

3. See also Michael Thompson's 1989 argument that engineering is 'tacit anthropology'.
4. See Bijker et al. 1987.
5. For a broad discussion of the relationship between nuclear power and theories of the risk society, see Irwin et al. 2000.
6. Sellafield crisis as BNFL is given safety ultimatum. *Independent*, 19 February 2000, pp. 1–3.
7. See also Durant 1992.
8. In *Innovation and Technology Transfer*, European Commission Innovation Programme 1998, p. 16.
9. See the discussion in Wajcman 1995.
10. See Macnaghten and Urry 1998.

Chapter 7 Society, Nature, Knowledge

1. Emphasis in original. With thanks to Christina Durkin.
2. Beck argues that 'the philosophies and theories . . . of so-called "post-modernity" . . . cannot answer very basic questions about how and in what ways everyday lives and professional fields are being transformed' (1999, p. 133).
3. Defined by Sokal and Bricmont as 'an intellectual current characterized by the more-or-less explicit rejection of the rationalist tradition of the Enlightenment, by theoretical discourses disconnected from any empirical test, and by a cognitive and cultural relativism that regards science as nothing more than a "narration", a "myth" or a social construction among many others' (1998, p. 1).
4. As it was put to me informally at a North American conference: 'Surely you can only be a constructivist if you don't care about the environment?'
5. 'The constructivist approach has had a pernicious effect on the sociology of environmental issues' (Murphy 1994a, p. 197).
6. For one science-studies based response to the question 'Do you believe in reality?', see Latour 1999.
7. See Collins and Yearley 1992.
8. As an illustration of this positive relationship between social science and environmental policy, see the output from the environmental programme of the UK ESRC: Economic and Social Research Council 2000.
9. See, for example, Kroll-Smith et al. 2000.

References

Abraham, J. 1995: *Science, Politics and the Pharmaceutical Industry: controversy and bias in drug regulation*. London: UCL Press.

Adam, B., Beck, U. and Van Loon, J. (eds) 2000: *The Risk Society and Beyond: critical issues for social theory*. London, Thousand Oaks, New Delhi: Sage.

Barry, J. 1999: *Environment and Social Theory*. London and New York: Routledge.

Bauman, Z. 1991: *Modernity and Ambivalence*. Cambridge: Polity.

Bauman, Z. 1992: *Intimations of Postmodernity*. London and New York: Routledge.

Beck, U. 1992: *Risk Society: towards a new modernity*. London, Newbury Park, New Delhi: Sage.

Beck, U. 1995a: *Ecological Enlightenment: essays on the politics of the risk society*. New Jersey: Humanities Press.

Beck, U. 1995b: *Ecological Politics in an Age of Risk*. Cambridge: Polity.

Beck, U. 1996: Risk society and the provident state. In Lash, S., Szerszynski, B. and Wynne, B. (eds), *Risk, Environment and Modernity: towards a new ecology*. London, Thousand Oaks, New Delhi: Sage, pp. 27–43.

Beck, U. 1999: *World Risk Society*. Cambridge: Polity.

Beck, U., Giddens, A. and Lash, S. (eds) 1994: *Reflexive Modernization: politics, tradition and aesthetics in the modern social order*. Cambridge: Polity.

Bell, M. M. 1998: *An Invitation to Environmental Sociology*. Thousand Oaks, CA: Pine Forge Press.

Benton, T. 1991: Biology and social science: why the return of the repressed should be given a (cautious) welcome. *Sociology* 25 (1), pp. 1–29.

Bijker, W. E. 1995: Sociohistorical technology studies. In Jasanoff, S., Markle, G. E., Petersen, J. C. and Pinch, T. (eds), *Handbook of Science and Technology Studies*. Thousand Oaks, London, New Delhi: Sage, pp. 229–56.

Bijker, W. E., Hughes, T. P. and Pinch, T. (eds) 1987: *The Social Construction of Technological Systems*. Cambridge, MA: MIT Press.

Bramwell, A. 1989: *Ecology in the Twentieth Century: a history*. New Haven, CT: Yale University Press.

Braun, B. and Castree, N. (eds) 1998: *Remaking Reality: nature at the millennium*. London and New York: Routledge.

Brickman, R., Jasanoff, S. and Ilgen, T. 1985: *Controlling Chemicals: the politics of regulation in Europe and the United States*. Ithaca: Cornell University Press.

Bronowski, J. 1973: *The Ascent of Man*. London: BBC.

Brooks, D. B. 1992: The challenge of sustainability: is integrating environment and economics enough? *Policy Sciences* 26, pp. 401–8.

Brown, P. 1992: Popular epidemiology and toxic-waste contamination: lay and professional ways of knowing. *Journal of Health and Social Behaviour* 33 (3), pp. 267–81.

Brown, P. and Mikkelsen, E. 1997: *No Safe Place: toxic waste, leukemia, and community action*. Berkeley: University of California Press.

Buckingham-Hatfield, S. 2000: *Gender and the Environment*. London and New York: Routledge.

Buckingham-Hatfield, S. and Evans, B. (eds) 1996: *Environmental Planning and Sustainability*. Chichester: John Wiley and Sons.

Buckingham-Hatfield, S. and Percy, S. (eds) 1999: *Constructing Local Environmental Agendas*. London: Routledge.

Burgess, J. 1990: The production and consumption of environmental meanings in the mass media: a research agenda for the 1990s. *Transactions of the Institute of British Geographers* 15, pp. 139–61.

Burke, T. 1997: The buck stops everywhere. *New Statesman*, 20 June, pp. 14–16.

Burningham, K. 1996: Us and them: the construction and maintenance of divisions in a planning dispute. In Samson, C. and South, N. (eds), *The Social Construction of Social Policy: methodologies, racism, citizenship and the environment*. Basingstoke: Macmillan, pp. 193–209.

Burningham, K. and Cooper, G. 1999: Being constructive: social constructionism and the environment. *Sociology* 33 (2), pp. 297–316.

Buttel, F. H. 1987: New directions in environmental sociology. *Annual Review of Sociology* 13, pp. 465–88.

Buttel, F. 1997: Social institutions and environmental change. In Redclift, M. and Woodgate, G. (eds), 1997: *The International Handbook of Environmental Sociology*. Cheltenham UK and Northampton MA: Edward Elgar, pp. 40–54.

Carson, R. 1991 [1962]: *Silent Spring*. Harmondsworth: Penguin.

Castree, N. and Braun, B. 1998: The construction of nature and the nature of construction: analytical and political tools for building survivable futures. In Braun and Castree, *Remaking Reality*, pp. 3–42.

Catton, W. R. and Dunlap, R. E. 1978: Environmental sociology: a new paradigm. *The American Sociologist* 13, pp. 41–9.

Catton, W. R. and Dunlap, R. E. 1980: A new ecological paradigm for post-exuberant sociology. *American Behavioral Scientist* 24, pp. 15–47.

Collingridge, D. and Reeve, C. 1986: *Science Speaks to Power: the role of experts in policymaking*. New York: St Martin's Press.

Collins, H. and Pinch, T. 1993: *The Golem: what everyone should know about science*. Cambridge: Cambridge University Press.

Collins, H. M. and Yearley, S. 1992: Epistemological chicken. In Pickering, A. (ed.), *Science as Culture and Practice*. Cambridge: Cambridge University Press, pp. 301–26.

Collins, R. 1986: *Max Weber: a skeleton key*. Newbury Park, London, New Delhi: Sage.

Cook, J. and Kaufman, C. 1982: *Portrait of a Poison: the 2,4,5-T story*. London: Pluto Press.

Couch, S. R. 1996: Environmental contamination, community transformation, and the Centralia mine fire. In Mitchell, J. K. (ed.), *The Long Road to Recovery: community responses to industrial disaster*. Tokyo, New York, Paris: United Nations University Press, pp. 60–85.

Couch, S. R. and Kroll-Smith, J. S. 1985: The chronic technical disaster: towards a social scientific perspective. *Social Science Quarterly* 66 (3), pp. 564–75.

Couch, S. and Kroll-Smith, J. S. (eds) 1991: *Communities at Risk: collective responses to technological hazards*. New York: Peter Lang.

Couch, S. R., Kroll-Smith, J. S. and Kindler, J. D. 2000: Discovering and inventing hazardous environments: sociological knowledge and publics at risk. In Cohen, M. (ed.), *Risk in the Modern Age: social theory, science and environmental decision-making*. Basingstoke: Macmillan. London: St Martin's Press, pp. 173–95.

Demeritt, D. 1996: Social theory and the reconstruction of science and geography. *Transactions of the Institute of British Geographers* 21, pp. 484–503.

Department of the Environment 1995: *British Government Panel on Sustainable Development. First Report*. London: HMSO.

Dickens, P. 1992: *Society and Nature: towards a green social theory*. Hemel Hempstead: Harvester Wheatsheaf.

Dickens, P. 1996: *Reconstructing Nature: alienation, emancipation and the division of labour*. London: Routledge.

Dickens, P. 1997: Beyond sociology: Marxism and the environment. In Redclift and Woodgate (eds), *The International Handbook of Environmental Sociology*, pp. 179–92.

Dobson, A. 1998: *Justice and the Environment: conceptions of environmental sustainability and dimensions of social justice*. Oxford: Oxford University Press.

Douglas, M. 1975: *Implicit Meanings: essays in anthropology*. London: Routledge and Kegan Paul.

Douglas, M. 1980: Environments at risk. In Dowie, J. and Lefrere, P. (eds), *Risk and Chance*. Milton Keynes: Open University Press, pp. 278–96.

Douglas, M. 1986: *Risk Acceptability According to the Social Sciences*. London: Routledge and Kegan Paul.

Douglas, M. and Wildavsky, A. 1983: *Risk and Culture: an essay on the selection of technological and environmental dangers*. Berkeley: University of California Press.

Dryzek, J. 1997: *The Politics of the Earth: environmental discourses*. Oxford: Oxford University Press.

Dunlap, R. E. 1997: The evolution of environmental sociology: a brief history and assessment of the American experience. In Redclift and Woodgate (eds), *The International Handbook of Environmental Sociology*, pp. 21–39.

Durant, J. (ed.) 1992: *Biotechnology in Public: a review of recent research*. London: Science Museum.

The Ecologist 1972: *Blueprint for Survival*. Harmondsworth: Penguin.

Economic and Social Research Council (ESRC) Global Environmental Change programme 2000: *Risky Choices, Soft Disasters: environmental decision-making under uncertainty*. University of Sussex, Brighton. *www.gecko.ac.uk*

Edelstein, M. R. 1988: *Contaminated Communities: the social and psychological impacts of residential toxic exposure*. Boulder, CO: Westview Press.

Eder, K. 1996: *The Social Construction of Nature*. London, Thousand Oaks, New Delhi: Sage.

Engels, F. 1968: *The Condition of the Working Class in England*. Oxford: Oxford University Press.

Erikson, K. T. 1976: *Everything in its Path: destruction of community in the Buffalo Creek flood*. New York: Simon and Schuster.

Freudenburg, W. R. and Pastor, S. 1992: Public responses to technological risks: towards a sociological perspective. *The Sociological Quarterly* 33, pp. 389–412.

Gerth, H. H. and Mills, C. W. (eds) 1993: *From Max Weber: essays in sociology*. London: Routledge.

Giddens, A. 1990: *The Consequences of Modernity*. Cambridge: Polity.

Giddens, A. 1991: *Modernity and Self-identity: self and society in the late modern age*. Cambridge: Polity.

Giddens, A. 1994a: *Beyond Left and Right: the future of radical politics*. Cambridge: Polity.

Giddens, A. 1994b: Living in a post-traditional society. In Beck, Giddens and Lash (eds), 1994: *Reflexive Modernization*, pp. 56–109.

Gill, D. A. and Picou, J. S. 1991: The social psychological impacts of a technological accident: collective stress and perceived health risks. *Journal of Hazardous Materials* 27, pp. 77–89.

Gillespie, B., Eva, D. and Johnston, R. 1979: Carcinogenic risk assessment in the United States and Great Britain: the case of aldrin/dieldrin. *Social Studies of Science* 18, pp. 265–301.

Gillespie, B., Eva, D. and Johnston, R. 1982: Carcinogenic risk assessment in the USA and UK: the case of aldrin/dieldrin. In Barnes, B. and Edge, D. (eds), 1982: *Science in Context: readings in the sociology of science*. Milton Keynes: Open University Press, pp. 303–35.

Goldblatt, D. 1996: *Social Theory and the Environment*. Cambridge: Polity.

Grint, K. and Woolgar, S. 1997: *The Machine at Work: technology, work and organization*. Cambridge: Polity.

Habermas, J. 1978: *Towards a Rational Society*. London: Heinemann.

Hajer, M. 1995: *The Politics of Environmental Discourse: ecological modernization and the policy process*. Oxford: Clarendon Press.

Hannigan, J. A. 1995: *Environmental Sociology: a social constructionist perspective*. London and New York: Routledge.

Haraway, D. J. 1991: *Simians, Cyborgs and Women: the reinvention of nature*. London: Free Association Books.

Haraway, D. 1995: Otherworldly conversations, terran topics, local terms. In Shiva, V. and Moser, I. (eds), *Biopolitics: a feminist and ecological reader on biotechnology*. London and New Jersey: Zed Books, pp. 69–92.

Her Majesty's Government 1990: *This Common Inheritance: Britain's environmental strategy*. London: HMSO.

Her Majesty's Government 1994: *Sustainable Development: the UK strategy*. London: HMSO.

Hobbelink, H. 1995: Biotechnology and the future of agriculture. In Shiva, V. and Moser, I. (eds), *Biopolitics: a feminist and ecological reader on biotechnology*. London and New Jersey: Zed Books, pp. 226–33.

Hooper, P. 1986: The Silksworth Colliery controversy: a case of undemocratic decision making? Unpublished undergraduate dissertation, University of Manchester.

Irwin, A. 1985: *Risk and the Control of Technology: public policies for road traffic safety in Britain and the United States*. Manchester: Manchester University Press.

Irwin, A. 1989: Deciding about risk: expert testimony and the regulation of hazard. In Brown, J. (ed.), *Environmental Threats: perception, analysis and management*. London and New York: Belhaven Press, pp. 19–32.

Irwin, A. 1995: *Citizen Science: a study of people, expertise and sustainable development*. London: Routledge.

Irwin, A. 1997: Risk, the environment and environmental knowledges. In Redclift and Woodgate (eds), *The International Handbook of Environmental Sociology*, pp. 218–26.

Irwin, A., Allan, S. and Welsh, I. 2000: Nuclear risks: three problematics. In Adam, Beck and Van Loon (eds), *The Risk Society and Beyond*, pp. 78–104.

Irwin, A., Mc Carthy, E., Rothstein, H. and Yearley, S. 1997a: Regulatory science and the European control of agrochemicals. In Bal, R. and Halffman, W. (eds), *The Politics of Chemical Risk: scenarios for a regulatory future*. Dordrecht, Boston, London: Kluwer, pp. 231–50.

Irwin, A., Rothstein, H., Yearley, S. and Mc Carthy, E. 1997b: Regulatory science – towards a sociological framework. *Futures* 29 (1), pp. 17–31.

Irwin, A., Simmons, P. and Walker, G. 1999: Faulty environments and risk reasoning: the local understanding of industrial hazards. *Environment and Planning A* 31, pp. 1311–26.

Irwin, A. and Wynne, B. (eds) 1996: *Misunderstanding Science? the public reconstruction of science and technology*. Cambridge: Cambridge University Press.

Jasanoff, S. 1990: *The Fifth Branch: science advisers as policymakers*. Cambridge, MA: Harvard University Press.

Jasanoff, S. 1999: STS and public policy: getting beyond deconstruction. *Science, Technology and Society* 4 (1), pp. 59–72.

Jasanoff, S., Markle, G. E., Petersen, J. C. and Pinch, T. (eds) 1995: *Handbook of Science and Technology Studies*. Thousand Oaks, London, New Delhi: Sage.

Kasperson, R. E., Golding, D. and Tuler, S. 1992: Social distrust as a factor in siting hazardous waste facilities and communicating risks. *Journal of Social Issues* 48 (4), pp. 161–87.

Krakauer, J. 1996: *Into the Wild*. New York: Anchor/Doubleday.

Kroll-Smith, J. S. and Couch, S. R. 1990: *The Real Disaster is Above Ground: a mine fire and social conflict*. Lexington: University Press of Kentucky.

Kroll-Smith, J. S. and Couch, S. R. 1993: Technological hazards: social responses as traumatic stressors. In Wilson, J. P. and Raphael, B. (eds), *International Handbook of Traumatic Stress Syndromes*. New York and London: Plenum Press, pp. 79–91.

Kroll-Smith, J. S., Gunter, V. and Laska, S. Spring 2000: Theoretical stances and environmental debates: reconciling the physical and the symbolic. *The American Sociologist*, pp. 44–61.

Kroll-Smith, J. S. and Hugh Floyd, H. 1997: *Bodies in Protest: environmental illness and the struggle over medical knowledge*. New York and London: New York University Press.

Lash, S., Szerszynski, B. and Wynne, B. (eds) 1996: *Risk, Environment and Modernity: towards a new ecology*. London, Thousand Oaks, New Delhi: Sage.

Latour, B. 1987: *Science in Action*. Milton Keynes: Open University Press.

Latour, B. 1992: *We Have Never Been Modern*. London: Harvester Wheatsheaf.

Latour, B. 1999: *Pandora's Hope: essays on the reality of science studies*. Cambridge, MA, and London: Harvard University Press.

Latour, B. and Woolgar, S. 1979: *Laboratory Life: the social construction of scientific facts*. Beverly Hills: Sage.

Law, J. and Callon, M. 1988: Engineering and sociology in a military aircraft project: a network analysis of technological change. *Social Problems* 35 (3), pp. 284–97.

Lear, L. 1997: *Rachel Carson: witness for nature*. New York: Henry Holt.

Levidow, L. 1995: Whose ethics for agricultural biotechnology? In Shiva, V. and Moser, I. (eds), *Biopolitics: a feminist and ecological reader on biotechnology*. London and New Jersey: Zed Books, pp. 175–90.

Macgill, S. 1987: *The Politics of Anxiety: Sellafield's cancer-link controversy*. London: Pion Press.

Macnaghten, P. and Urry, J. 1998: *Contested Natures*. London, Thousand Oaks, New Delhi: Sage.

Martell, L. 1994: *Ecology and Society: an introduction*. Cambridge: Polity.

Marx, K. 1976: *Capital: Volume 1*. Harmondsworth: Penguin.

McKechnie, R. 1996: Insiders and outsiders: identifying experts on home ground. In Irwin and Wynne (eds), *Misunderstanding Science?*, pp. 126–51.

McSorley, J. 1990: *Living in the Shadow: the story of the people of Sellafield*. London, Sydney and Auckland: Pan.

Meadows, D. H., Meadows, D. L., Randers, J. and Behrens, W. W. 1972: *The Limits to Growth*. London: Pan Books.

Meehan, R. L. 1984: *The Atom and the Fault*. Cambridge, MA: MIT Press.

Michael, M. 1992: Lay discourses of science: science-in-particular, science-in-general, and self. *Science, Technology and Human Values* 17 (3), pp. 313–33.

Mills, C. W. 1973: *The Sociological Imagination*. Harmondsworth: Penguin.

Milton, K. 1996: *Environmentalism and Cultural Theory: exploring the role of anthropology in environmentalist discourse*. London: Routledge.

Moffatt, S., Phillimore, P., Bhopal, R. and Foy, C. 1995: If this is what it's doing to our washing, what is it doing to our lungs? Industrial pollution and public understanding in North-East England. *Social Science and Medicine* 41, pp. 883–91.

Moser, I. 1995: Introduction. Mobilizing critical communities and discourses in modern biotechnology. In Shiva, V. and Moser, I. (eds), *Biopolitics: a feminist and ecological reader on biotechnology*. London and New Jersey: Zed Books, pp. 1–24.

Mulkay, M. 1991: *Sociology of Science: a sociological pilgrimage*. Milton Keynes: Open University Press.

Murphy, R. 1994a: *Rationality and Nature: a sociological inquiry into a changing relationship*. Boulder, San Francisco, Oxford: Westview Press.

Murphy, R. 1994b: The sociological construction of science without nature. *Sociology* 28 (4), pp. 957–74.

Myers, G. and Macnaghten, P. 1998: Rhetorics of environmental sustainability: commonplaces and places. *Environment and Planning A* 30 (2), pp. 333–53.

Myerson, G. and Rydin, Y. 1996: Sustainable development: the implications of the global debate for land use planning. In Buckingham-Hatfield and Evans (eds), *Environmental Planning and Sustainability*, pp. 19–34.

Neocleous, M. 1997: *Fascism*. Buckingham: Open University Press.

Newby, H. 1991: One world, two cultures: sociology and the environment. BSA bulletin. *Network* 50, pp. 1–8.

Novo Nordisk 1997: *Environment and Bioethics Report 1997*. Bagsvaerd, Denmark. *http://www.novo.dk*

O'Connor, J. 1994: Is sustainable capitalism possible? In O'Connor, M. (ed.), *Is Capitalism Sustainable? Political economy and the politics of ecology.* New York: The Guildford Press, pp. 152–75.

O'Riordan, T. and Cameron, J. (eds) 1994: *Interpreting the Precautionary Principle.* London: Earthscan.

Phillimore, P. and Moffatt, S. 1994: Discounted knowledge: local experience, environmental pollution and health. In Popay, J. and Williams, G. (eds), *Researching the People's Health.* London: Routledge, pp. 134–53.

Pickering, K. T. and Lewis, A. O. 1994: *An Introduction to Global Environmental Issues.* London and New York: Routledge.

Picou, J. S. and Gill, D. A. 1996: The *Exxon Valdez* oil spill and chronic psychological stress. *American Fisheries Society Symposium* 18, pp. 879–93.

Picou, J. S., Gill, D. A., Dyer, C. L. and Curry, E. W. 1992: Disruption and stress in an Alaskan fishing community: initial and continuing impacts of the *Exxon Valdez* oil spill. *Industrial Crisis Quarterly* 6 (3), pp. 235–57.

Polt, R. 1999: *Heidegger: an introduction.* London: UCL Press.

Ratzan, S. C. (ed.) 1998: *The Mad Cow Crisis: health and the public good.* London: UCL Press.

Redclift, M. 1992: *Sustainable Development: exploring the contradictions.* London and New York: Routledge.

Redclift, M. and Benton, T. (eds) 1994: *Social Theory and the Global Environment.* London and New York: Routledge.

Redclift, M. and Woodgate, G. 1994: Sociology and the environment: discordant discourse? In Redclift and Benton (eds), *Social Theory and the Global Environment,* pp. 51–66.

Redclift, M. and Woodgate, G. (eds) 1997: *The International Handbook of Environmental Sociology.* Cheltenham UK and Northampton MA: Edward Elgar.

Reid, D. 1996: *Sustainable Development: an introductory guide.* London: Earthscan.

Rifkin, J. 1998: Apocalypse when? *New Scientist,* 31 October 1998, pp. 34–7.

Rosa, E. A. 1998: Metatheoretical foundations for post-normal risk. *Journal of Risk Research* 1, pp. 15–44.

Rothstein, H., Irwin, A., Yearley, S. and Mc Carthy, E. 1999: Regulatory science, Europeanisation, and the control of agrochemicals. *Science, Technology and Human Values* 24 (2), pp. 241–64.

Royal Society 1992: *Risk: analysis, perception and management.* London: Royal Society.

Sachs, W. 1997: Sustainable development. In Redclift and Woodgate (eds), *The International Handbook of Environmental Sociology,* pp. 71–82.

Schama, S. 1995: *Landscape and Memory.* London: Fontana.

Schwarz, M. and Thompson, M. 1990: *Divided We Stand: redefining politics, technology and social choice.* Hemel Hempstead: Harvester Wheatsheaf.

Shiva, V. 1995: Biotechnological development and the conservation of biodiversity. In Shiva, V. and Moser, I. (eds), *Biopolitics: a feminist and ecological reader on biotechnology*. London and New Jersey: Zed Books, pp. 193–213.

Shiva, V. 1998: *Biopiracy: the plunder of nature and knowledge*. Dartington Totnes: Green Books.

Sokal, A. and Bricmont, J. 1998: *Intellectual Impostures: postmodern philosophers' abuse of science*. London: Profile Books.

Soper, K. 1995: *What is Nature?* Oxford: Blackwell.

Stehr, N. and Grundmann, R. 1996: 'Classical social science discourse and the impact of climate on society.' Mimeo. Wall Institute for Advanced Studies, The University of British Columbia, Vancouver and Max-Planck-Institut für Gesellschaftsforschung, Köln.

Studholme, M. 1997: British sociology and the issue of the environment. Unpublished PhD thesis, University of Bristol, UK.

Thompson, M. 1989: Engineering and anthropology: is there a difference? In Brown, J. (ed.), *Environmental Threats: perception, analysis and management*. London and New York: Belhaven Press, pp. 138–50.

Tönnies, F. 1955 [1887]: *Community and Association*. London: Routledge.

United Nations 1992: *Agenda 21*. Geneva: United Nations.

Vogel, D. 1986: *National Styles of Regulation*. Ithaca: Cornell University Press.

Wajcman, J. 1995: Feminist theories of technology. In Jasanoff, Markle, Petersen and Pinch (eds), *Handbook of Science and Technology Studies*, pp. 189–204.

Walker, G., Simmons, P., Wynne, B. and Irwin, A. 1998: *Public Perceptions of Risk Associated with Major Accident Hazards*. London: HSE Books. Contract research report: 194/1998.

Waterton, C. and Wynne, B. 1996: Building the European Union: science and the cultural dimensions of environmental policy. *Journal of European Public Policy* 3 (3), pp. 421–40.

Webster, A. 1991: *Science, Technology and Society*. Basingstoke and London: Macmillan.

Welsh, I. 1993: The NIMBY syndrome and its significance in the history of the nuclear debate in Britain. *British Journal for the History of Science* 26, pp. 15–32.

Welsh, I. 2000: *Mobilising Modernity: the nuclear moment*. London and New York: Routledge.

Wilkinson, E. 1939: *The Town that was Murdered*. London: Victor Gollancz.

Woolgar, S. 1988: *Science – the very idea*. London: Tavistock.

World Commission on Environment and Development (WCED) 1987: *Our Common Future* (The Brundtland Report). Oxford and New York: Oxford University Press.

Worster, D. 1977: *Nature's Economy: a history of ecological ideas*. Cambridge: Cambridge University Press.

Wynne, B. 1982: *Rationality and Ritual: the Windscale Inquiry and nuclear decisions in Britain*. Chalfont St Giles: British Society for the History of Science.

Wynne, B. 1989: Frameworks of rationality in risk management: towards the testing of naïve sociology. In Brown, J. (ed.), *Environmental Threats: perception, analysis and management*. London and New York: Belhaven Press, pp. 33–47.

Wynne, B. 1992: Uncertainty and environmental learning: reconceiving science and policy in the preventive paradigm. *Global Environmental Change* 2 (2), pp. 111–27.

Wynne, B. 1996: Misunderstood misunderstandings: social identities and public uptake of science. In Irwin and Wynne (eds), *Misunderstanding Science?*, pp. 19–46.

Yearley, S. 1991: *The Green Case: a sociology of environmental issues, arguments and politics*. London: HarperCollins.

Yearley, S. 1996: *Sociology, Environmentalism, Globalization*. London, Thousand Oaks, New Delhi: Sage.

Zonabend, F. 1993: *The Nuclear Peninsula*. Cambridge: Cambridge University Press.

Index